Sunset
Seafood
Cook Book

By the
Editors of
Sunset Books
and
Sunset Magazine

LANE PUBLISHING CO.
Menlo Park, California

ACKNOWLEDGMENTS

We wish to acknowledge with thanks the checking and consultation of Bertha V. Fontaine, Seafood Consumer Specialist, and Melvin Waters, Food Technologist, both of the National Marine Fisheries Service in Pascagoula, Mississippi. We also extend special thanks to Robert Pata, Fisheries Marketing Specialist of the San Francisco office of the NMFS, and Gene Cope, Consumer and Trade Education Specialist of the Seafood Quality and Inspection Division of the NMFS in Washington, D.C. Finally, we extend thanks and recognition to Cynthia Scheer for her culinary assistance with our seafood photography.

Supervising Editor:
Holly Lyman Antolini

Assistant Editor: **Denise Van Lear**

Special Consultant:
Linda Anusasananan
Staff Home Economist,
Sunset Magazine

Design: **Cynthia Hanson**
Photo Editor: **Lynne B. Morrall**
Illustrations: **John Lytle, Susan Jaekel**

Photography: **Tom Wyatt:** 35, 38, 43, 46, 51, 54, 59, 62, 67, 70, 75, 78, 83, 91, 94, 99, 102, 110, 115, 118, 123, 126. **Glenn Christiansen:** 86, 107.

Cover: The splendor and variety of seafood cookery are exemplified in two main-dish specialties. Lightly sautéed sole fillets are decked with hot buttered grapes and a river of delicately seasoned cream sauce (recipe on page 50). In ripe red tomatoes, a salad of smoked salmon boasts a curry-lemon-yogurt dressing; it's garnished with small shrimp (recipe on page 68). Photographed by Tom Wyatt.

Editor, Sunset Books: David E. Clark

Second printing February 1982

CONTENTS

SPECIAL FEATURES

THE SIMPLY ELEGANT ART OF SEAFOOD COOKERY

Fish are a wondrous food; their multiple advantages have been known and cultivated among the world's cuisines from time immemorial, and today their appeal, both practical and gastronomical, is as great as ever.

It is easy to point to the reasons. First of all, fish are remarkably adaptable. Whether cooked in utter simplicity in a pan of butter and served with a squeeze of lemon, or elaborately poached, sauced and served with a graceful garnish, they are awarded accolades of elegance. They can accommodate an astonishing variety of seasonings and can be cooked by a number of different methods without losing their integrity.

They cook quickly, compared with most meats—a 1-inch-thick piece of fish, such as a salmon steak, cooks in 10 minutes—so serving fish can be an important time saver. They are generally low in fat content (again compared with other proteins) and yet high in nutrition —added attractions in these days of dietary consciousness. Finally, once you have learned to cook one fish, you are well on your way to cooking *any* fish, so nearly interchangeable are they in their response to heat.

With these attractions, and the wealth of fresh and frozen seafood available in markets, why are many Americans hesitant to cook fish? Why are they reluctant to venture outside the familiar terrain of boiled lobster, broiled salmon, and sole à la meunière?

Chances are that many people feel intimidated by the confusion of fish names in the markets, where there's such an overlap in terms that three different fish may share one name, or where half the names are unfamiliar and odd-sounding, like "croaker," "drum,"
or "lingcod." Or they may think that a whole fish—fins, scales, and all—seems too hard to handle. Even concern about the perishability of fish plays a part in people's hesitation. And underneath it all is the wide-spread assumption that fish cookery is just too difficult to be done well.

It is to dispel the mystery and confusion surrounding fish cookery and to encourage the enjoyment of our many fine fish that we present this book. It is both a manual for beginners and a smörgåsbord of ideas for the experienced fish cook.

Included are charts to help you identify and select from the fish available in your market, giving you their most common names, forms (whole, steaks, fillets, etc.), and cooking characteristics. We also have illustrations that show how to handle a whole fish or any of the most common shellfish, and you'll find information on the important aspects of storing and freezing fish.

There's a whole chapter packed with step-by-step cooking techniques (including precise timing instructions) which, once understood, provide the remarkably simple basis for the whole art of fish cookery, with all its variations. And you'll find an extensive selection of the fish and shellfish most commonly available in eastern, southern, and western seaboard markets (plus several common fresh-water fish), presented with recipes and cooking suggestions tailored to their individual characteristics. Tucked into the various chapters are numerous sauce suggestions to dress up simple fish, and directions for doing your own smoking of fish. We even tell you some ways to serve it raw.

WHEN THE FISH FLAKES

By nature, fish is tender and free of tough fibers that need to be softened by cooking. Cooking a fish is therefore somewhat like cooking an egg—the heat should be allowed just to firm the delicate protein—for, like an egg, fish becomes tough and dry when overcooked. The delicate fibers break down, letting all the fish's moisture and flavor drain away.

Recognizing when a fish is done is the essential step in learning to cook it well. Most recipes tell you to cook fish "until it flakes readily when prodded with a fork." This is because the fish flakes at the precise moment of doneness, when the heat has broken down the connective fibers just enough to permit the tender flesh to slide apart along its natural divisions at the gentle probing of a fork, but not so much that the flavor and moisture have escaped. Another moment or two and the fish will be overcooked. When a fish is badly overcooked, it will, of its own accord, fall into pieces along its natural divisions, and the flesh will be very tough and tasteless.

Be sure you probe with your fork into the center of the thickest portion of the fish or piece of fish, because the thinner parts may appear done when the thicker part is still raw inside. (If this is the case, the inside of the thicker portion will feel resistant to the fork and appear translucent, while the thinner portion will be opaque and tender.)

Because of the speed with which fish cooks, and because its delicate flesh will retain enough heat to continue to cook itself after removal from the heat source, it is most often cooked just before serving, so that it can be served the minute it is done. In cases where it's served cold, though, or where specific "cook-ahead" directions are given, some fish may be cooked in advance.

Also due to fish's brief cooking time, we have called for a preheated oven (in cases when the oven is used), so that the proper temperature is maintained throughout the cooking of the fish, making under or overcooking less likely.

THE FAT & THE LEAN

Though fish in general is considered a low-fat source of protein, there are differences in fat content from species to species. These differences affect the flavor and texture of the fish and dictate the best choice of cooking method for it.

In a fish of moderately high fat content (5 percent or over), such as swordfish or salmon, oil is distributed throughout the flesh of the fish, causing it often to have a more pronounced and distinctive flavor, a more meatlike texture, and a tinted or darker color than a leaner fish (one with less than 5 percent fat content). The leaner fish, on the other hand, tends to concentrate its oils in the liver, which is removed when the fish is cleaned. Anyone who has ever tasted cod liver oil can attest to the fact that the liver carries the strong flavors away, leaving the lean fish much milder in flavor and whiter in color than the fattier fish.

The difference in the amount of oil a fish retains in its flesh affects your choice of cooking method slightly, but importantly. The fattiest fish is more likely to remain moist when subjected to searing heat, so it is best adapted to such methods as broiling, barbecuing, and baking at high temperatures.

The leaner fish may dry out too much when cooked by these methods, unless basted frequently with butter or oil to keep it moist; moreover, its usually mild flavor may be overpowered by barbecuing because of the penetratingly strong smoky taste. But lean fish poaches beautifully, because its flesh firms as it cooks gently in simmering liquid; it doesn't fall apart as easily as fattier fish, which must be handled with great care in poaching if its shape is to be retained.

For the same reason, lean fish is delicious in soups or sauced dishes, or in fried dishes involving butter or oil, because in these methods its moisture is retained or replenished.

THE FORM...

Unlike the bewildering array of meat cuts you face as a shopper, the forms of fish you can buy are quite simple and straightforward. But choosing the right one is important, to suit your recipe and ease the preparation.

Whole or round. This form is the fish as it comes from the water, scales and all. To cook it, you must at least eviscerate, scale, and dress it yourself (see directions on page 7—some fish, such as smelt, need only eviscerating). Fish tends to be least expensive in whole form, but remember that only 45 percent of it, on average, is edible meat.

Cleaned or drawn. It is possible to buy whole fish that are already eviscerated or "drawn." These are about 48 percent edible. However, you must still scale, dress, and, if necessary, cut up the fish yourself.

Dressed or pan-dressed. A dressed fish is a whole fish that has been drawn and scaled and usually has had its fins and often its head and tail removed. It is ready to cook and is about 67 percent edible meat.

Chunks and steaks. These pieces are cross-section slices of a large, dressed fish. A chunk is usually 4 to 6 inches thick; a steak is ¾ to 1 inch thick. Because the only bone is a cross-section piece of backbone, these cuts are about 84 percent edible, and they are ready to cook.

Fillets. This is the most common form of fish available, fresh or frozen. It is the fleshy sides of the fish, cut away from the backbone and ribs. Fillets are practically boneless. A "butterfly fillet" is a double fillet formed by both sides of the fish, still joined by the uncut flesh and skin of the belly. A single fillet is just one side of the fish and is generally skinless. Both butterfly and single fillets are almost totally edible.

Portions and fish sticks. Frozen fish is available in uniform, ready-to-cook rectangles cut from boneless frozen fish blocks and breaded. These may be raw or partially cooked; in either case, they require no preparation for cooking.

Scraps. If your fish dealer dresses or bones a whole fish for you, you can claim the bones, head, and scraps—they make excellent fish stock (see recipe on page 32) to be used in fish sauces, casseroles, or soups. If you don't need the scraps immediately, wrap them airtight in freezer paper or heavy-duty aluminum foil and freeze them until ready to use.

Shellfish. Forms of shellfish are discussed individually in Chapter 4, "A Cook's Catalog of Common Shellfish."

...& THE FRESHNESS

In some cultures where fish is a staple of the diet, freshness is prized so highly that people will refuse any fish that is more than 6 hours out of the water. With modern methods of storage and transportation, such selectivity isn't necessary, but for dishes that are both tasty and healthful, it is important that you know how to choose a fresh fish. Once you know the signs, it's easy to judge the freshness of fish.

Fresh fish

In a fresh fish, the flesh is firm and springs back when pressed gently; it hasn't begun separating from the bones. Fillets and steaks are moist and firm, look freshly cut, and have no traces of either browning at the edges or a dried-out look. The odor of the fish, whole or in pieces, should be fresh and mild when you buy it. Never buy a fish whose odor is disagreeably strong.

The eyes of a really fresh whole fish are clear, full, and often protruding. When the fish is old and spoiling, the eyes look cloudy and sunken. The gills of a whole fish should be pinkish red and free of slime; as the fish ages, the gills turn gray, and then brownish or greenish. And finally, the skin of a whole fish should be shiny, with unfaded color and pronounced markings.

Frozen fish

Frozen fish should be checked for spoilage also—if fish has not been frozen correctly, it probably will have had ample opportunity to spoil before you buy it. The flesh should be solidly frozen. There should be no discoloration, no brownish tinge, and no white, cottony appearance. The odor, if any, should be very slight. Packaging should be airtight and undamaged. (The best-protected frozen fish is that which has been covered completely in a glazing of ice, so that it is totally shielded from contact with the air.)

Shellfish

Shellfish also have distinguishing characteristics of freshness; these will be discussed under the individual shellfish in Chapter 4, "A Cook's Catalog of Common Shellfish."

HANDLING FISH: FREEZING & THAWING

Fish are known for their perishability. If you conscientiously follow some conservative guidelines for handling and storage, though, you need never fear that your fish is spoiled. (If you *do* have doubts about a fish's freshness after storage, the best rule is to throw it away and get another one.)

Refrigerating

Fresh fish should be eviscerated, if necessary, and refrigerated at 35°-40° in a leakproof wrapper as soon as possible after purchase; even a couple of hours at room temperature could start spoilage. It should be cooked within 2 days. Once cooked, the fish can be kept in the refrigerator—covered—for 2 or 3 more days at most.

Fresh shellfish should be refrigerated in the coldest part of the refrigerator and eaten the day you buy it.

Freezing

Though fish is most delicious when it is eaten fresh (the process of freezing and thawing causes the expansion and contraction of ice crystals, which breaks down the delicate fish fibers just enough to cause a slight but noticeable loss of moisture and flavor when cooked), it can be frozen and stored for extended periods of time, if necessary.

To freeze it, make sure it is eviscerated; then wrap it airtight in freezer paper or heavy-duty foil, seal it, and date it. Store it in the freezer at 0° or lower. Fish of moderate fat content, as well as crab and lobster, can be stored 3 months this way. Leaner fish and other shellfish (shells removed) can remain frozen up to 6 months. (For information on fat content, see page 5 and see charts on pages 8-11.)

Thawing

When you want to thaw a frozen fish, schedule it so that you can cook the fish as soon as possible after it has thawed—never store thawed fish for more than a day, because the freezing and thawing will have broken down the delicate fish fibers slightly, thus speeding the process of spoilage. For the same reason, never refreeze a partially or completely thawed fish—its flesh cannot weather the freezing and thawing process twice.

Thaw fish in the refrigerator for best results, allowing 18 to 24 hours for a 1-pound package. If quicker thawing is necessary, place the package, *unopened,* in *cold* water; allow 1 to 2 hours. *Do not thaw fish at room temperature or in warm water;* it would only speed the breakdown process, resulting in loss of flavor and moisture.

THE FISH DISMANTLED

Scaling. *Hold fish firmly by the tail under running water. Position knife almost vertically; draw it from tail to head, scraping off scales as you go.*

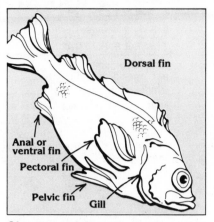

Cleaning and dressing. *Cut along belly from pelvic to anal fins; remove and discard entrails. Then cut around pelvic fins; remove and discard.*

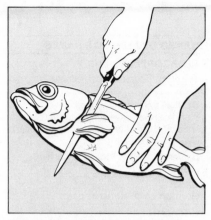

Dressing. *Cut behind gills and collarbone to remove head and pectoral fins. (If backbone is large, cut down to it on both sides; bend to snap, or saw off.)*

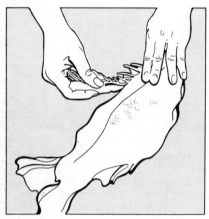

Dressing to use whole. *Remove dorsal fin by cutting flesh along both sides, then giving a quick pull toward head to remove fin with root bones attached. Remove rest of fins in same way.*

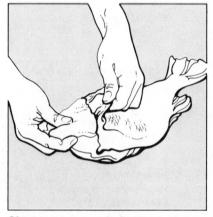

Skinning to use whole. *With knife, free a corner of skin at head end of fish. Holding head end down with one hand, grasp skin with other and pull gently toward tail. Skin all of one side, then other.*

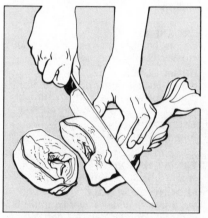

Cutting steaks. *Cut cross-section slices to make fish steaks (do not skin). If backbone is large, cut down to it on both sides, then saw through it with a coping saw.*

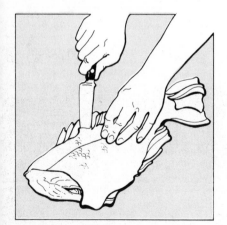

Filleting. *Cut through flesh along backbone of a cleaned, scaled fish (head removed), beginning at tail end, cutting along both sides of dorsal fin, and ending at head end. Cut off tail; trim off ventral fins.*

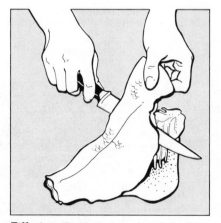

Filleting. *Turn knife flat and cut flesh of fish's side from bone, sliding blade along backbone and over rib bones to release flesh in one piece. Lift entire side (fillet) off bones. Turn fish over; repeat process.*

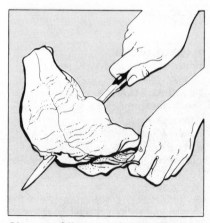

Skinning fillets. *Lay fillet flat, skin side down. With knife, free a corner of skin from flesh at wider end of fillet. Grasp free corner and, holding knife flat against skin, cut horizontally to release flesh from skin.*

A PROFILE OF COMMON FISH

NAMES & ALTERNATE NAMES	FLAVOR & TEXTURE	FAT CONTENT*	SIZE RANGE
ALBACORE, PACIFIC longfin tuna	Rich flavor; soft flesh becomes firm and meaty when cooked	Moderate	10 to 25 pounds
BLUEFISH blue snapper, skipjack, tailor, fatback, snapping mackerel	Mild flavor; tender flesh	Low	1 to 7 pounds
BUTTERFISH harvestfish, silver dollar, dollarfish, pumpkin seed	Mild, delicate flavor; soft, melting flesh	Moderate	¼ to 1¼ pounds
CARP German carp, summer carp	Mild flavor; firm flesh	Low to moderate	2 to 8 pounds
CATFISH channel catfish, flathead catfish, yaqui, headwater catfish, blue catfish, white catfish, madtom, widemouth and toothless blindcats, stonecats, gafftopsail catfish	Mild flavor; tender flesh	Low	1 to 40 pounds
COD, ATLANTIC OR PACIFIC codfish	Mild flavor; tender-firm flesh that flakes easily when cooked	Very low	1½ to 20 pounds
CROAKER crocus, hardhead, Texas croaker, chut, golden croaker, corvina, roncadina, drum	Mild flavor; tender flesh	Low	½ to 2 pounds
DRUM, BLACK oyster cracker, oyster drum, sea drum, gray drum, channel bass, barbed drum, big drum, striped drum, drumfish, sheepshead	Mild flavor; tender-firm flesh	Low	1 to 40 pounds
EEL, COMMON American eel, silver eel	Mild flavor; tender-firm flesh	Moderate	1 to 5 pounds
FINNAN HADDIE smoked haddock, smoked cod	Rich, smoky flavor; tender texture	Low	½ to 3 pounds per fillet
FLOUNDER OR SOLE blackback flounder, winter flounder, fluke, summer flounder, dab, sea dab, lemon sole, gray sole, southern flounder, yellow-tail flounder, petrale sole, rex sole, sand dab, sand sole, Dover sole, English sole	Mild, delicate, distinctive flavor; tender, flaky flesh	Low	¾ to 12 pounds
GROUPER sea bass	Mild flavor; tender-firm flesh	Low	5 to 12 pounds
HADDOCK scrod	Mild flavor; tender-chewy, flaky flesh	Low	1½ to 7 pounds
HALIBUT, PACIFIC northern halibut; if 6 to 10 pounds, chicken halibut	Mild flavor; tender-firm flesh	Very low	6 to 100 pounds
HERRING, ATLANTIC sea herring	Pronounced flavor; tender flesh	Moderate	⅛ to ¼ pound
KINGFISH king mackerel, cero	Pronounced flavor; firm flesh	Moderate	5 to 20 pounds
LINGCOD cultus cod, blue cod, buffalo cod; not a true cod	Delicate flavor; tender flesh	Very low	5 to 10 pounds
MACKEREL Boston mackerel, Atlantic mackerel, Spanish mackerel, Pacific mackerel, blue mackerel, American mackerel	Rich, pronounced flavor; firm flesh	High	1 to 4 pounds
MULLET jumping mullet, striped mullet, silver mullet, black mullet, liza, sand mullet, white mullet	Mild flavor; tender flesh	Moderate	½ to 3 pounds

*Very Low: Less than 2 percent fat; Low: 2-5 percent fat; Moderate: 6-10 percent fat; High: More than 10 percent fat

FORMS AVAILABLE	WHERE AVAILABLE	WHEN AVAILABLE	HOW TO COOK*
Whole (sometimes steaks, chunks)	Western coast (on request from market)	Summer (in Northwest, midsummer through October)	Steaks: butter-sauté, pan-fry, oven-fry, broil, barbecue. Chunks: poach or bake
Whole, drawn	Eastern, Gulf coasts	All year	Oven-fry, broil, bake
Whole, drawn	Eastern coast	Spring to late autumn	Butter-sauté, pan-fry, oven-fry, broil, smoke
Whole, dressed, steaks, fillets	Great Lakes, other U.S. lakes, inland rivers	All year (best from October to March)	Oven-fry, broil, poach, bake
Whole, dressed, dressed and skinned	Great Lakes, other U.S. lakes, inland rivers	All year	Pan-fry, oven-fry, broil, barbecue, smoke
Drawn, dressed, steaks, fillets, dried and salted	Northeastern, mideastern, western coasts (available frozen in rest of U.S.)	All year	Poach, or cook in soups, stews, casseroles, fish cakes
Whole, drawn, fillets	Mideastern and southeastern coasts	March to October, especially summer and autumn	Butter-sauté, pan-fry, oven-fry, broil
Whole, drawn, steaks	Mideastern, south-eastern, Gulf coasts	October through February	Oven-fry, poach, bake
Whole, dressed, dressed and skinned	Eastern coast	All year (less in winter)	Butter-sauté, pan-fry, poach, smoke, or cook in soups, stews, or casseroles
Fillets	Eastern coast	All year	Oven-fry, broil, poach, bake in casseroles
Whole, dressed, fillets	Northeastern, mideastern, western coasts	All year	Butter-sauté, pan-fry, oven-fry, broil, poach
Drawn, dressed, steaks, fillets	Southeastern coast	November to May	Pan-fry, deep-fry, oven-fry, broil, poach, steam, bake
Drawn, fillets	Northeastern coast (available frozen in rest of U.S.)	All year	Butter-sauté, pan-fry, deep-fry, oven-fry, broil, poach, smoke, steam, bake
Steaks, fillets (chicken halibut available whole, on request from market)	Western coast (available frozen in rest of U.S.)	May to September (available frozen the rest of the year)	Butter-sauté, pan-fry, oven-fry, broil, poach
Whole, drawn, packed in brine	Northeastern, mideastern, western coasts	All year	Pan-fry, oven-fry,
Drawn, fillets, steaks	Southeastern, Gulf coasts	November to March	Oven-fry, broil, barbecue, poach
Whole, fillets, steaks	Western coast	All year (best April to October on California coast, October to May in Northwest)	Butter-sauté, pan-fry, deep-fry, oven-fry, broil, poach
Whole, fillets	Northeastern, mideastern, western coasts	All year (spring and summer in East)	Broil, barbecue, bake
Whole	Southeastern, Gulf coasts	April to November	Pan-fry, oven-fry, broil, barbecue, smoke, bake

*Basic methods described on pages 14–31

(Continued on next page)

NAMES & ALTERNATE NAMES	FLAVOR & TEXTURE	FAT CONTENT*	SIZE RANGE
OCEAN PERCH, ATLANTIC redfish, red perch, rosefish	Mild flavor; tender, flaky flesh	Very low	½ to 2 pounds
PIKE common pike, pickerel, muskellunge, yellow pike perch, walleyed pike, blue pike perch, sauger, sand pike	Mild flavor, firm flesh	Low	1 to 30 pounds
POMPANO great pompano, permit, golden pompano, Carolina permi, cobblerfish, butterfish, palmenta	Rich, distinctive flavor; firm flesh	Moderate	½ to 3½ pounds
PORGY/SCUP fair maid, northern porgy, paugy, porgee, white snapper	Mild flavor; tender, flaky flesh	Low	½ to 1½ pounds
ROCKFISH rock cod, sea bass, rosefish, grouper, red snapper, Pacific ocean perch	Mild flavor; firm flesh	Very low	2 to 5 pounds
SABLEFISH black cod, Alaska cod, butterfish	Buttery, mild flavor; very soft, melting flesh	Moderate to high	4 to 20 pounds
SALMON, PACIFIC king (chinook, spring), and coho (silver, silverside); also sockeye or red salmon, pink or humpback salmon, chum or keta or calico salmon	Rich, distinctive flavor; firm flesh of a light pink to bright red	Moderate	6 to 30 pounds
SEA BASS black sea bass (black jewfish, giant seabass, grouper bass, California black seabass), white sea bass	Mild flavor; tender flesh	Very low	Black: 50 to 600 pounds White: Up to 50 pounds
SEA BASS, COMMON blackfish, black sea bass	Mild flavor; tender flesh	Low	½ to 4 pounds
SEA TROUT, GRAY OR SPOTTED weakfish, gray trout, squeteague, speckled trout, spotted sea trout, spotted trout, sand sea trout	Mild flavor; tender-firm flesh	Low	1 to 6 pounds
SHAD & ROE American shad, white shad (roe are the eggs of the shad)	Mild flavor; firm, meatlike flesh, quite bony	High	1½ to 7 pounds
SHARK greyfish, grayfish, dogfish, pinback, soupfin, thresher, leopard, tiger, bull, mako	Pronounced flavor (like swordfish); firm, meatlike flesh	Low	Western variety: 12 to 30 pounds (except dogfish: 12 to 18 pounds); Southeastern and Gulf variety: up to 200 pounds
SMELT whitebait, icefish, frostfish, candlelight fish	Rich flavor; tender-firm flesh	Low to moderate	8 to 12 per pound
SNAPPER, RED snapper	Mild, distinctive flavor; tender-firm flesh	Low	2 to 20 pounds
SPOT	Mild flavor; tender flesh	Low	¼ to 1¼ pounds
STRIPED BASS rockfish, striper	Mild flavor; tender-firm flesh	Low	2 to 50 pounds
SWORDFISH broadbill	Rich, distinctive flavor; firm, meatlike flesh	Moderate	200 to 600 pounds
TROUT rainbow trout, brook trout, brown trout	Mild, distinctive flavor; firm flesh	Moderate to high	⅓ to 2 pounds
TURBOT, GREENLAND	Mild flavor; tender, soft, flaky flesh	Low	5 to 15 pounds
WHITEFISH cisco, lake whitefish, chub	Delicate flavor; tender flesh	Moderate	2 to 6 pounds
WHITING silver hake	Mild, delicate flavor; tender, flaky flesh	Low	¾ to 3 pounds

*Very Low: Less than 2 percent fat; Low: 2–5 percent fat; Moderate: 6–10 percent fat; High: More than 10 percent fat

FORMS AVAILABLE	WHERE AVAILABLE	WHEN AVAILABLE	HOW TO COOK*
Whole, fillets	Northeastern coast (available frozen in rest of U.S.)	All year	Butter-sauté, pan-fry, oven-fry, broil, poach
Whole, drawn, fillets	Great Lakes, other U.S. lakes	All year	Butter-sauté, pan-fry, deep-fry, oven-fry, broil, barbecue, poach, steam, bake
Whole, drawn	Gulf coast	All year (especially March through May)	Butter-sauté, pan-fry, oven-fry, broil, barbecue, bake
Whole, drawn	Eastern coast	September to May (especially January to April)	Pan-fry, oven-fry, broil, barbecue
Whole, fillets	Western coast	All year	Butter-sauté, pan-fry, deep-fry, oven-fry, broil, barbecue, poach, bake
Whole, fillets, steaks	Western coast	All year (best in summer on California coast; August to November in Northwest)	Oven-fry, broil, barbecue, poach, smoke
Whole, drawn, steaks, fillets	Western coast (available frozen in rest of U.S.)	Varies by areas (available frozen all year)	Butter-sauté, pan-fry, deep-fry, oven-fry, broil, barbecue, poach, smoke
Steaks, chunks, fillets	Western coast	All year	Butter-sauté, pan-fry, oven-fry, broil, poach
Whole, drawn, dressed, fillets	Eastern coast	All year	Butter-sauté, pan-fry, oven-fry, broil, poach
Whole, drawn, fillets	Mideastern, southeastern coasts	April to November	Butter-sauté, pan-fry, oven-fry broil, barbecue, bake
Whole, drawn	Eastern, northwestern coasts	March through May	Oven-fry, barbecue, poach
Steaks, chunks, fillets	Western, southeastern, Gulf coasts	All year, especially in summer	Oven-fry, broil, barbecue, poach
Whole, drawn, sometimes boneless	Northeastern, western coasts	All year	Butter-sauté, pan-fry, deep-fry, oven-fry, broil
Whole, drawn, steaks, fillets	Gulf coast	All year	Butter-sauté, pan-fry, oven-fry, broil, poach
Whole, drawn	Mideastern, southeastern coasts	All year	Butter-sauté, pan-fry, oven-fry, broil
Whole, drawn, steaks, fillets	Mideastern, southeastern coasts	All year	Butter-sauté, pan-fry, oven-fry, broil, barbecue, poach, bake
Steaks, chunks	Northeastern, mideastern, western coasts	August through October (frozen the rest of the year)	Oven-fry, broil, barbecue
Drawn, dressed	Inland rivers and fish farms	All year (frozen or fresh)	Butter-sauté, pan fry, deep-fry, oven-fry, broil, barbecue, poach, smoke
Fillets (frozen)	Imported (available frozen throughout the U.S.)	All year	Butter-sauté, pan-fry, oven-fry, poach,
Whole, drawn, fillets, smoked	Great Lakes, other U.S. lakes	April to December	Butter-sauté, pan-fry deep-fry, oven-fry, broil, barbecue, poach, smoke, steam, bake
Drawn, dressed, steaks, fillets	Northeastern, mideastern coasts	All year, especially in summer	Butter-sauté, pan-fry, deep-fry, oven-fry, broil, poach

*Basic methods described on pages 14–31

A PROFILE OF COMMON SHELLFISH

NAMES & ALTERNATE NAMES	FORMS AVAILABLE	SIZE RANGE	WHERE AVAILABLE
ABALONE	Steaks (pounded to tenderize)	3 to 8 per pound	Western coast
CLAM Butter clam	Live in shell Shucked meats	100 per sack, live 25 to 30 per quart, shucked	Western coast
Geoduck clam (king clam, gooey-duck, gweduc)	Live, fresh on request from market Frozen steaks, minced meats, chunks	Each clam: 3 pounds (yields 1½ lb. meat)	Northwestern coast
Hard clam (quahog, sharp clam, hard-shell clam, littleneck clam, cherrystone clam)	Live in shell Shucked, whole Shucked, minced	80 pounds per bushel 25 to 30 per quart	Eastern coast
Razor clam	Live in shell Shucked, whole Shucked, minced	80 per box	Western coast
Soft-shell clam (manninose clam)	Live in shell Shucked, whole	45 pounds per bushel 50 to 175 per quart	Eastern coast
Surf clam (skimmer clam, beach clam, giant clam, sea clam, hen clam, bar clam)	Shucked, whole	25 to 75 per quart	Eastern coast
CRAB Blue crab (hard-shell crab, soft-shell crab)	Live in shell Steamed and picked from shell; sold in ½ or 1-pound tins as lump meat, flake meat (from body), or claw meat	Hard-shell: ¼ to 1 pound Soft-shell: ⅐ to ⅓ pound	Mideastern, southeastern, Gulf coasts
Dungeness crab	Live in shell Cooked in shell, fresh or frozen Cooked and picked from body, claws	1¼ to 2½ pounds	Western coast
Alaska king crab	Cooked in shell, frozen Legs cooked in shell, frozen	6 to 20 pounds	Eastern, western coasts
Rock crab	Live in shell	⅓ pound	Northeastern coast
CRAYFISH Crawfish, crawdad, ecrevisse, mudbug	From western coast: Live in shell Cooked in shell Frozen in shell From rivers of Louisiana and Mississippi: Live in shell Cooked in shell Tail meat in 5-pound cans	Western variety: 4 to 7 inches long Southern variety: less than 3 inches long	Western rivers, southern rivers, particularly in Louisiana and Mississippi
LOBSTER Northeastern lobster	Live in shell Cooked, shelled	¾ to 4 pounds	Eastern, western coasts
Spiny Pacific lobster	Live in shell Frozen raw in shell	1 to 4 pounds	Southwestern coast
MUSSEL	Live in shell	55 pounds per bushel	Northeastern, mideastern coasts

NAMES & ALTERNATE NAMES	FORMS AVAILABLE	SIZE RANGE	WHERE AVAILABLE
OCTOPUS Polpi, pulpi, devilfish	Whole on request from market	Imported: frozen 1 to 4 pounds Western: fresh or frozen 3 to 5 pounds	Western coast, imported
OYSTER Eastern oyster (cove oyster)	Live in shell Shucked, whole	80 pounds per bushel 40 to 50 per quart	Eastern, Gulf coasts
Olympia oyster (western oyster)	Live in shell Shucked, whole	120 pounds per sack 300 to 400 per quart	Northwestern coast
Pacific Oyster (Japanese oyster)	Live in shell Shucked, whole	80 pounds per sack 12 to 60 per quart	Western coast
SCALLOP Bay scallop (cape scallop)	Shucked, whole	62 to 85 per quart	Eastern, Gulf coasts
Sea scallop	Shucked, whole	25 to 30 per quart	Eastern coast (available frozen in rest of U.S.)
SHRIMP Prawn, ocean shrimp, bay shrimp, northern shrimp, Alaska shrimp	Raw in shell Cooked in shell Cooked, shelled; fresh or frozen	Ocean shrimp: 150 to 180 per pound Small: 45 to 65 per pound Medium: 30 per pound Large (or jumbo or prawn): 6 to 15 per pound	Northern, southeastern, Gulf coasts Ocean shrimp: western coast (available frozen in rest of U.S.)
SQUID Inkfish, calamari	Whole Cleaned, frozen	10 to 12 inches long	Northeastern, mideastern, and western coasts

A HANDY METRIC CONVERSION TABLE

To change	To	Multiply by
ounces (oz.)	grams (g)	28
pounds (lbs.)	kilograms (kg)	0.45
teaspoons	milliliters (ml)	5
tablespoons	milliliters (ml)	15
fluid ounces (oz.)	milliliters (ml)	30
cups	liters (l)	0.24
pints (pt.)	liters (l)	0.47
quarts (qt.)	liters (l)	0.95
gallons (gal.)	liters (l)	3.8
inches	centimeters (cm)	2.5
Fahrenheit temperature (°F)	*Celsius temperature (°C)*	*5/9th after subtracting 32*

EIGHT
BASIC
METHODS
OF
COOKING
FISH

BAKING • BARBECUING • BROILING • BUTTER-SAUTÉING
DEEP-FRYING • OVEN-FRYING • PAN-FRYING • POACHING

All fish cookery rests on a foundation of eight classically simple preparation methods—once you've mastered them, you can master any recipe that has been devised for the treatment of fish.

The basic techniques—baking, barbecuing, broiling, butter-sautéing, deep-frying, oven-frying, pan-frying, and poaching—have, in their simplicity, such subtle and delicious results that they need no elaboration at all. In themselves, they constitute an extensive repertoire of fish dishes, especially if you take advantage of the seasoning suggestions included in each technique, the flavored butters appearing on page 29, and the selection of sauces given on pages 20 – 21. Any of these will add a finishing touch to your simple masterpiece.

Almost any fish in the market can be used in each of these techniques, because the adaptability of fish is practically endless. Some revisions in basic technique (such as length of cooking time or level of heat) may be necessary, and some methods may be preferred for particular kinds of fish, because of differences in fat content, size, or thickness of fish pieces. Where adaptations are required, or where there is a reason to prefer one fish over another, you'll find specific instructions included under the individual methods. Also, under some of the preparation methods, you'll find sections called "Dishes to Suit Any Fish." These include recipes whose methods, seasonings, and sauces make them particularly adaptable to any fish you may wish to use.

Because the tender and delicate fibers of a fish cook quickly, you will usually want to have the rest of the meal ready before you start to cook the fish. Then bear in mind the cardinal rule of fish cookery: *don't overcook.* A good rule of thumb is to *allow 10 minutes cooking time for a piece of fish that is 1 inch thick in the thickest portion, measured when the piece is lying flat.* If the piece is thicker or thinner, just vary the cooking time to maintain a ratio of 10:1; for example, a ½-inch-thick fillet will cook in 5 minutes.

These basic techniques are simple, but performing them with finesse requires some skill. We've done our best to give precise guidelines for heat levels and lengths of cooking time in each case, but the best advice, ultimately, is this: *practice!*

For a good introduction to the basics of fish cookery, buy a couple of pounds of lean, mild, white-fleshed fish fillets, such as whiting, Greenland turbot, or rockfish. Then choose one method you like, such as butter-sautéing or broiling, and use it several times in succession.

As you experiment, keep an eye on the appearance of your fish while it cooks; test it often by prodding it gently in the thickest portion with a fork to see if it flakes readily (see "When the Fish Flakes," page 5); then sample the texture and flavor of the fish. Familiarize yourself with how it tastes, feels, and looks when done to your liking. You'll soon develop your own intuitive knack for these basic methods…and *that's* the real secret of fish cookery.

BAKING

On the days when both your time and energy are in short supply, you'll find baking can be an appealingly quick, no-nonsense approach to fish cookery.

Baking covers a wide range of fish preparations, from simple, low calorie fare to creations with rich sauces. Many of the recipes in the following two chapters involve baking with sauces and can be adapted to a variety of different fish. Here, though, we'll concentrate on the simplest method for baking fish, with some basic flavorings.

We recommend baking plain fish at a high temperature (though not as high as oven-frying)—it shortens the cooking time and locks in the fish's juicy freshness.

HOW TO BAKE

Unlike oven-fried fish, baked fish needs no coating, nor must it be immersed in liquid as for oven-poaching. The baking method adapts to any size, shape, or kind of fish: fillets, steaks, chunks, and small or large whole fish.

>   **Fish fillets or steaks (up to 1½ inches thick), or
>   small whole fish (up to 3 lb.), cleaned and scaled**
>   **Half butter or margarine and half salad oil**
>   **Seasoning liquid (optional—suggestions follow)**
>   **Chopped herbs (optional—suggestions follow)**
>   **Salt and pepper**
>   **Lemon wedges (optional)**

Preheat oven to 425°. Put a large, shallow baking pan in oven to preheat. Wipe fish with damp cloth. Cut into serving-size pieces (3 by 5 inches), if desired.

Remove pan from oven. Put butter and oil in pan and swirl until butter is melted (fat should be about ⅛ inch deep).

Lay a piece of fish in pan; turn to coat with melted butter and oil. Repeat with rest of fish, arranging as many pieces in pan as will fit without crowding. (If using thin fillets—½ inch thick or less—you can layer them two deep. Drizzle top layer with a little butter and oil and adjust cooking time accordingly.)

Drizzle seasoning liquid over fish, if desired (liquid should be about ¼ inch deep). Sprinkle with chopped herbs, if desired.

Return pan to oven and bake, uncovered, until fish flakes readily when prodded in thickest portion with a fork. For a 1-inch-thick piece of fish (measured in thickest portion; if fish fillets are layered, measure total thickness of both layers), allow 10 minutes. (Allow same ratio of thickness to time—1 inch: 10 minutes—for fish of all thicknesses.)

When fish is done, transfer to warm serving platter. Add salt and pepper to taste and serve immediately, garnished with lemon wedges, if desired. Spoon seasoning liquid (if any remains) over servings.

Seasoning liquids. Use chicken broth, dry white wine, or dry sherry. For 4 to 6 servings of fish (1½ to 2½ lb. fish pieces), you'll need about ½ cup.

Chopped herbs. Select one or two of the following: chopped parsley, dry basil, dry tarragon, savory leaves, thyme or marjoram leaves, or finely chopped green onion.

Baking a large whole fish

If you count any avid anglers among your family and friends, the chances are that sooner or later one of them will present you with the prize catch of the day—a large, whole fish.

It could be anything from a 5-pound striped bass to a 20-pound king salmon, but whatever it is, you may want to preserve its handsome appearance by cooking and serving it whole. Even if you don't have a barbecue or poaching pan, you can still prepare a large, whole fish —just bake it in your oven.

If the fish weighs 6 pounds or more, see if it fits in your oven. If the fish is too long, cut it in half, crosswise, through the backbone and bake the halves, side by side, in the oven. After they're done, you can reassemble the fish on a serving platter and disguise the cut with a garnish of parsley or a sauce (for sauces, see pages 20 – 21). If the fish is small enough to fit in your oven whole, you may want to bake it with a tangy lemon rice stuffing.

>   **Lemon rice stuffing (optional
>   —see recipe on page 66)**
>   **1 large whole fish (3 to 20 lb.),
>   cleaned and scaled**
>   **Melted butter**

Preheat oven to 425°. Prepare lemon rice stuffing, if desired.

Wipe fish with damp cloth, inside cavity and outside. If using stuffing, lightly pack it into cavity; sew opening

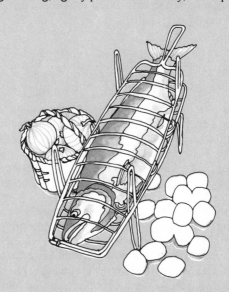

closed with heavy thread (wrap any leftover stuffing in foil and heat in oven while fish cooks). If fish is too large for oven, cut it in half, crosswise, through the backbone; do not stuff halves.

Cut a piece of heavy-duty foil to fit one side of whole fish, or cut two pieces to fit one side of each half. Coat fish well with melted butter; lay on foil and press foil smoothly to fit fish. Lay whole fish, foil side down, in shallow, well-greased baking pan large enough to contain fish (tail may turn up, if necessary). Or lay fish halves, foil side down, on two well-greased overlapping rimless cooky sheets.

If desired, insert a thermometer into fish in thickest portion (next to, but not touching, dorsal fin). If cooking fish halves, you need only one thermometer, inserted in thickest half.

Bake, uncovered, until fish flakes readily when prodded in thickest portion with a fork or until thermometer registers 120°. For a 3-inch-thick fish (measured in thickest portion after stuffing), allow at least 30 minutes. (Allow same ratio of thickness to time—1 inch: 10 minutes—for fish of all thicknesses.) If, when slit with a small, sharp knife, flesh is still dark or translucent near backbone, continue cooking, cutting a new slit every 5 minutes to check for doneness.

When fish is done, remove pan or cooky sheets from oven. Hold a warm serving platter near fish. Slide wide metal spatulas under foil at each end of fish and lift carefully onto platter. Arrange halves on platter to resemble whole fish.

Serve immediately, cutting directly to bone, crosswise, then sliding wide metal spatula between meat and ribs and lifting off each serving. Spoon out some of the stuffing, if used, to accompany each serving. When top half has been served, lift and remove backbone (sever from head, if necessary) and cut down to skin to serve bottom half (be careful not to catch foil). A 4-pound fish makes 6 to 8 servings.

BARBECUING

When you barbecue fish, the tantalizing aroma of sizzling fish and smoky charcoal is all you need as an appetizer. Fish is delicious just butter-basted on the barbecue, but we've also included lots of flavor ideas in the form of bastes and marinades to dress up your fish.

Moderately fat and full-flavored fish, such as salmon, trout, mackerel, and bluefish, are recommended for the barbecue because the smoke enhances their flavor; smoke might overpower a delicately flavored fish, such as sole (see charts on pages 8-11).

Following, you'll find directions for barbecuing serving-size fillets, steaks, and small whole fish, and sections on how to make fish skewers (called "kebabs") and how to handle a large whole fish or large fillet on

the grill. (Before you begin barbecuing, be sure to read manufacturer's directions carefully, as your barbecue may require a slight adaptation of the following general directions.)

HOW TO BARBECUE FILLETS & STEAKS

If your fillets and steaks are ¾ inch thick or thicker, they can cook directly on the greased grill of your barbecue, as can small whole fish. But thinner fish pieces will be easier to handle and turn if held inside a hinged wire broiler. Every form or variety of fish must be brushed with a butter-baste or a marinade while barbecuing, to prevent it from drying out.

> **Fish fillets or steaks, or small whole fish (up to 1½ inches thick), cleaned and scaled**
> **Baste or marinade (suggestions follow)**
> **Salt and pepper**
> **Lemon wedges (optional)**

About 30 to 45 minutes before you plan to begin cooking, ignite coals (for 1½ to 2½ lb. fish you will need about 20 to 30 long-burning briquets).

Wipe fish with damp cloth. Cut into serving-size pieces (about 3 by 5 inches), if desired. Refrigerate until ready to cook, or, if using marinade, prepare marinade (directions follow) and pour over fish; cover and chill for at least 30 minutes (some marinades require up to 2 hours).

When coals are covered with gray ash, arrange in a single, solid layer to underlie entire area to be used on grill. Knock ash off coals and let burn down until moderately hot (about 5 to 10 minutes longer). Adjust grill height to 4 to 6 inches above coals.

Remove fish from refrigerator. If marinated, remove fish from marinade and reserve marinade for use as baste. If using a plain baste, prepare baste; have ready near barbecue.

Grease grill. Arrange as many fish pieces on grill as will fit over coals without crowding (if pieces are less than ¾ inch thick, arrange them in a hinged wire broiler and place on grill). Generously brush with baste or marinade. Continue grilling, basting frequently and turning once to brown evenly, until fish is browned and flakes readily when prodded in thickest portion with a fork. For a 1-inch-thick piece of fish, measured in thickest portion, allow about 10 minutes total—5 minutes on each side. (Allow same ratio of thickness to time—1 inch: 10 minutes—for fish of all thicknesses).

Note: Length of cooking time can be affected by varying barbecuing conditions such as heat of coals or temperature of air.

When done, transfer cooked fish to warm serving platter. Keep warm if more fish will be cooked; if not, add salt and pepper to taste and serve immediately, garnished with lemon wedges, if desired.

Bastes and marinades. Bastes and marinades keep fish moist as it grills on the barbecue, and they also help to season the fish. Bastes will impart a mild flavor; marinades, a stronger one. If using a marinade, you

can vary the intensity of flavoring by varying the length of time the fish remains in the marinade. All of the following recipes are adapted to 4 to 6 servings of fish (1½ to 2½ lb. fish pieces).

Seasoned butter-baste. For the simplest baste, use ¼ cup melted butter or margarine. Other possibilities are: ¼ cup melted butter combined with ¼ cup lemon juice or dry sherry or dry vermouth, and, if desired, ¼ teaspoon dry rosemary and ¼ teaspoon thyme leaves, or ½ teaspoon tarragon leaves. If you have rosemary growing in your garden, you might like to cut a few sprigs and tie them together to make an aromatic basting brush.

All-purpose barbecue marinade. Combine ¼ cup salad oil, ¼ cup bourbon or dry sherry, 2 tablespoons soy sauce, 1 teaspoon Worcestershire, 1 teaspoon garlic powder, and ⅛ teaspoon pepper. For a mild flavor, use marinade just as a basting sauce; for a stronger seasoning, pour it over fish, cover, and chill from 30 minutes to 2 hours, turning fish occasionally to marinate all sides.

Teriyaki marinade. In a bowl, stir together ½ cup soy sauce, 1 tablespoon sugar, 2 teaspoons minced fresh ginger root or ½ teaspoon ground ginger, 2 teaspoons lemon juice, 1 clove garlic (minced or pressed), and 2 tablespoons dry sherry or sake. Add fish pieces to marinade; turn to coat all sides. Cover and chill 30 minutes, turning fish in marinade occasionally to marinate all sides.

Italian-style marinade. Combine ¾ cup olive oil or salad oil, ¼ cup white wine vinegar, 1 clove garlic (minced or pressed), and ¼ teaspoon oregano leaves. Pour over fish; cover and chill 30 minutes, turning fish occasionally to marinate all sides.

Herb-wine marinade. In a pan, combine 1 cup dry white wine, ¼ cup lemon juice, 2 tablespoons white wine vinegar, 2 cloves garlic (minced or pressed), 1 teaspoon salt, 1 teaspoon tarragon leaves or dry rosemary, and 2 tablespoons melted butter or margarine or salad oil. Heat just to a simmer; remove from heat. Cover and let stand for 1 hour to allow flavors to blend. Pour over fish; cover and chill 30 minutes to 1 hour, turning fish occasionally to marinate all sides.

FISH KEBABS ON THE BARBECUE

To make fish kebabs, we recommend that you use a firm, meaty-textured fish (see buying guide charts on pages 8-11), so that when cubed and cooked, the fish will not flake off the skewers. Ignite about 30 to 40 long-burning briquets. Wipe 1½ to 2½ pounds fish with a damp cloth and cut fish into 1-inch cubes. Refrigerate until ready to use or marinate as directed in "Bastes and marinades," using any of the marinades.

When coals are covered with gray ash, remove fish cubes from marinade (if used). Thread cubes on skewers, alternating fish with your choice of at least two of the following vegetables, if desired (quantities of vegetables, along with fish, make 4 to 6 servings): 1 large onion, cut in 1-inch cubes; 2 medium-size green peppers, seeded and cut in 1-inch squares; 1 basket cherry tomatoes; 2 small zucchini, cut crosswise in 1-inch-thick slices; or 1 dozen tiny, cooked new potatoes (about 1 to 2 inches in diameter). Barbecue kebabs as you would other fish (see directions that precede), basting with reserved marinade or with a baste (suggestions precede).

BARBECUING A LARGE WHOLE FISH
(Barbecued whole salmon pictured on page 59)

Large whole fish—such as salmon, rockfish, mackerel, sea trout, striped bass, or one of the larger fresh-water trout—can be delicious when barbecued, but because of their size and weight, they require special handling. The following directions can be used for any fish weighing 3 to 8 pounds. You'll find directions, too, for handling a large fish fillet, such as that of a butterflied salmon, on the barbecue.

Whole fish (3 to 8 lb.), cleaned and scaled, with head removed, if desired
Salt and pepper
1 **lemon, sliced**
1 **small onion, sliced**
Parsley

Ignite coals about 45 minutes before you plan to begin cooking. You will need about 25 to 50 long-burning briquets, depending on length of fish.

Wipe fish with damp cloth, inside body cavity and out. Sprinkle salt and pepper inside cavity; tuck in lemon and onion slices and several sprigs of parsley.

Cut one piece of heavy-duty foil which, when doubled, will fit exactly against one side of fish from head to tail to provide two layers of protection and support. Fold foil and press smoothly to fish.

When coals are completely covered with gray ash, divide them in half and arrange one half in a long row, two briquets wide and the length of the fish. Arrange remaining briquets in same manner, parallel to first row, but leaving an empty channel the width of the fish

When coals are covered with gray ash, arrange in a single, solid layer, and adjust grill height to 6 inches above coals. When coals are moderately hot, lay fish on grill, foil side down; baste (see suggestions in "Bastes and marinades," page 16). Cover barbecue with lid or heavy-duty foil as directed for whole fish (preceding). Cook without turning, about 20 minutes, lifting lid or foil to baste occasionally. Fish is done if it flakes readily when prodded in thickest portion with a fork. To serve, cut down to skin and lift off fish with a wide spatula.

...Barbecuing (cont'd.)

down center of barbecue. This will allow fish to receive indirect heat from coals, rather than direct heat, which could burn fish on the bottom before it cooks on top. Adjust grill height to 6 inches above coals.

When coals are moderately hot, place fish, foil side down, on center of grill, between rows of coals. Arrange a wad of foil under tail to support it and protect it slightly from heat. If desired, insert a thermometer into fish in thickest portion (not touching dorsal fin).

If you have a covered barbecue, place lid over barbecue and adjust dampers to maintain high heat according to manufacturer's directions. If your barbecue is uncovered, tear off enough heavy-duty aluminum foil to cover grill *completely*, and tuck foil over edges of barbecue to seal in heat and smoke.

Allow 10 minutes cooking time per 1-inch thickness of fish, measured in thickest portion. (*Note:* Length of cooking time can be affected by varying barbecuing conditions such as heat of coals or temperature of air.) At the end of that time (30 minutes for a 3-inch-thick fish, for example), lift cover or foil and test for doneness. Thermometer should register about 120°. Cut a narrow slit in thickest portion of fish with a sharp knife; when done, flesh will be firmer and less translucent than when raw. If flesh is still dark or translucent near backbone, re-cover barbecue and continue cooking, checking for doneness every 5 minutes (cut a new slit).

When fish is done, hold a warm serving platter close to fish on barbecue. Slide a wide metal spatula carefully under foil-lined fish and ease onto platter (if one person holds platter and another uses two spatulas to move fish, the job is easier).

To serve, lift off top layer of skin, if you wish. Cut directly to bone, slide a wide spatula between flesh and ribs, and lift off each serving. When top half has been served, lift and remove backbone (sever from head, if necessary) and cut down to skin to serve remaining half (be careful not to catch foil lining when you serve).

BARBECUING A LARGE FILLET

To barbecue a large fish fillet (3 to 5 lb.), light 20 to 35 long-burning briquets. Wipe fish with damp cloth. Leave skin on fillet and line skin side of fillet with heavy-duty foil; press smoothly to fit.

BROILING
(Broiled halibut steaks pictured on page 35)

A platter of fish grilled briefly under the broiler is simplicity itself. It's a quick, nongreasy method of cookery (the only fat involved is a brush-on baste) that's often done without even coating the fish. The fish develops its own rich flavor under the intense heat, but if you like, it can be well complemented by a lemon, wine, or teriyaki baste or a crunchy coating of cornmeal or nuts.

HOW TO BROIL

Thick fish pieces seem to fare better under a broiler than very thin ones (¼ inch or less), particularly if no coating is used. A thicker piece of fish has plenty of time to develop a golden surface before the inside is cooked, but the high heat penetrates and cooks a thin, uncoated piece too fast for browning to occur. However, any fish fillet or steak or any small whole fish can be cooked by this method; just make sure that you baste a leaner fish with plenty of butter or oil to keep it from drying out.

> **Fish fillets or steaks, or small whole fish (up to 1½ inches thick), cleaned and scaled**
> **Baste or marinade (suggestions follow)**
> **Coating (optional—suggestions follow)**
> **Salt and pepper**
> **Lemon wedges (optional)**

Wipe fish with damp cloth. Cut into serving-size pieces (about 3 by 5 inches), if desired. Cover with marinade, if you wish, and chill for at least 30 minutes (some marinades may require up to 2 hours).

Turn on broiler and preheat broiler pan. Coat fish, if desired and if marinade is not used. Prepare baste if marinade is not used. (If coating is used, just baste with melted butter.)

Remove pan from broiler; grease lightly. Arrange as many fish pieces on pan as will fit without crowding. Brush with baste or marinade (if coating is used, drizzle with baste instead of brushing).

Return pan to broiler. (Adjust pan to proper distance from heat source: 2 inches for pieces up to ¼ inch thick; 3 inches for pieces up to ¾ inch thick; 4 inches for pieces up to 1½ inches thick; 6 inches for thicker pieces. If nut coating is used, place 1 or 2 extra inches from heat source to prevent burning.) Broil, basting once or twice, until lightly browned and fish flakes readily when prodded in thickest portion with a fork (pieces thicker than ¼ inch will need to be turned once to brown evenly). For a 1-inch-thick piece of fish (measured in thickest portion), allow 10 minutes total—5 minutes on each side. (Allow same ratio of thickness to time—1 inch:10 minutes—for fish of all thicknesses.)

When done, transfer cooked fish to warm serving platter. Keep warm if more fish will be cooked; if not, add salt and pepper to taste and serve immediately, garnished with lemon wedges, if desired.

Bastes and marinades. To make the simplest baste for 4 to 6 servings of fish (1½ to 2½ lb. fish pieces), melt ¼ cup butter or margarine, or use ¼ cup salad oil or olive oil. For a seasoned baste, combine ¼ cup melted butter and ¼ cup lemon juice, dry sherry, or dry vermouth. Marinades given under "Barbecuing" (see page 17) are excellent for use in broiling. Try the teriyaki marinade or one of the herbed ones.

Coatings. For 4 to 6 servings of fish (1½ to 2½ lb. fish pieces), have ready 1 cup yellow cornmeal, wheat germ, or finely minced or ground almonds (to grind nuts, whirl ¾ cup nut meats, about half at a time, in blender until finely ground). Spread coating on a shallow pan or piece of wax paper. Rub salad oil or olive oil, or melted butter or margarine all over fish pieces. Coat pieces in cornmeal, wheat germ, or nuts; shake off excess.

DISHES TO SUIT ANY FISH: BROILING

Once you are acquainted with broiling, try the following all-purpose broiling recipe with your next fish. The recipe—selected from among our favorites because it will accommodate any variety of fish, easily and flavorfully—includes the information you need to adapt it to your fish.

Broiled Fish in Yogurt Curry

Curry-laden butter is both a base for the sauce and a baste for the fish in this Indian-inspired dish. The sauce is finished with yogurt while the fish broils; then they're served together with an assortment of typical condiments.

> ½ cup (¼ lb.) butter or margarine
> 1 cup *each* finely chopped onion and green pepper
> 2 tablespoons curry powder
> ½ teaspoon ground ginger
> 2 tablespoons firmly packed brown sugar
> 3 tablespoons lemon juice
> 2 tablespoons water
> ¼ teaspoon liquid hot pepper seasoning
> 2 pounds fish fillets or steaks
> 1 cup (8 oz.) unflavored yogurt
> 6 thin lemon slices
> 3 eggs, hard-cooked and coarsely chopped
> ⅔ cup *each* raisins, chopped cashews, and Major Grey's chutney
> 1 cucumber, peeled and coarsely chopped

In a wide frying pan, melt butter over medium heat and cook onion, green pepper, curry powder, and ginger until onion is soft and golden (about 15 minutes). Stir in brown sugar, lemon juice, water, and hot pepper seasoning; then remove from heat.

Turn on broiler and preheat broiler pan. Wipe fish with damp cloth; cut into serving-size pieces (3 by 5 inches), if desired. Push vegetables to one side of frying pan and dip each fish piece in curry butter, turning to coat all sides. Arrange fish in single layer on wax paper within reaching distance of range.

Remove pan from broiler. Arrange as many fish pieces on pan as will fit without crowding.

Return pan to broiler (adjust pan to proper distance from heat source: 2 inches for pieces up to ¼ inch thick; 3 inches for pieces up to ¾ inch thick; 4 inches for pieces up to 1½ inches thick; 6 inches for thicker pieces). Broil until fish flakes readily when prodded in thickest portion with a fork (pieces thicker than ¼ inch will need to be turned once to brown evenly). For a 1-inch-thick piece of fish (measured in thickest portion), allow 10 minutes total—5 minutes on each side. (Allow same ratio of thickness to time—1 inch:10 minutes—for fish of all thicknesses.)

When done, transfer the cooked fish pieces to a warm serving platter. Keep the fish warm while the remaining pieces cook.

Meanwhile, stir yogurt into curry butter and vegetables; cook, stirring, over low heat until hot; do not boil.

Arrange fish on serving platter and garnish with lemon slices. Place eggs, raisins, cashews, chutney, and cucumber in individual serving bowls and arrange on a tray. Offer hot yogurt curry sauce in bowl to spoon over fish; pass condiments to sprinkle on top. Makes 4 to 6 servings.

THE SECRET IS THE SAUCE

How do you transform a simply cooked fish into the highlight of a special dinner? The secret is the sauce you choose to dress it in! Whip up a delectable hollandaise to slather over poached salmon, or nestle broiled sea bass in a Portuguese tomato sauce. Add a vigorous note to a platter of seafoods with a thick, garlicky Provençale sauce, or serve barbecued swordfish with herb-scented, homemade mayonnaise. All these sauces and more, both hot and cold, appear here—mix and match them to suit your taste, with fish cooked by any of the "Basic Methods" on pages 14-31, and you'll have a whole repertoire of irresistible dishes at your command.

Hollandaise Sauce

3 egg yolks
1 tablespoon lemon juice
1 teaspoon Dijon mustard
1 cup (½ lb.) butter or
   margarine, melted

In top of a double boiler, combine egg yolks, lemon juice, and mustard; beat until well blended with portable electric mixer or a wire whip.

Place pan over gently simmering water (water should not boil or touch bottom of pan) and, beating rapidly and constantly, gradually add butter, mixing in just a few drops at a time at first, then increasing to a slow, steady stream (about 1/16 inch wide).

After all butter is added, continue to cook, beating constantly, until sauce is thick enough to hold shape briefly when dropped from beater. Remove at once from heat and serve with hot or cold fish or shellfish. If made ahead, you can let stand at room temperature for as long as several hours, or cover and chill up to 1 week; in either case, rewarm to serving temperature.

To warm hollandaise to serving temperature, stir with wire whip over hot (not boiling) water until warm to touch (5 to 10 minutes). Makes 1⅓ cups.

Blender hollandaise sauce. In a blender, combine egg yolks, mustard,

and lemon juice. Cover and whirl until well blended. Turn blender on high speed and add butter, mixing in just a few drops at a time at first, then increasing to a slow, steady stream (about 1/16 inch wide). After all butter has been added, making sauce thick and opaque, continue to whirl just until well blended (if whirled too long, sauce may break). Serve at once with hot or cold fish or shellfish. If made ahead, you can let stand at room temperature for as long as several hours, or cover and chill up to 1 week; in either case, rewarm to serving temperature (directions precede).

Lemon Butter Mayonnaise

½ cup (¼ lb.) butter or
   margarine
3 egg yolks
2 tablespoons lemon juice
1 tablespoon white wine vinegar
2 teaspoons Dijon mustard
1 teaspoon grated lemon peel
¾ teaspoon sugar
½ teaspoon salt
½ cup salad oil

In a small pan over medium heat, melt butter. Remove from heat; let cool to lukewarm.

In a blender, combine egg yolks, lemon juice, wine vinegar, mustard, lemon peel, sugar, and salt. Cover and whirl at high speed until blended. Combine lukewarm butter with oil and, with blender on high speed, add oil mixture in a slow, steady stream (about 1/16 inch wide) until all mixture has been incorporated.

As sauce thickens and oil mixture becomes hard to incorporate, turn blender off frequently; blend in oil mixture briefly with a rubber spatula and turn blender on again. Continue until all oil mixture is incorporated. Serve immediately with hot or cold fish or shellfish. (Sauce can stand at room temperature for several hours, if necessary, before serving; do not chill, or sauce will become hard.) Makes 1 cup.

Aioli

4 large cloves (or 6 to 8 medium
   cloves) garlic, minced or
   pressed
1½ tablespoons lemon juice
½ teaspoon salt
3 egg yolks
½ cup *each* salad oil and olive oil
   Water

In a blender, combine garlic, lemon juice, salt, and egg yolks. Cover and whirl for about 1 minute or until mixture is smooth. Continuing to blend at high speed, combine salad and olive oil and add to egg mixture, just a few drops at a time at first; then when mixture thickens, increase oil to a slow, steady stream (about 1/16 inch wide—oil should never be added so quickly that it collects in puddles).

When sauce becomes so thick that oil is hard to incorporate (usually after you've added about ½ the oil), blend in 1 or 2 tablespoons water; then add remaining oil slowly. (If sauce ceases to take up oil, shut off blender, stir sauce, adding a little more oil or a little more water, and blend again; repeat as necessary until all oil is incorporated.)

Chill sauce, covered, for at least 3 to 4 hours to mellow flavors; it keeps for about 4 days, after which garlic flavor deteriorates. Serve with hot or cold fish or shellfish. Makes 1¾ cups.

Simple Cucumber Sauce

3 large cucumbers
2 teaspoons salt
1 cup sour cream or unflavored
   yogurt
1 cup mayonnaise
1 tablespoon dill weed

Peel cucumbers; cut in half lengthwise. With a metal spoon, scrape out and discard seeds. Chop cucumbers finely; place in bowl and sprinkle evenly with salt. Chill for at least 2 hours; drain well. Mix thoroughly with sour cream, mayonnaise, and dill weed. Cover and chill well; serve over cold fish. Makes 3 to 4 cups.

Brown Butter Almond Sauce

½ cup slivered almonds
1 cup (½ lb.) butter or margarine
2 egg yolks
1 tablespoon lemon juice
½ teaspoon dry mustard
Dash of cayenne
1 tablespoon dry sherry
Hot water

Place almonds in shallow baking pan; bake in a 350° oven, shaking occasionally, for 10 minutes or until lightly browned. Remove from oven and let cool.

In a small pan over medium heat, melt butter and cook, swirling, until it foams and then turns a golden brown; remove from heat immediately and cool to lukewarm. In a blender, combine egg yolks, lemon juice, mustard, and cayenne. Cover and whirl at high speed until blended. Continuing to blend at high speed, add butter just a few drops at a time at first; then as mixture begins to thicken, increase butter to a slow, steady stream (about 1/16 inch wide) until all butter has been incorporated.

Stir in sherry and 1 tablespoon hot water; then stir in toasted almonds. If mixture becomes too stiff, add a little more hot water. Serve immediately with hot or cold fish or shellfish. (Sauce can stand at room temperature for several hours, if necessary, before serving; do not chill, or sauce will become hard.) Makes about 2 cups.

Portuguese Tomato Sauce

¼ cup butter or margarine
1 medium-size onion, chopped
1 clove garlic, minced or pressed
½ teaspoon thyme leaves
¼ teaspoon dry rosemary, crushed
1 can (1 lb.) stewed tomatoes
Salt and pepper

In a frying pan, melt butter over medium-high heat; add onion and sauté, stirring occasionally, until soft. Stir in garlic, thyme, rosemary, and tomatoes (break tomatoes up with a spoon). Simmer, uncovered, stirring occasionally, until reduced by half (about 15 minutes). Add salt and pepper to taste.

Serve hot over hot fish—this sauce is best suited for fish having assertive flavor and/or firm, meatlike texture (see buying guide charts on pages 8-11). Makes about 2½ cups.

Herbed Mayonnaise or Rémoulade Sauce

2 egg yolks
2 tablespoons *each* lemon juice and chopped parsley
1 tablespoon chopped chives (fresh, frozen, or freeze-dried)
1 teaspoon *each* dry mustard, salt, thyme leaves, and tarragon leaves
Dash of cayenne
1 cup salad oil or olive oil
Hot water

In a blender, combine egg yolks, lemon juice, parsley, chives, mustard, salt, thyme, tarragon, and cayenne. Cover and whirl at high speed until blended. Continuing to blend at high speed, add oil, just a few drops at a time at first; then, as mixture begins to thicken, increase oil to a slow, steady stream (about 1/16 inch wide), until all oil has been incorporated. Beat in enough water until sauce is consistency you like. Serve with hot or cold fish or shellfish. Makes 1½ cups.

Rémoulade sauce. Prepare Herbed Mayonnaise, omitting chives, salt, and thyme and adding 1 teaspoon anchovy paste and ½ teaspoon dry chervil to egg mixture before adding oil. After all oil has been incorporated (omit water), stir in ¼ cup finely chopped dill pickle, 1 tablespoon drained chopped capers, and 2 chopped hard-cooked eggs. Serve with hot or cold fish or shellfish.

Shellfish Cocktail Sauce

½ cup catsup
¼ cup *each* tomato-based chili sauce and grapefruit juice
2 tablespoons lemon juice
1 tablespoon thinly sliced green onion (including some tops)
1 teaspoon *each* prepared horseradish and Worcestershire
2 or 3 drops liquid hot pepper seasoning
1½ pounds cold, cooked, shelled shellfish
Thinly sliced green onions (including some tops—optional)

Combine catsup, chili sauce, grapefruit juice, lemon juice, onion, horseradish, Worcestershire, and hot pepper seasoning. Makes about 1 cup.

To serve cold, cover and chill sauce for several hours to blend flavors. Pour into serving bowl and serve as a dip, accompanied by shellfish. Or combine shellfish with sauce and serve in small bowls, garnished with green onion.

To serve hot, combine ingredients in a small pan and bring to simmering; add shellfish to sauce and simmer just until heated through. Serve immediately in small individual serving bowls, garnished with green onion slices. Makes 8 appetizer servings.

Quick Tartare Sauce

½ cup mayonnaise (or ¼ cup *each* mayonnaise and sour cream)
¼ cup sweet pickle relish, well drained
1 teaspoon instant minced onion
¼ teaspoon Worcestershire
4 drops liquid hot pepper seasoning
½ teaspoon lemon juice

Combine mayonnaise, pickle relish, onion, Worcestershire, hot pepper seasoning, and lemon juice; mix well. Cover and chill for at least 30 minutes to blend flavors. Serve with hot or cold fish. Makes about ¾ cup.

BUTTER-SAUTÉING

In French cuisine, there is a quick and easy method of cooking fish that has elegantly appealing results—crisply golden pieces of fish with meltingly tender flesh. The French call it *à la meunière;* our word for it is *butter-sautéing.* Steaks, fillets, even small whole fish such as trout, smelt, or butterfish go into a pan of foaming hot butter to be quickly sautéed to doneness.

Served in the classical manner, the butter-sautéed fish are arranged on a platter and garnished only with a little chopped parsley and some lemon wedges to squeeze over. For a more elaborate presentation, serve the fish with one of the garnishes on page 26 and 29, or with a creamy mustard pan sauce, as in the recipe "Fish with Mustard Sauce" under the section on "Pan-frying" on page 26.

HOW TO BUTTER-SAUTÉ

The term suggests that butter-sautéing takes place over high heat, but this is true only for thin fish pieces (no more than ⅝ inch thick) that must brown quickly before they cook through. Thicker pieces should be done over medium heat, allowing time for the heat to penetrate the interior of the fish before burning the surface.

Whatever thickness of fish you cook, you will need a frying pan that distributes heat evenly.

Though butter is the preferred fat for reasons of flavor, it burns easily at the temperatures required for butter-sautéing. To avoid burning but retain the buttery flavor, we recommend using a combination of half butter and half salad oil.

> **Fish fillets or steaks, or small whole fish (up to 1½ inches thick), cleaned and scaled**
> **All-purpose flour**
> **Half butter or margarine and half salad oil**
> **Salt and pepper**
> **Chopped parsley and lemon wedges**

Wipe fish with damp cloth. Cut into serving-size pieces (about 3 by 5 inches), if desired. Coat fish with flour; shake off excess. Arrange in a single layer on wax paper within reaching distance of range.

In a wide frying pan, heat butter and oil (about ⅛ inch deep) until it foams but doesn't brown. Promptly add as many of the fish pieces as will fit without crowding. Cook until lightly browned—over medium-high heat if pieces are ⅝ inch thick or less; over medium heat if pieces are thicker than ⅝ inch.

Turn each piece carefully with a wide spatula to brown other side. For a 1-inch-thick piece of fish (measured in thickest portion), allow 10 minutes total—5 minutes on each side, turning only once. (Allow same ratio of thickness to time—1 inch:10 minutes—for fish of all thicknesses.) Fish is cooked if it flakes readily when prodded in the thickest portion with a fork. Remove each piece as it is done; arrange on a warm serving platter and keep warm until all fish is cooked.

Salt and pepper to taste. Serve immediately, sprinkled with chopped parsley and garnished with lemon wedges.

DEEP-FRYING

(Deep-fried fish and chips pictured on page 38)

From familiar golden puffs of British "fish 'n' chips" to ethereally lacy morsels of Japanese fish tempura, deep-fried fish is a favorite the world over. The deep-frying process may be a bit messy, but it produces a thicker, crustier coating than any other technique for frying fish.

HOW TO DEEP-FRY

This method of cooking can be done in a deep-fryer, a large pan, a deep frying pan, or a wok (because of its round bottom, the wok requires less oil for deep-frying than the other utensils). You will also need a deep-frying thermometer to help you achieve the best temperature for browning with the least fat absorption. To deep-fry, you can start with any form of fish—fillets, steaks, small or large whole fish.

> **Garnish or sauce (optional—suggestions follow)**
> **Salad oil**
> **Fish fillets or steaks, or small or large whole fish, cleaned and scaled**
> **Coating (suggestions follow)**
> **Salt and pepper**

Prepare garnish or sauce, if desired, before you begin to cook fish; set aside.

In a pan (see suggestions above) heat 1½ to 2 inches salad oil (pan should not be more than half full) to 375° on a deep-frying thermometer.

Meanwhile, wipe fish with damp cloth. Cut into serving-size pieces (about ½ to ¾ inch thick, 3 inches wide, and 5 inches long; for tempura, cut into strips 1½ inches wide, 3 inches long, and ¼ inch thick). Prepare coating (directions follow).

When oil has reached 375°, coat pieces of fish, one at a time, and gently lower into hot fat. Cook several pieces at a time, but be careful not to add too much fish at once—to do so lowers temperature of oil, and fish will not brown properly on outside before cooking through; also, if temperature is too low, fish absorbs too much oil and becomes greasy.

Cook fish pieces, turning occasionally, until they are golden brown (for tempura, just lightly browned—about 2 or 3 minutes) and flake readily when prodded in thickest portion with a fork. (Frequently skim off and discard any bits of batter from oil.) Remove fish with slotted spoon, tongs, or chopsticks, and drain briefly. Keep warm until all fish is cooked. Or, if you prefer, serve immediately, accompanied with garnish or sauce, if desired, and then repeat process with more fish, cooking and serving until all fish is cooked (tempura is best when served immediately).

Coating. Included here are three quite different coatings for deep-fried fish: a basic crumb coating, a puffy beer batter, and a light Japanese tempura batter. Any of these can be used on any kind of fish; each recipe makes enough to coat 4 to 6 servings of fish (1½ to 2½ lb. fish pieces).

Basic crumb coating. In a shallow pan, combine 2 eggs and 2 tablespoons milk; beat slightly. Have ready about 1 cup fine dry bread crumbs, cracker crumbs, or wheat germ; spread on a shallow pan or piece of wax paper. Dip each piece of fish in egg mixture to coat all over. Drain briefly; then roll in crumbs or wheat germ to coat all sides before adding to hot oil.

Beer batter. In a bowl, combine 1 cup all-purpose flour (unsifted), ½ teaspoon paprika, ¼ teaspoon salt, and ⅛ teaspoon pepper. Gradually stir in ¾ cup beer; beat until smooth. Dip fish in batter and let excess drip off before adding to hot oil.

Tempura batter. In a bowl, combine 1 cup ice-cold water, 1 egg, and ¼ teaspoon *each* soda and salt; beat slightly. Add 1 cup cake flour (unsifted); mix until just blended (batter will be lumpy). Sprinkle ⅓ cup cake flour (unsifted) over top of batter. Stir lightly one or two strokes—*do not* blend thoroughly; most of the flour should be floating on top of batter. Fill a larger bowl half full of ice; set bowl of batter in it to keep batter cold while you dip and cook fish. Dip fish in batter and let excess drip off before adding to hot oil. (For tempura, you can use large raw shrimp, shelled and deveined, as well as fish. To prepare shrimp for cooking, see directions on page 116.)

Garnishes and sauces. Deep-fried fish can be served most simply with just a garnish of lemon wedges and a shaker of salt. Accompany with a bowl of tartare sauce, if you like (see recipe on page 21). For fish coated in beer batter, you might follow the British tradition and provide a bottle of malt vinegar to shake over. Japanese tempura has its own special sauce and garnish (directions follow).

Tempura sauce. In a pan, combine 1 bottle (8 oz.) clam juice, ½ cup soy sauce, and ½ cup sake or dry sherry. Bring to a boil; remove from heat and let cool to room temperature. Serve in small individual dishes. Finely shred enough fresh ginger root and daikon (Japanese radish) or regular radish (squeeze out excess liquid) to make about 3 tablespoons *each*; pass ginger and radish to add to individual bowls of sauce.

OVEN-FRYING

Pop a panful of fish into a superhot oven, and in a very short time the fish toasts to a buttery doneness, golden brown on the outside, moist and tender inside. The high temperature of the oven in oven-frying produces results that are similar to those of pan-frying, but the oven technique is almost foolproof, takes little effort, and yields no spattering of fat.

HOW TO OVEN-FRY

This method works well with any fish fillets or steaks or with small whole fish (though pieces thinner than ½ inch tend to overcook before they brown nicely). They all go into a preheated, butter-coated pan, then into a 500° oven to cook. As in butter-sautéing, the high temperature of oven-frying causes butter to burn easily, so we recommend that you try a combination of half butter and half oil.

> **Fish fillets or steaks, or small whole fish (up to 1½ inches thick), cleaned and scaled**
> **Coating (suggestions follow)**
> **Half butter or margarine and half salad oil**
> **Salt and pepper**
> **Chopped parsley and lemon wedges (optional)**

Preheat oven to 500°. Wipe fish with damp cloth. Cut into serving-size pieces (3 by 5 inches), if desired.

Put a large, shallow baking pan in oven to preheat. Meanwhile, coat fish (directions follow); arrange in a single layer on wax paper within reaching distance of range.

Remove pan from oven. Put butter and oil in pan and swirl until butter is melted (fat should be about ⅛ inch deep).

Lay a piece of fish in pan; turn to coat with melted butter. Repeat with rest of fish, arranging as many pieces in pan as will fit without crowding.

(Continued on next page)

Return pan to oven and bake, uncovered, until fish is browned and flakes readily when prodded in thickest portion with a fork (pieces thinner than ¼ inch may have to be turned once to brown evenly). For a 1-inch-thick piece of fish (measured in thickest portion), allow 10 minutes total—5 minutes on each side. (Allow same ratio of thickness to time—1 inch:10 minutes—for fish of all thicknesses.)

When done, transfer cooked fish to warm serving platter. Keep warm if more fish is to be cooked; if not, add salt and pepper to taste and serve immediately, sprinkled with chopped parsley and garnished with lemon wedges, if desired.

Coatings. For oven-fried fish, you can choose from a variety of coatings, ranging from simple and light to more substantial and elaborate. Any of the following can be used on any kind of fish; each recipe makes enough to coat 4 to 6 servings of fish (1½ to 2½ lb. fish pieces).

Basic crumb coating. In a shallow pan, combine 2 eggs and 2 tablespoons milk; beat slightly. Have ready about 1 cup fine dry bread crumbs, cracker crumbs, or wheat germ. Or try one of the following combinations: ½ cup all-purpose flour (unsifted) mixed with ½ cup yellow cornmeal; or ½ cup fine dry bread crumbs mixed with ½ cup finely shredded Swiss, Gruyère, or Parmesan cheese; or ⅓ cup fine dry bread crumbs mixed with ⅔ cup finely minced or ground walnuts, ¼ teaspoon black pepper, and ¼ teaspoon ground allspice. (To grind nuts, whirl ½ cup nut meats in blender until finely ground.) Spread crumbs or crumb mixture on a shallow pan or piece of wax paper.

Dip each piece of fish in egg mixture to coat all over. Drain briefly; then roll in crumbs to coat all sides.

Green onion coating. Coat fish with all-purpose flour; shake off excess. Have ready ½ cup thinly sliced green onion (include some tops). You can use olive oil instead of butter to coat baking pan; when fish is arranged in pan, sprinkle evenly with green onion.

Sesame seed coating. Sprinkle fish with paprika and coat with all-purpose flour; shake off excess. When fish is arranged in baking pan, sprinkle each serving of fish evenly with about 2 tablespoons sesame seed.

Filbert crust coating. Have ready about ½ cup sour cream and 1 cup finely minced or ground filberts (to grind nuts, whirl ¾ cup nut meats, about half at a time, in blender until finely ground). Spread nuts on a shallow pan or piece of wax paper.

Spread one side of a fish piece with sour cream; lay carefully in nuts. Spread other side with sour cream and turn to coat in nuts. Repeat with remaining pieces. Follow directions in "How to oven-fry," but when laying fish pieces in baking pan, don't turn to coat second side with butter. Instead, drizzle a little melted butter over tops of pieces.

DISHES TO SUIT ANY FISH: OVEN-FRYING

Once you are acquainted with oven-frying, try one of the following all-purpose oven-frying recipes with your next fish. The recipes were selected from among our favorites because they will accommodate any variety of fish, easily and flavorfully. Each recipe includes the information you need to adapt it to your fish.

Fish Oven-fried in Sour Cream

For a cook in a hurry, nothing could be more convenient than a dish that goes together in less than half an hour. You can do it with this easily assembled dish: chunks of fish oven-fried under a rich coating of Parmesan-topped sour cream and chives.

> 2 **pounds fish fillets or steaks (***each* **about ¾ to 1 inch thick)**
>   **Salt and pepper**
> ¾ **cup sour cream**
> ¼ **cup fine dry bread crumbs**
> ¼ **teaspoon garlic salt**
> 1½ **tablespoons fresh, frozen, or freeze-dried chopped chives**
> ⅓ **cup grated Parmesan cheese**
> 1 **teaspoon paprika**
>   **Chopped parsley and lemon wedges (optional)**

Preheat oven to 400°. Put a large, shallow baking pan in oven to preheat. Wipe fish with damp cloth; cut into serving-size pieces (about 3 by 5 inches), if desired. Remove pan from oven, grease it, and arrange fish pieces in single layer, without crowding. Sprinkle lightly with salt and pepper.

In a bowl, mix together sour cream, bread crumbs, garlic salt, and chives. Spread mixture evenly over fish; sprinkle evenly with Parmesan and paprika.

Bake, uncovered, until fish flakes readily when prodded in thickest portion with a fork. For a 1-inch-thick piece of fish (measured in thickest portion), allow 10 minutes. (Allow same ratio of thickness to time—1 inch: 10 minutes—for fish of all thicknesses.)

Serve immediately, garnished with chopped parsley and lemon wedges, if desired. Makes 4 to 6 servings.

PAN-FRYING

If the thought of fish conjures up a big pan of them sizzling over a glowing campfire, you are already familiar with one form of pan-frying. But pan-frying is an equally convenient method of cooking fish right on the range in your kitchen, and it has a varied flavor potential, depending on your choice of coating, fat, and seasonings.

A pan-fried fish is any fish that has been given a coating and has then been cooked in a small amount of fat, in a wide pan on top of the range. (Deep-frying has different results; for directions, see page 22.)

HOW TO PAN-FRY

You can fry any fish fillets or steaks, or any small whole fish using this method. The results will be most successful if you have a frying pan that distributes the heat evenly. Though the simplest pan-fried fish is delicious, you can vary the dish by trying some of the seasoning and coating suggestions that follow the basic instructions. If you like, you can add a special garnish, too (directions follow). Garnishes, sautéed in the pan before the fish is cooked, can be an intriguing flavor addition.

> **Garnish (optional—directions follow)**
> **Fish fillets or steaks, or small whole fish (up to 1½ inches thick), cleaned and scaled**
> **Eggs**
> **Milk**
> **Coating (suggestions follow)**
> **Half butter or margarine and half salad oil *or* all salad oil or olive oil**
> **Seasoning liquid (optional—suggestions follow)**
> **Salt and pepper**

Prepare garnish, if you like; set aside.

Wipe fish with damp cloth. Cut into serving-size pieces (about 3 by 5 inches), if desired. For 4 to 6 servings of fish (1½ to 2½ lb. fish pieces), combine 2 eggs and 2 tablespoons milk in a shallow pan; beat slightly. Have ready 1 cup of coating (suggestions follow), spread on a shallow pan or piece of wax paper.

Dip each piece of fish in egg mixture; drain briefly. Then roll in coating to cover all sides evenly; arrange in a single layer on wax paper within reaching distance of range.

In a wide frying pan, heat butter and oil (about ⅛ inch deep) until it foams but doesn't brown (or, if using only oil, heat until it ripples when pan is tilted). Promptly add as many fish pieces as will fit without crowding. Cook until lightly browned—over medium-high heat if pieces are ⅝ inch thick or less; over medium heat if pieces are thicker than ⅝ inch.

Turn each piece carefully with a wide spatula to brown other side. As soon as all fish pieces have been turned, sprinkle seasoning liquid evenly over them, if

Oven-fried Fish with Olive Sauce

While a clove-seasoned tomato sauce simmers on the stove, you sear the fish quickly in a very hot oven. The olives go into the sauce at the last minute.

> 2 tablespoons olive oil
> 1 small onion, chopped
> 1 can (1 lb.) stewed tomatoes
> 2 teaspoons sugar
> ⅛ teaspoon ground cloves
> 2 pounds fish fillets, steaks, or small whole fish (*each* about ½ to 1 inch thick), cleaned and scaled
> Half butter or margarine and half salad oil (about 2 tablespoons each)
> ½ cup pimento-stuffed green olives, sliced
> 1 tablespoon capers, drained
> 1 tablespoon chopped parsley

Preheat oven to 500°. In a large pan, heat olive oil over medium-high heat; add onion and sauté until soft. Add tomatoes, sugar, and cloves. Simmer, uncovered, stirring often, until thickened (about 15 minutes).

Meanwhile, put a large, shallow baking pan in oven to preheat. Wipe fish with damp cloth; cut into serving-size pieces (about 3 by 5 inches), if desired. Remove pan from oven; put butter and oil in pan and swirl until butter is melted.

Lay a piece of fish in pan; turn to coat with melted butter. Repeat with remaining fish, arranging to fit in single layer without crowding.

Return pan to oven and bake, uncovered, until fish is browned and flakes readily when prodded in thickest portion with a fork (pieces thicker than ¼ inch may have to be turned once to brown evenly). For a 1-inch-thick piece of fish (measured in thickest portion), allow 10 minutes total—5 minutes on each side. (Allow same ratio of thickness to time—1 inch: 10 minutes —for fish of all thicknesses.)

When done, transfer cooked fish to warm serving platter and keep warm. Pour any fish juices from pan into sauce. Remove from heat, stir in olives and capers, and spoon sauce over fish. Garnish with parsley. Makes 4 to 6 servings.

...Pan-frying (cont'd.

desired (seasoning liquid is not recommended, though, if a nut or cornmeal coating is used on fish). For a 1-inch-thick piece of fish (measured in thickest portion), allow 10 minutes total—5 minutes on each side, turning only once. (Allow same ratio of thickness to time—1 inch: 10 minutes—for fish of all thicknesses.) Fish is cooked if it flakes readily when prodded in thickest portion with a fork.

Remove each piece as it is done; arrange on a warm serving platter and keep warm until all fish is cooked.

When last fish piece is removed from pan, stir garnish into pan juices, if desired, and heat through. Meanwhile, salt and pepper fish to taste. Spoon garnish over fish and serve immediately.

Coatings. To coat your fish for pan-frying, choose from among the following: fine dry bread crumbs, cracker crumbs, flour, cornmeal, wheat germ, or finely ground walnuts, filberts, or almonds. (To grind nuts, whirl ¾ cup nut meats, about half at a time, in blender until finely ground, to make 1 cup.)

Seasoning liquids. For 4 to 6 servings of fish (1½ to 2½ lb. fish pieces), you can choose one of the following: 2 tablespoons lemon juice; 2 to 3 tablespoons dry white wine or dry vermouth; 2 to 3 tablespoons dry sherry or dry madeira; 2 tablespoons brandy or gin. If using sherry, madeira, brandy, or gin, set aflame by holding a match close to pan edge as soon as liquor is added (be sure pan is *not* beneath a ventilating exhaust or flammable items); shake pan until flame dies.

Garnishes. Almost any butter-sautéed or pan-fried fish can be enhanced by a garnish (though if you plan to use a cornmeal or nut coating on the fish, then garnishes are *not* recommended). For 4 to 6 servings of fish (1½ to 2½ lb. fish pieces), melt ¼ cup butter or margarine in a small pan (or a wide frying pan, if papaya or peaches are used) over medium-low heat. Add one of the following: 1 large onion, thinly sliced; 1 papaya or 2 large peaches, peeled, seeded or pitted, and thickly sliced; ½ to 1 cup thinly sliced mushrooms; ¼ to ½ cup whole pine nuts; ¼ to ½ cup chopped, slivered, or sliced almonds, filberts, cashews, or pecans.

Cook onion, stirring frequently, until golden (15 to 20 minutes); cook fruit, turning occasionally, until heated through (5 to 10 minutes); cook mushrooms until limp and liquid is evaporated (about 15 minutes); cook nuts until lightly browned (about 10 minutes). Remove from heat.

DISHES TO SUIT ANY FISH: PAN-FRYING

Once you are acquainted with pan-frying, try one of the following all-purpose pan-frying recipes with your next fish. The recipes were selected from among our favorites because they will accommodate any variety of fish, easily and flavorfully. Each recipe includes the information you need to adapt it to your fish.

Fish with Mustard Sauce

Pan-fry the fish until golden and then bathe them in a creamy vermouth-laced mustard sauce made in the same pan.

> 2 **pounds fish fillets or steaks**
> **Salt and white pepper**
> **About ¼ cup all-purpose flour, unsifted**
> **Half butter or margarine and half salad oil (about 2 tablespoons each)**
> ¾ **cup dry vermouth**
> ⅛ **teaspoon ground nutmeg**
> 2 **tablespoons Dijon mustard**
> ¾ **cup whipping cream**
> **Chopped parsley (optional)**

Wipe fish with damp cloth. Cut into serving-size pieces (about 3 by 5 inches), if desired. Lightly sprinkle fish with salt and pepper on both sides. Coat with flour; shake off excess. Arrange in a single layer on wax paper within reaching distance of range.

In a wide frying pan, heat butter and oil (about ⅛ inch deep) until it foams but doesn't brown. Promptly add as many fish pieces as will fit without crowding. Cook until lightly browned—over medium-high heat if pieces are ⅝ inch thick or less; over medium heat if pieces are thicker than ⅝ inch. Turn each piece carefully with a wide spatula to brown other side. For a 1-inch-thick piece of fish (measured in thickest portion) allow 10 minutes total—5 minutes on each side, turning only once. (Allow same ratio of thickness to time—1 inch: 10 minutes—for fish of all thicknesses.) Fish is cooked if it flakes readily when prodded in thickest portion with a fork.

Remove cooked fish to a warm serving platter and keep warm; add more butter and oil and cook remaining fish in same manner.

When last fish is removed from pan, remove pan from heat and pour vermouth into pan; stir and scrape to blend with pan drippings. Return pan to medium-high heat and stir in nutmeg, mustard, and cream until smooth. Bring sauce to a boil and cook, stirring, until sauce thickens slightly and is reduced to about 1 cup. Pour sauce over fish and sprinkle with parsley, if desired. Makes 4 to 6 servings.

Fish with Garlic Sauce

A generous quantity of chopped garlic slowly cooked to sweetness in butter is transformed into a robust sauce for fish. Watch the garlic carefully while it cooks; if it burns, it will taste very bitter.

>   **About ½ cup (¼ lb.) butter or margarine**
> **½   cup finely chopped garlic (about 24 large**
> **   cloves)**
> **2   pounds fish fillets or steaks, or small whole**
> **   fish (up to 1½ inches thick), cleaned and**
> **   scaled**
> **   Salt and pepper**
> **2   eggs**
> **   About 2 tablespoons milk or water**
> **2   tablespoons salad oil**
> **   Lemon wedges**

Melt 6 tablespoons of the butter in a small pan over medium-low heat. Add garlic and cook, stirring occasionally, until garlic just begins to turn golden (about 15 to 20 minutes). Remove from heat and keep warm.

Wipe fish with damp cloth. Cut into serving-size pieces (about 3 by 5 inches), if desired. Lightly sprinkle with salt and pepper on both sides. Also lightly beat eggs together with milk in shallow pan.

In a wide frying pan, heat 1 tablespoon of remaining butter and 1 tablespoon oil (fat should be about ⅛ inch deep) until it foams but doesn't brown. Promptly dip fish pieces, one at a time, in egg mixture; drain briefly and place in frying pan. Continue to add as many fish pieces as will fit without crowding. Cook until lightly browned—over medium-high heat if pieces are ⅝ inch thick or less; over medium heat if pieces are thicker than ⅝ inch.

Turn each piece carefully with a wide spatula to brown other side. For a 1-inch-thick piece of fish (measured in thickest portion) allow 10 minutes total—5 minutes on each side, turning only once. (Allow same ratio of thickness to time—1 inch: 10 minutes—for fish of all thicknesses.) Fish is cooked if it flakes readily when prodded in thickest portion with a fork. Remove cooked fish to a warm serving platter and keep warm; add rest of butter and oil and cook remaining fish in same manner.

When last fish is removed from pan, pour warm garlic sauce over fish and serve with lemon wedges. Makes 4 to 6 servings.

POACHING

Poaching is unmatched as a versatile method of preparing fish. Just as an egg poaches in water, a fish simmers to firmness in a gently bubbling, savory liquid that delicately flavors as it cooks the fish.

Poached fish can be served steaming hot, napped in a sauce made from the poaching liquid. Or it can be chilled and served in a variety of salads and sandwiches or as part of an elegant cold entrée for a hot summer's day. In addition, poaching is an easy way to produce an unusually tasty and nutritious low-calorie dish, because no fat is used.

Though any fish can be poached, the method is particularly well suited to fish of low fat content, as well as to some of the fatter fish with a mild flavor, such as salmon or trout. The poaching technique can be used for any *form* of fish as well, whether fillets, steaks, small whole fish, or even large ones (we include a section on how to manage a 3 to 8-pound whole fish in the poaching pan). When fish or pieces are large, we recommend that cheesecloth be wrapped around them to help support and maintain their shape.

If you poach large fish frequently, you might like to get one of the special pans designed for poaching; they come in a wide range of sizes, all long and oval to fit a whole fish, and equipped with a rack for lowering and raising the fish from the liquid.

HOW TO POACH

To poach serving-size fish pieces, all you really need are a wide spatula and a wide frying pan or other pan just deep enough to immerse the pieces in simmering liquid. You can poach on top of the range or in the oven.

Our basic poaching liquid is designed to enhance the natural flavor of the fish, not mask it. The stock that remains after the fish has been poached can either be reserved to make a fish soup (freeze it if you plan to keep it longer than 24 hours) or it can become the base of one of the flavorful sauce suggestions we offer, to be served with the poached fish.

>   **Fish fillets or steaks, or small whole fish,**
> **   cleaned and scaled**
> **Basic poaching liquid (recipe follows)**
> **Fish velouté sauce (optional—suggestions**
> **   follow)**

If fish is to be oven-poached, preheat oven to 425°.

Wipe fish with damp cloth. Cut into serving-size pieces (about 3 by 5 inches), if desired. If using pieces much larger than the surface area of your spatula, wrap in cheesecloth, folding edges together on top of fish, to make handling easier after cooking.

For oven-poaching, arrange fish in a single layer in a greased wide baking pan. Bring poaching liquid to a boil and pour over fish—there should be just enough liquid to cover fish; if not, add equal parts water and dry white wine (or all water) just to cover fish. Cover pan and place in preheated oven.

For poaching on top of range, bring poaching liquid to a boil in poaching pan. Lower fish into simmering liquid—there should be just enough liquid to cover fish; if not, add equal parts water and dry white wine (or all water) just to cover fish. Reduce heat, cover, and simmer gently (water should never be allowed to boil).

Cook, either in oven or on top of range, until fish flakes readily when prodded in thickest portion with a fork—for a 1-inch-thick piece of fish (measured in thickest portion), allow 10 minutes from the moment simmering resumes after fish has been added. (Allow same ratio of thickness to time—1 inch: 10 minutes—for fish of all thicknesses.)

When done, lift fish from liquid with a wide spatula, supporting it with the cheesecloth if necessary. Drain well; then open cheesecloth, if used, and gently remove from beneath fish (fish may break easily after cooking, so be especially careful).

If fish is to be served with a fish velouté sauce, arrange on warm serving platter and keep warm while sauce is made. If it is to be used in salads, sandwiches, or cold entrées, cool, cover, and chill until ready to use.

To serve fish with sauce, pour some of the sauce evenly over fish; pass remaining sauce in a bowl at table.

Basic poaching liquid. In a 3-quart pan (or in poaching pan, if you like), combine 1 medium onion (sliced), 6 whole black peppers, 2 whole allspice, 3 tablespoons lemon juice or white wine vinegar, 1 bay leaf, 1 teaspoon salt, about ½ cup dry white wine (or water), and about 1 quart water (you will need just enough to cover fish pieces, so amount of water and wine may be varied accordingly). Cover and simmer ingredients for at least 20 minutes.

Recipe may be doubled or tripled if larger amounts are needed (if so, simmer ingredients for 30 minutes to 1 hour). Poaching liquid may be reused several times—it will simply acquire more flavor, the more often it is used. However, liquid should not be stored in the refrigerator longer than 2 days; freeze in an airtight container if longer storage is necessary.

SAUCES FROM THE POACHING LIQUID

We begin with a basic fish velouté sauce made from the poaching liquid that remains after the fish have been poached. The sauces that follow it are simply flavorful variations on the basic one: an estragon sauce with a whiff of tarragon; a cheesy mornay sauce; a spicy curry sauce; and a rich and creamy shrimp sauce, all based on the savory stock from the poaching pan.

Basic fish velouté sauce. Melt 3 tablespoons butter or margarine in a pan over low heat. With a wire whip, stir in 3 tablespoons all-purpose flour and cook until

bubbly. Remove from heat and gradually stir in 2 cups poaching liquid. Continue cooking, stirring, until thickened. Add salt and pepper if needed, and a dash of nutmeg. Sprinkle with some finely chopped parsley, if you wish. Makes 2 cups.

Estragon sauce. Melt 3 tablespoons butter or margarine in a pan over low heat. Using a wire whip, stir in 3 tablespoons all-purpose flour and ¼ teaspoon tarragon leaves and cook until bubbly. Remove from heat and gradually stir in 1½ cups poaching liquid and ½ cup whipping cream. Continue cooking, stirring, until thickened. Add salt, pepper, and finely chopped parsley, if desired. Makes 2 cups.

Mornay sauce. Melt 3 tablespoons butter or margarine in a pan over low heat. Using a wire whip, stir in 2 tablespoons all-purpose flour and cook until bubbly. Remove from heat and gradually stir in 1½ cups poaching liquid and ½ cup whipping cream. Continue cooking, stirring, until thickened; then stir in ¾ cup shredded Gruyère or Swiss cheese and ¼ cup grated Parmesan. Continue cooking over low heat just until cheese has melted. Makes 2½ cups.

Curry sauce. Melt ½ cup butter or margarine in a small pan over medium-high heat. Add 2 tablespoons minced onion and sauté until golden brown. Reduce heat to medium-low; using a wire whip, stir in ⅓ cup all-purpose flour (unsifted) and cook until bubbly. Gradually blend in 1½ cups poaching liquid. Add 1½ teaspoons curry powder and ½ cup half-and-half (light cream); cook, stirring, until thickened. Makes 2 cups.

Shrimp sauce. After removing fish from poaching liquid, set 2½ cups liquid in pan over high heat and boil rapidly, uncovered, until liquid is reduced by half (you should have about 1¼ cups of reduced stock). While liquid is boiling, shell and devein ¼ pound medium-size raw shrimp (see directions on page 116). Drop shrimp into liquid; cook 3 minutes and remove from liquid with slotted spoon. (Or instead of cooking raw shrimp, use ¼ pound small cooked shrimp, thawed if frozen.) Chop coarsely and set aside.

Meanwhile, melt 3 tablespoons butter or margarine in another pan over low heat. Stir in 3 tablespoons all-purpose flour and cook until bubbly. Using a wire whip, gradually stir in 1¼ cups reduced poaching liquid and ¼ cup whipping cream. Cook until thickened; stir in shrimp. Add salt, if necessary. Makes 2 cups.

POACHING A LARGE WHOLE FISH

The size and weight of large whole fish such as salmon, carp, or sea bass require special handling during poaching, whether done in the oven or on top of the range. The following directions can be used for any fish weighing 3 to 8 pounds.

If you don't have a conventional poaching pan, you'll need a large roasting or broiling pan to poach in; make sure it's large enough to permit the fish to lie flat (tail can turn up, if necessary) and deep enough to allow

(Continued on page

SEASONED BUTTERS

Butter is the base for a variety of saucy seasonings to spark up your simplest fish. Whether butter is whipped or melted, its nutty flavor is an ideal background for a host of herbs, flavorful sautéed vegetables, and crunchy nuts and seeds. Additionally, it goes well on any simply cooked fish, whether baked, barbecued, broiled, butter-sautéed, oven-fried, pan-fried, or poached.

Butter sauces have the advantage of being quick and easy to make from ingredients you probably have on hand. (For those who prefer it, margarine can take the place of butter in any of the sauces.) All of the following recipes make enough to cover 4 to 6 servings of fish (1½ to 2½ lb. fish pieces).

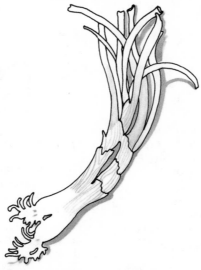

Whipped, Chilled Butters

These light, herbed confections are blended from creamy butter, whipped with savory seasonings. Serve them as a topping to melt over hot fish; the remainder becomes a spread for French bread.

Lemon butter aux fines herbes. Combine ½ cup (¼ lb.) butter or margarine (at room temperature), 1 tablespoon *each* minced parsley and chopped chives (fresh, frozen, or freeze-dried), 2 teaspoons lemon juice, ½ teaspoon *each* tarragon and chervil leaves, ¼ teaspoon salt, and a dash of pepper; beat until fluffy. Cover and refrigerate until ready to serve.

Mustard butter. Combine ½ cup (¼ lb.) butter or margarine (at room temperature), 1 tablespoon minced parsley, 2 teaspoons lemon juice, ¼ teaspoon salt, and ⅛ teaspoon pepper; beat until fluffy. Beat in 2 tablespoons Dijon mustard. Cover and refrigerate until ready to serve.

Garlic butter. Combine ½ cup (¼ lb.) butter or margarine (at room temperature), 2 to 3 cloves garlic (minced or pressed), and 2 tablespoons minced parsley; beat until fluffy. Cover and refrigerate until ready to use.

Basil butter. Combine ½ cup (¼ lb.) butter or margarine (at room temperature), ½ cup lightly packed, chopped, fresh basil leaves (or 2 tablespoons dry basil), ¼ cup grated Parmesan cheese, 2 tablespoons minced parsley, and 1 tablespoon lemon juice; beat until fluffy. Cover and refrigerate until ready to use.

Dill butter. Press yolks of 2 hard-cooked eggs through a wire strainer (reserve whites for other uses); combine with ½ cup (¼ lb.) butter or margarine, 3 teaspoons dill weed, ½ teaspoon salt, and ⅛ teaspoon pepper; beat until fluffy. Cover and refrigerate until ready to use.

Hot Herb-Lemon or Nut Butters

Hot butters can be made either in a small pan or in the pan the fish has cooked in (make sure you wipe out any fat that may have burned in the pan; keep the fish warm while you make the butter sauce). The lemon and herbs will add a hint of piquancy, the nuts a touch of crunch.

Classic lemon butter. Melt ¼ cup butter or margarine over medium heat; add juice of 1 lemon. Heat until butter bubbles; stir lightly and pour over hot fish.

Parsley lemon butter. Make classic lemon butter as directed preceding, adding 1 or 2 tablespoons minced parsley along with lemon juice.

Sage lemon butter. Make classic lemon butter as directed preceding, adding ½ teaspoon mace, ¼ teaspoon rubbed sage, a dash of pepper, and grated peel of 1 lemon along with lemon juice.

Nut butter. Melt ¼ cup butter or margarine over medium heat. Add ¼ to ½ cup nuts (use whole pine nuts; or use chopped, slivered, or sliced almonds, cashews, filberts, macadamia nuts, or pecans). Heat until butter bubbles and nuts are lightly browned (about 5 to 10 minutes).

Hot Butter Garnishes

Sliced mushrooms or green onions tossed in hot butter with seasonings create sauces that should really be called garnishes, they're so full of good things. Make them before you cook your fish; then heat briefly to serve.

Crunchy onion garnish. Melt ¼ cup butter or margarine over medium heat and add 1 cup minced green onion (about 7 onions), including some tops, and 3 tablespoons sesame seed. Stir until butter bubbles and sesame seed browns lightly (about 3 to 5 minutes). Remove from pan; set aside while fish cooks. When fish is done, return garnish to pan; heat through and spoon over fish.

Mushroom tarragon garnish. Melt 6 tablespoons butter or margarine over medium-high heat and add ½ teaspoon tarragon leaves; stir lightly. Add 3 tablespoons chopped shallots or onion and 2 cups sliced fresh mushrooms; sauté, stirring, until mushrooms are limp. Sprinkle 2 tablespoons dry white wine or regular-strength chicken broth over mushrooms and cook, stirring, 1 minute longer. Remove from pan; set aside while fish cooks. When fish is done, return garnish to pan; heat through and spoon over fish.

the poaching liquid to just cover the fish. You'll also need a good deal of cheesecloth to help lower and raise the fish from the liquid, if you don't have the rack that is supplied with a conventional poaching pan.

> **Basic poaching liquid, uncooked (directions precede; double or triple the amount)**
> **Whole fish (3 to 8 lb.), cleaned and scaled, with head removed, if desired**
> **Parsley and lemon wedges (optional)**

Wipe fish with damp cloth, inside body cavity and out, and place in poaching pan (on rack, if one is supplied with pan).

Make poaching liquid as directed (preceding); before heating, measure quantity by pouring over fish in poaching pan. If you need more liquid, add 1 part water to 1 part dry white wine (or all water) just to cover fish.

Remove fish and rack and set aside. Cover poaching pan with lid or foil and simmer poaching liquid for 30 minutes to 1 hour. Strain liquid and discard vegetables and whole spices; return liquid to poaching pan. If oven-poaching, preheat oven to 400°.

Meanwhile, place fish on rack or, if you don't have a rack, wrap snugly in cheesecloth, folding edges together on top of fish. Bring poaching liquid to boiling in poaching pan and lower fish on rack or in cheesecloth into boiling liquid. (If some liquid has boiled away, add just enough dry white wine or water to cover fish.) Cover pan with lid or foil.

Simmer on top of range (you may need to use two burners at once) or, if oven-poaching, place pan in preheated oven. Allow 10 minutes cooking time per 1-inch thickness of fish (measured in thickest portion). To test for doneness, cut a narrow slit in thickest portion of fish (through cheesecloth, if necessary) with a sharp knife. When done, flesh will be firmer and look lighter in color and less translucent than when raw. If flesh is still dark or translucent near backbone, recover pan and continue cooking, checking for doneness every 3 minutes (make a new slit).

When fish is done, lift out of liquid on rack (or lift cheesecloth-wrapped fish out of liquid, supporting with two spatulas). Open cheesecloth and gently remove from beneath fish (fish may break easily after cooking, so be especially careful). Arrange fish on warm serving platter; cover with foil and keep warm if you intend to make one of the fish velouté sauces (preceding—you should double recipe for amount needed to serve with a large whole fish). If not, serve immediately, garnished with parsley and lemon wedges, if desired. Or cool, cover, and chill at least 3 hours; serve, garnished with parsley and lemon wedges and accompanied by one of the sauces given on pages 20-21.

To serve, cut directly to bone, then slide a wide spatula between flesh and ribs and lift off each serving. When top half has been served, lift and remove backbone (sever from head, if necessary) before serving remaining half.

DISHES TO SUIT ANY FISH: POACHING

Once you are acquainted with poaching, try one of the following all-purpose poaching recipes with your next fish. The recipes were selected from among our favorites because they will accommodate any variety of fish, easily and flavorfully. Each recipe includes the information you need to adapt it to your fish.

Oven-poached Fish in Mushroom Sauce

A delicate, wine-laced mushroom sauce, made from the stock in which the fillets were oven-poached, masks the fish for a second quick, bubbling bake in the oven. You can do the preliminary poaching and saucing ahead of time, if you like.

> 2 **pounds fish fillets or steaks**
> **About ½ cup dry white wine**
> 1 **tablespoon lemon juice**
> **Salt**
> ¼ **cup butter or margarine**
> ½ **pound mushrooms, thinly sliced**
> 3 **tablespoons all-purpose flour**
> ½ **cup half-and-half (light cream)**
> **Ground nutmeg**
> ¾ **cup shredded Swiss cheese**

Preheat oven to 400°. Wipe fish with damp cloth. Arrange fish in single layer in large shallow baking pan. Pour ½ cup wine and the lemon juice evenly over fish; sprinkle lightly with salt. Cover and bake until fish flakes readily when prodded in thickest portion with a fork. For a 1-inch-thick piece of fish (measured in thickest portion), allow 10 minutes. (Allow same ratio of thickness to time—1 inch:10 minutes—for fish of all thicknesses.) Remove from oven; let cool slightly.

Holding fish in place with a wide spatula or pan lid, drain poaching liquid from baking pan into a measuring cup; set aside. Cover and chill fish.

You should have about 1 cup poaching liquid, but this varies with the fish; therefore, either boil liquid over high heat to reduce to 1 cup or add dry white wine to make cup; reserve.

In a pan, melt 2 tablespoons butter over medium-high heat; add mushrooms and cook, stirring, until mushrooms are limp and liquid has evaporated. Remove mushrooms from pan and set aside. Melt remaining butter in pan and blend in flour. Remove from heat and, using a wire whip, gradually stir in reserved poaching liquid, the half-and-half, and ⅛ teaspoon ground nutmeg. Bring to a boil and cook, stirring, for 1 or 2 minutes or until thickened. Remove from heat, add mushrooms, and salt to taste. Let cool.

Spoon cooled sauce evenly over cold poached fish, covering completely. Scatter cheese evenly over fish. (At this point you can cover and chill fish until next day, if you wish.)

To bake fish, preheat oven to 400°. Place pan, uncovered, in oven for 10 to 12 minutes (20 to 24 minutes if chilled) or until sauce around edges is bubbling and cheese has melted. Dust very lightly with ground nutmeg and serve. Makes 4 to 6 servings.

Baked Fish with Vegetable Sauce

Cover the bake-and-serve pan tightly, and these fish will literally steam in their own juices in a very hot oven. The creamy vegetable sauce has a fresh note: green peas and a nip of lemon juice.

2 pounds fish fillets or steaks
¼ cup butter or margarine
¼ pound mushrooms, sliced
½ cup finely chopped green pepper
¼ cup all-purpose flour, unsifted
½ teaspoon salt
¼ teaspoon pepper
Milk
1 package (10 oz.) frozen peas, thawed
1 tablespoon lemon juice
¼ cup grated Parmesan cheese

Preheat oven to 425°. Wipe fish with damp cloth. Arrange fish in single layer in greased large, shallow baking pan; cover with foil and bake until fish flakes readily when prodded in thickest portion with a fork. For a 1-inch-thick piece of fish (measured in thickest portion), allow 10 minutes. (Allow same ratio of thickness to time—1 inch:10 minutes—for fish of all thicknesses.) Remove from oven and let stand, covered, about 5 minutes.

Melt butter in a frying pan over medium-high heat and add mushrooms and green pepper; sauté just until mushrooms are limp. Stir in flour, salt, and pepper; reduce heat to medium and cook until bubbly, then remove from heat.

Holding fish in pan with a wide spatula or pan lid, drain liquid from fish into a measuring cup; add milk to make 1½ cups liquid. Using wire whip, gradually stir liquid into mixture in frying pan and cook over medium heat, stirring, until it boils and thickens. Stir in peas and lemon juice; spoon over fish in baking pan and sprinkle evenly with cheese. Broil about 4 inches from heat until top is golden. Makes 4 to 6 servings.

Oven-poached Fish with Horseradish Cream Sauce

Horseradish adds a touch of Scandinavian piquancy to the simple velouté sauce that masks this oven-poached fish. The dish can be assembled in advance, then baked at the last minute just long enough to heat through.

2 pounds fish fillets or steaks
About ½ cup regular-strength chicken broth
1 tablespoon lemon juice
Salt
3 tablespoons butter or margarine
2 tablespoons all-purpose flour
⅓ cup half-and-half (light cream)
1 tablespoon prepared horseradish
Chopped parsley or sliced green onion (including some tops)

Preheat oven to 400°. Wipe fish with damp cloth. Arrange fish evenly in large, shallow baking pan. Pour ½ cup chicken broth and the lemon juice over fish; sprinkle lightly with salt. Cover and bake until fish flakes readily when prodded in thickest portion with a fork. For a 1-inch-thick piece of fish (measured in thickest portion), allow 10 minutes. (Allow same ratio of thickness to time—1 inch:10 minutes—for fish of all thicknesses.) Remove from oven; let cool slightly.

Holding fish in place with a wide spatula or pan lid, drain poaching liquid into a measuring cup. Cover and chill fish.

You should have about 1 cup liquid, but this varies with the fish; therefore, either boil liquid to reduce to 1 cup or add broth to make 1 cup.

In a pan, melt butter over medium heat and blend in flour; cook until bubbly. Remove from heat and, using a wire whip, gradually add reserved 1 cup poaching liquid, half-and-half, and horseradish. Bring to a boil and cook, stirring, until thickened (1 or 2 minutes). Let cool.

Spoon sauce evenly over cold poached fish, covering completely. (At this point you can cover and chill fish up to 12 hours before baking.)

To bake fish, preheat oven to 400°. Place pan, uncovered, in oven for 10 to 12 minutes or until sauce around edges is bubbling and fish is heated through. Garnish with parsley or green onion. Makes 4 to 6 servings.

CLASSIC SEAFOOD SOUPS & STEWS

An air of pleasant informality pervades any meal in which the main dish is a fragrant, bubbling soup or stew. Here we offer recipes for a variety of such dishes, each one easy to assemble and having the added attraction of cooking in a brief time.

Serve your favorite brew of seafood morsels, vegetables, and herbs in bowls or mugs, along with crusty French bread, crisp lettuce or citrus salad, and perhaps a light, dry wine.

Basic Fish Stock

Fish stock is often used as a base for soups and stews or as a substitute for poaching liquid in poaching fish and making velouté sauces. You can make it in quantity (just double or triple the recipe) and then freeze it in the amounts needed for individual recipes. Fish markets often have bones, heads, and trimmings you can buy to supplement bones and trimmings saved from previous fish meals and frozen in airtight containers.

- 2 tablespoons butter or margarine
- 1 cup *each* finely chopped onion and parsley
- 4 pounds fish bones, trimmings, and heads (preferably those of lean, mild, white-fleshed fish—see charts on pages 8–11)
- 3 tablespoons lemon juice
- 1½ cups dry white wine
- 2 quarts water

Melt butter in large kettle over medium-high heat; sauté onion and parsley just until onion is soft. Lay fish bones, trimmings, and heads over vegetables; add lemon juice and cook over low heat, shaking occasionally, for 5 minutes. Add wine and simmer, uncovered, until liquid is reduced by half (about 20 to 30 minutes). Then add water, bring to a boil, and boil rapidly for 30 minutes or until reduced by half; strain. Makes 4 cups.

Spanish Seafood Soup

In a spicy tomato broth redolent of lemon, wine, and garlic, the Spanish cook chunks of mild fish, curls of tender pink shrimp, and clams in their shells to make a hearty main-dish soup. If you can't get clam juice for the broth, substitute regular-strength chicken broth.

- 3 tablespoons olive oil or salad oil
- 2 medium-size onions, finely chopped
- 2 cloves garlic, minced or pressed
- 1 large green pepper, seeded and chopped
- 1 small can (10½ oz.) tomato purée
- 2 bottles (*each* 8 oz.) clam juice
- ¾ cup dry white or red wine
- 2 cans (*each* about 14 oz.) regular-strength chicken broth
- 2 bay leaves
- ½ teaspoon *each* crushed red pepper, dry basil, thyme leaves, and whole coriander seed, crushed
- 1 lemon, thinly sliced
- 2 medium-size carrots, thinly sliced
- About 8 small hard-shelled clams, cleaned (see "Cleaning and opening clams," page 88)
- ½ to ¾ pound medium-size raw shrimp, shelled and deveined (see directions on page 116)
- About 1½ pounds fish fillets or steaks
- Chopped parsley (optional)

Heat oil in a 5-quart kettle over medium-high heat; sauté onions, garlic, and green pepper until onion is soft. Stir in tomato purée, clam juice, wine, broth, bay leaves, red pepper, basil, thyme, coriander, lemon slices, and carrots. Reduce heat to low. Simmer, uncovered, for 10 minutes. Add clams; cover and simmer until clams begin to open (about 7 minutes). Meanwhile, wipe fish with damp cloth; cut into 1-inch cubes. When clams begin to open, add shrimp and

fish to broth; cover and simmer until shrimp turn pink and clams are fully opened (about 7 minutes more). Sprinkle servings with chopped parsley, if desired. Makes 6 to 8 servings.

Lemon Fish Soup with Skordalia

The broth of this soup is blended with eggs and lemon juice to give it the savor and the delicate soft-custard texture of Greek avgolemono sauce. Serve the soup in mugs. The fish is arranged separately on a platter, along with a potent garlic almond mayonnaise called "skordalia."

- 2 stalks celery, sliced
- 2 carrots, sliced
- 1 medium-size onion, cut in chunks
- ½ bay leaf
- 2 teaspoons chicken stock base or 2 chicken bouillon cubes
- 2 teaspoons salt
- 2 quarts water
- 2 dozen medium-size raw shrimp Skordalia (recipe follows)
- ½ cup dry white wine
- 12 small new potatoes
- 2 pounds fish fillets or steaks
- 2 tablespoons butter or margarine
- 2 tablespoons *each* cornstarch and water
- 4 eggs
- ⅓ cup lemon juice

In a large kettle (about 6-quart size or larger), combine celery, carrots, onion, bay leaf, stock base, salt, and water. Shell and devein shrimp (see "Shelling and deveining shrimp," page 116)—reserve shrimp, covered and chilled, and add shells to kettle. Bring to a boil. Reduce heat, cover, and simmer 1 hour; strain, discarding vegetables, seasonings, and shells.

Meanwhile, prepare skordalia. Return broth to kettle, add wine, and bring to a boil; add potatoes and simmer 10 minutes. Wipe fish with damp cloth; cut

·into serving-size pieces (about 3 by 5 inches), if desired. Add fish and shrimp to broth and simmer gently 5 to 10 minutes more or until fish flakes readily when prodded in thickest portion with a fork and shrimp turn pink.

Carefully lift out fish, shrimp, and potatoes; arrange on a warm serving platter and dot generously with butter. Keep warm.

Bring broth to a boil; blend cornstarch and water and stir into boiling broth. Cook, stirring, until thickened. Set aside about ⅓ cup of the broth.

Beat eggs until light; then beat in lemon juice. Using a wire whip, gradually stir some of the hot broth from kettle into beaten eggs. Stir egg mixture back into broth in kettle and place over very low heat; cook, stirring, until soup is thickened to a soft-custard consistency (do not boil). Pour into a serving bowl. Drizzle reserved ⅓ cup broth evenly over platter of fish to moisten; serve soup and fish side by side, along with a serving bowl of skordalia to spoon over fish. Makes 6 servings.

Skordalia (garlic almond mayonnaise). Place ⅓ cup blanched almonds in a shallow baking pan; bake in a 350° oven, shaking occasionally, for 10 minutes or until lightly browned. Place in a blender and whirl until finely ground; remove nuts and set aside.

Without washing blender container, put in 1 egg, 2 cloves garlic, ½ teaspoon salt, and 1½ tablespoons *each* lemon juice and wine vinegar. Whirl for a few seconds to combine; then very gradually add ⅔ cup salad oil, mixing in just a few drops at a time at first. As mixture begins to thicken, increase oil to a slow, steady stream, about 1/16 inch wide. Whirl until smooth.

Add almonds and whirl until thoroughly mixed. Spoon into serving bowl, cover, and chill. Makes 1½ cups sauce.

Fish & Potato Selyanka

Country fare, plain and simple, is this substantial Finnish soup, fragrant with dill and brimming with chunks of potato and fish. Each bowl is seasoned with chopped raw onion and melted butter.

> **6 cups regular-strength chicken broth**
> **2 pounds fish fillets or steaks**
> **1 pound small new potatoes, peeled and cut in ½-inch cubes**
> **1 large onion, finely chopped**
> **1 teaspoon dill weed**
> **1 medium-size white or red onion (mild flavor, if available), chopped**
> **6 tablespoons butter or margarine, melted**
> **Salt and pepper**
> **Dill weed**

In a kettle, heat broth to boiling. Wipe fish with damp cloth; add to broth. When broth returns to a boil, reduce heat and simmer until fish flakes readily when prodded in thickest portion with a fork. For a 1-inch-thick piece of fish (measured in thickest portion), allow 10 minutes. (Allow same ratio of thickness to time—1 inch:10 minutes—for fish of all thicknesses.) Set aside for at least 20 minutes (or you can chill fish in broth to intensify flavor); then lift out fish with a slotted spoon. Remove and discard any skin and bones; cut fish in bite-size chunks.

Return broth to high heat. Add potatoes, the large chopped onion, and the 1 teaspoon dill weed. Boil, covered, for about 10 minutes or until potatoes are tender when pierced. Add fish and cook just until heated through.

To serve, ladle soup into bowls; season individual servings with the chopped white onion, melted butter, salt and pepper to taste, and an additional sprinkling of dill weed. Makes 5 or 6 main-dish servings.

North Beach Fish Stew

First you brown the fish chunks, then stew them, along with prawns, in a luscious tomato sauce subtly seasoned with lemon and wine.

> **2 pounds fish fillets or steaks**
> **About ½ cup all-purpose flour, unsifted**
> **½ teaspoon garlic salt**
> **Half butter or margarine and half salad oil (about 2 tablespoons *each*)**
> **1 medium-size onion, thinly sliced**
> **1 large can (1 lb. 12 oz.) whole tomatoes**
> **½ teaspoon thyme leaves**
> **1 bay leaf**
> **¾ cup *each* catsup and white wine**
> **1 whole lemon, thinly sliced**
> **2 teaspoons *each* sugar and Worcestershire**
> **Salt and pepper**
> **1 pound large raw shrimp or prawns, shelled and deveined (see directions on page 116)**
> **Chopped parsley**
> **Hot cooked rice**

Wipe fish with damp cloth; cut into 1½-inch chunks. Combine flour and garlic salt; coat fish and shake off excess. Arrange in single layer on wax paper within reaching distance of range. In a wide frying pan, heat butter and oil (⅛ inch deep) over medium-high heat until it foams but doesn't brown. Promptly add fish and sauté for about 10 minutes until browned but not completely cooked; remove from pan and set aside.

Add onion to pan and sauté until soft (about 5 minutes). Add tomatoes (break them up with a spoon) and their liquid, thyme, bay leaf, catsup, wine, lemon, sugar, and Worcestershire. Simmer, uncovered, stirring often, until thickened (about 15 minutes).

Add fish and shrimp, spooning some of the sauce over them. Cover and simmer 6 to 10 minutes or until fish flakes readily when prodded in thickest portion with a fork. Add salt and pepper to taste; garnish with chopped parsley and serve over hot cooked rice in wide soup plates. Makes 6 servings.

A COOK'S CATALOG OF COMMON FISH

HOW TO SELECT, PREPARE & COOK TO PERFECTION

What do you do when a friend gives you a freshly caught fish and it's a kind you've never learned to cook? Where do you turn when the fish on special sale at the market is unfamiliar to you, or when you're looking for a new way to serve an old favorite?

For mouthwatering ideas and answers, turn to this chapter. Here you'll find a selection of the most common fish sold in regional markets across the U.S. Arranged in alphabetical order, from albacore to whiting, each fish is presented to you with information on where it's sold, how big it is, what form (whole steaks, fillets) it comes in, and how to prepare it for cooking. Each also has a section called "Choosing your method,"

which gives general hints on basic cooking methods—such as pan-frying or poaching—best suited to the individual fish. Page references help you apply the information in Chapter 2, "Eight Basic Methods of Cooking Fish."

Best of all are the delectable recipes developed especially to suit the unique flavor, texture, and appearance of each fish in this chapter. Ideas for seasonings, sauces, and presentations come from cuisines the world over and are planned with every sort of occasion in mind, from family dinners to grand buffets. For the adventurous, we feature recipes for serving the great delicacy, raw fish.

ALBACORE, PACIFIC

The albacore is an aristocratic member of the tuna family, rarely seen beyond the western summer markets except in cans. The basic guidelines for cooking albacore may be applied to other kinds of tuna (such as yellowfin and bluefin) that appear in both eastern and western fresh fish markets at different times of year.

Choosing your method. There are many ways to cook albacore besides the recipes that follow. For ideas, see "Basic Methods" (pages 14-31), particularly the sections on barbecuing, broiling, butter-sautéing, oven-frying, pan-frying, and poaching. You'll find sauce pos-

sibilities on page 20 and seasoned butters on page 29.

How to prepare for cooking. An albacore is an especially messy fish to clean, so if you buy a whole one, ask your fish dealer to trim, clean, and scale it. Have it cut into 1-inch-thick steaks if you intend to barbecue or fry, into fillets if you want to poach the fish.

Handling steaks. You'll notice that albacore steaks have distinct areas of dark red meat on each side of the bone. (In other red-meated varieties of tuna, these areas will be almost black.) Strong fish oils are concentrated in these areas; if you cut them out before cooking the meat, the flavor will be milder. Use a small, sharp knife to cut around and lift out the dark areas; while you're at it, lift out the bone as well.

Because albacore meat is soft when

raw, your steak may look as though you've ruined it; but don't be concerned. Push the steak back together; if any small pieces have fallen off, poke them into the center.

If you plan to fry or broil steaks, leave the skin on and use 3 or 4 wooden picks to hold the pieces together. If barbecuing, remove the skin, wrap a strip of bacon around the circumference of each steak, and secure it with a wooden pick; the bacon adds flavor and helps hold the piece neatly on the grill. (Whether you're frying, broiling, or barbecuing, the biggest steaks should be divided into 2 servings.) As soon as the fish begins to cook, the meat firms and welds into neat, easy-to-handle pieces.

Handling fillets. The term "loin" is used to describe the boneless section of solid white meat in the fillet of an alba-

Hale and hearty houseboat fare boasts thick broiled halibut steaks
(see broiling instructions on pages 18–19) wreathed with steamed carrots, Brussels sprouts, and new potatoes.
For the zesty cucumber sauce recipe, see page 20.

core. These loins poach very well, if prepared as follows: Carefully pull the skin off each fillet, using a knife when needed to free it from the soft flesh. Cut each fillet in half lengthwise along the bone and remove the center bone. You will see streaks of dark red meat running the length of the fillets. With a small, sharp knife, cut out and discard the dark red portions. Now the loins are ready to poach (see directions on page 27).

Barbecued Albacore with Lemon Butter

Take your choice of three ways to serve barbecued albacore, all using the same lemon baste. Bacon strips hold the soft flesh together until it cooks firm.

- **6 serving-size pieces albacore steak (*each* about ½ pound and all about the same thickness), skin removed**
- **6 slices bacon**
- **½ cup (¼ lb.) butter or margarine**
- **1 medium-size clove garlic, minced or pressed**
- **¼ cup lemon juice**
- **2 tablespoons chopped parsley Salt and pepper**

About 30 to 45 minutes before you plan to begin cooking, ignite coals (you'll need about 35 long-burning briquets).

Prepare steaks as directed in "Handling steaks." Wrap a strip of bacon around circumference of each and secure it with a wooden pick.

Melt butter in a small pan; stir in garlic, lemon juice, and parsley; set aside. When coals are covered with gray ash, arrange in a single, solid layer to underlie entire grill area to be used. Knock ash off coals and let burn down until moderately hot (about 5 to 10 minutes longer). Adjust grill height to 6 inches above coals.

Grease grill and arrange steaks on it, directly above the coals. Brush with lemon-butter baste and cook, turning once and basting several times, until fish is browned and flakes readily when prodded in thickest portion with a fork. For a 1-inch-thick piece of fish (measured in thickest portion), allow about 10 minutes. (Allow same ratio of thickness to time—1 inch:10 minutes—for fish of all thicknesses.) Transfer to a warm serving platter, sprinkle with salt and pepper to taste, and serve immediately. Makes 6 servings.

Smoke-barbecued albacore. Prepare coals, fish, and lemon-butter baste according to preceding directions. Adjust grill height to 6 inches above coals. Arrange steaks on grill on a piece of heavy-duty foil with several holes poked in it; brush with baste. Cover barbecue completely with lid or heavy-duty foil (as directed under "Barbecuing a Large Whole Fish," page 17) and adjust drafts for slow cooking.

Cook, lifting lid to baste several times (but don't turn fish), until fish flakes readily when prodded in thickest portion with a fork. Allow about twice the normal cooking time—for a 1-inch-thick piece of fish (measured in thickest portion), allow about 20 minutes. (Allow same ratio of thickness to time—1 inch:20 minutes—for fish of all thicknesses.) Transfer to a warm platter and sprinkle with salt and pepper to taste.

Oyster-topped albacore. Prepare coals, fish, and lemon-butter baste as directed in "Smoke-barbecued albacore." Arrange steaks on grill on a piece of heavy-duty foil with several holes poked in it. Top each steak with several thin slices of sweet onion, 1 thin slice of a large tomato, 1 thin lemon slice, and 1 or 2 shucked oysters; drizzle with baste. Smoke-barbecue, drizzling several times with baste. Transfer to a warm serving platter, sprinkle with salt and pepper to taste, and serve immediately.

BLUEFISH

Silvery-blue markings give the bluefish its name. Sold in eastern markets in whole form, it can be cooked whole with appealing results. It is possible to fillet the larger bluefish (see directions on page 7), making certain cooking methods—such as broiling—much easier.

Choosing your method. Bluefish is especially good when baked, broiled, or oven-fried (see directions in "Basic Methods," pages 14–31). For these treatments, fillets or the smaller whole fish are recommended. You'll find sauce possibilities on page 20 and seasoned butters on page 29.

Baked Bluefish with Spinach Stuffing

Dill-seasoned spinach and mushrooms make a flavorful stuffing for whole bluefish—they bake together in a sauce of lemon butter.

- **½ cup (¼ lb.) butter or margarine**
- **⅓ pound mushrooms, thinly sliced**
- **6 cups chopped fresh spinach, lightly packed (about 1½ lb.), or 3 packages (*each* 10 oz.) frozen chopped spinach, thawed**
- **1 medium-size onion, chopped**
- **3 teaspoons dill weed**
- **½ cup fine dry bread crumbs**
- **1½ teaspoons salt Pepper**
- **4 whole bluefish (*each* about 1 pound—to substitute larger fish, see directions that follow), cleaned and scaled**
- **¼ cup lemon juice**

Preheat oven to 375°. Melt ¼ cup of the butter in a wide frying pan over medium-high heat; add mushrooms and sauté until limp. If using fresh spinach, add to mushrooms in pan, along with onion, dill, bread crumbs, salt, and a dash of pepper; stir until thoroughly mixed. Cook just until spinach is wilted but still bright green. (If using thawed frozen spinach, place in colander; press out most of moisture before adding to pan. Mix thoroughly with other ingredients but do not cook.)

Wipe fish with damp cloth, inside cavities and outside. Fill each fish cavity with spinach mixture (lightly packed);

ALBACORE, PACIFIC

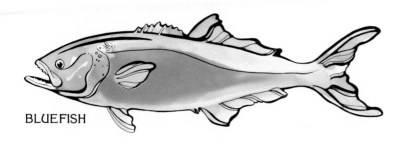

BLUEFISH

skewer edges together or sew with heavy thread. Spread remaining spinach mixture evenly in bottom of greased large, shallow baking pan. Arrange fish on top of spinach in pan.

Melt remaining butter; add lemon juice. Brush fish with lemon butter and bake, uncovered, basting several times with more lemon butter until fish flakes readily when prodded in thickest portion with a fork. For 3-inch-thick fish (measured in thickest portion after stuffing), allow 30 minutes. (Allow same ratio of thickness to time—1 inch:10 minutes —for fish of all thicknesses.)

Remove from oven; pour any remaining lemon butter over fish and serve immediately. Makes about 4 servings.

For larger bluefish. If you wish, you may make the same dish using two bluefish, *each* 2 to 3 pounds, or use one 4 to 5-pound bluefish. Follow preceding directions, making sure each fish is well filled with stuffing.

BUTTERFISH

Nothing could describe the eastern butterfish more aptly than its nickname: "silver dollar." These delightful, flavorful, tender little fish are round and coinlike in shape, and they gleam with a silver iridescence. Several of them make a single serving, and they're best cooked whole.

Choosing your method. In addition to the suggestions that follow, good methods for cooking butterfish include baking, broiling, butter-sautéing, and oven-frying (see directions in "Basic Methods," pages 14–31). You'll find sauce possibilities on page 20 and seasoned butters on page 29. Butterfish can also be smoked deliciously (see directions in "Building a Simple Smoker," page 120).

Basil Butterfish Sauté

The delicate flavor of butterfish demands only the lightest of seasonings: butter, basil, and dry white wine.

2 **pounds small, whole, dressed butterfish (***each* **fish about 6 oz.)**
   All-purpose flour
   Half butter or margarine and half salad oil (about 2 tablespoons *each*)
1½ **teaspoons dry basil leaves, crushed**
⅓ **cup dry white wine**

Wipe fish with damp cloth, inside cavities and outside. Coat with flour; shake off excess. Arrange in single layer on wax paper within reaching distance of range.

In a wide frying pan, heat butter and oil (about ⅛ inch deep) over medium heat until it foams but doesn't brown. Promptly add as many fish as will fit in pan without crowding (about half the fish); sprinkle with half the basil. Cook, turning once, until the fish is lightly browned and flakes readily when prodded in thickest portion with a fork. For a ¾-inch-thick fish (measured in thickest portion), allow 7 to 8 minutes total—3½ to 4 minutes on each side. (Allow same ratio of thickness to time—1 inch : 10 minutes—for fish of all thicknesses.)

When done, transfer fish to a warm

serving platter; keep warm. Repeat process with remaining fish and remaining basil, adding more butter and oil, if necessary.

When the last fish is removed from pan, add wine to pan; quickly stir and scrape to release browned particles and blend wine with pan juices. Pour liquid evenly over fish. Makes 4 servings.

Broiled Butterfish with Mustard Sauce

There's a hint of mustard in the creamy, stir-together sauce swirled atop these broiled butterfish.

1 **cup sour cream**
½ **cup finely chopped green onion**
1½ **tablespoons Dijon mustard**
1 **tablespoon chopped parsley**
½ **teaspoon *each* salt, thyme leaves, and marjoram leaves**
   Dash of pepper
2 **pounds whole, dressed butterfish (***each* **fish about 6 to 8 oz.), heads removed**
   Salt

Stir together sour cream, onion, mustard, parsley, salt, thyme, marjoram, and pepper; set aside.

Place a shallow baking pan in broiler; turn on broiler. Wipe fish with damp cloth, inside cavities and outside. With a sharp knife, cut 2 or 3 shallow, diagonal slashes in sides of each fish; salt lightly. Remove pan from broiler; grease lightly.

Arrange fish in single layer in pan; return pan to broiler, adjusting to proper distance from heat: 3 inches for fish up to ¾ inch thick, 4 inches if any of the fish are thicker. Broil for 4 minutes or until lightly browned on side closest to heat; remove pan from broiler and turn fish over.

Spread top of each fish generously with sour cream mixture. Return to broiler and broil 4 minutes longer or until fish flakes readily when prodded in

(Continued on page 39)

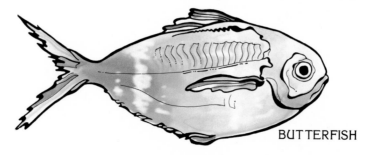

BUTTERFISH

The British are coming! They'll feel right at home with
this basket of golden brown, crispy fish and chips, sprinkled with malt vinegar
and washed down with English ale. The beer batter recipe and deep-frying
instructions are on pages 22–23.

thickest portion with a fork. For a 1-inch-thick fish (measured in thickest portion), allow 10 minutes total—5 minutes on each side. (Allow same ratio of thickness to time—1 inch:10 minutes—for fish of all thicknesses.) Transfer to a warm serving platter and serve immediately. Makes 4 servings.

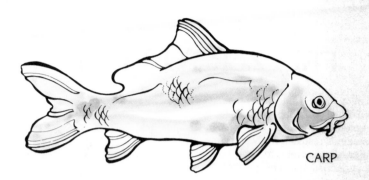

CARP

CARP

To many people, "carp" means a Japanese paper fish kite with a gaping mouth, or a decorative fish for a fish pond. But the carp is also a fresh-water food fish that can be bought whole or in steaks or fillets almost anywhere in the United States. A firm-fleshed fish, it is reputed to have a slightly "muddy" flavor that is least strong in the colder season, making October through March the ideal time to buy carp.

Choosing your method. When whole, a carp can be poached; as steaks or fillets, it can be baked, broiled, or oven-fried as well as poached (see directions in "Basic Methods," pages 14–31). You'll find sauce possibilities on page 20 and seasoned butters on page 29.

Stuffed Carp with Tomatoes

A whole carp bakes with a stuffing of buttery toasted crumbs and onions, topped with a thyme-scented tomato sauce.

  1 **whole carp (about 3 lb.), cleaned and scaled**
  ½ **cup (¼ lb.) butter or margarine**
  ½ **cup finely chopped onion**
  1 **cup coarsely crushed unseasoned croutons**
  2 **teaspoons salt**
  ¾ **teaspoon thyme leaves**
  2 **medium-size onions, sliced**
  1 **large can (1 lb. 12 oz.) whole tomatoes**
  ½ **teaspoon pepper**

Preheat oven to 400°. Wipe fish with damp cloth, inside cavity and outside. In a frying pan, melt ¼ cup of the butter over medium-high heat; add finely chopped onion and sauté until golden. Add croutons, ½ teaspoon of the salt, and ½ teaspoon of the thyme; mix well. Fill cavity of fish with stuffing and

skewer edges together or sew with heavy thread. Place fish in greased shallow baking pan large enough to contain fish (tail may turn up, if necessary).

To frying pan add remaining ¼ cup butter and sliced onions; sauté over medium-high heat until golden. Add tomatoes and their liquid (break up tomatoes with a spoon), remaining 1½ teaspoons salt, pepper, and remaining ¼ teaspoon thyme. Cook, stirring, over medium-high heat until thickened (about 15 minutes).

Pour over fish and bake, uncovered, until fish flakes readily when prodded in thickest portion with a fork. For a 3-inch-thick fish (measured in thickest portion after stuffing), allow about 30 minutes. (Allow same ratio of thickness to time—1 inch:10 minutes—for fish of all thicknesses.) Serve immediately, cutting directly to bone, then sliding a wide spatula between flesh and ribs and lifting off each serving. When top half has been served, lift and remove backbone (sever from head, if necessary) before serving bottom half. Spoon extra tomato sauce from pan over servings. Makes 4 to 6 servings.

CATFISH

Fish with whiskers? The fresh-water catfish certainly looks as though he has whiskers—they're the barbels growing on either side of his mouth. Among the numerous shapes, sizes and varieties of catfish available in all parts of the United States are many fish of exceptionally delicate flavor and pleasant texture. These versatile fish are sold whole, skinned and dressed, and occasionally as steaks or fillets.

Choosing your method. The catfish is delicious whether baked, barbecued, broiled, butter-sautéed, oven-fried,

pan-fried, or poached (see directions in "Basic Methods," pages 14–31). You'll find sauce possibilities on page 20 and seasoned butters on page 29. Catfish may also be smoked (see directions in "Building a Simple Smoker," page 120).

How to prepare for cooking. It is advisable to buy your catfish already skinned, but if you're faced with the job of removing the tough hide yourself, we recommend cutting off the head first, including the pectoral fins (be careful of the spines). Then cut the skin along the full length of the fish, following the backbone and cutting around both sides of the dorsal fin (do not cut through the flesh). Finally, using a pair of pliers to grip the slippery skin, ease it back from "shoulders" to tail, cutting away from the flesh where necessary with a sharp knife. Cut off the tail along with the skin. Now the fish may be cooked as it is or sliced into steaks or fillets (see directions on page 7).

Tangy Lemon Catfish Fry

You steep these fish morsels for half an hour in a pungent marinade.

  2 **pounds skinless catfish fillets (to skin, see directions in "How to prepare for cooking," preceding)**
  ¼ **cup lemon juice**
  1 **teaspoon salt**
  1 **clove garlic, minced or pressed**
  ¼ **teaspoon oregano leaves**
  1 **cup cornmeal**
  ½ **cup all-purpose flour**
      Half butter or margarine and half salad oil (about 2 tablespoons *each*)

Wipe fish with damp cloth; cut into serving-size pieces (about 3 by 5 inches), if desired. Combine lemon juice, salt, garlic, and oregano. Pour

(Continued on page 41)

FREEZER TO TABLE: ONE QUICK STEP

In general, fresh fish is better than frozen, but if you poach or bake today's processed-at-sea frozen fish, you can get delicious results quickly and conveniently. The secret is to cook the fish without defrosting it. This retains the succulent texture and saves you lots of thawing time. In fact, you can have a fit-for-company meal ready in an hour or less. (If you want to pan-fry, broil, or butter-sauté the fish instead, thaw and separate the fillets first. Then follow directions on pages 14–33.)

In many areas, frozen fish is more available than fresh, and it's usually less expensive (up to 25 percent less for many varieties). But be sure the fish you buy is well frozen (see page 6).

Sole, cod, perch, and haddock are the most common varieties. You'll find the fillets packaged in 1-inch thick, 1-pound blocks in the frozen-food section of most supermarkets. They're boned and skinned, ready to cook.

Here's an easy rule for poaching and baking frozen fish—for each inch of thickness, allow 20 to 24 minutes of cooking time (add a few extra minutes if the fish cooks with a sauce or topping).

In these recipes, you can use sole, cod, perch, and haddock interchangeably.

Carrot-topped Baked Fish

Shredded carrots and a hint of lemon make an unusually light, fresh accompaniment for fish.

- **2 packages (1 lb. *each*) frozen fish fillets**
- **2 cups coarsely shredded carrots**
- **6 tablespoons melted butter or margarine**
- **1 teaspoon grated lemon peel**
- **2 tablespoons lemon juice**
- **¼ teaspoon *each* thyme leaves and salt**
- **3 tablespoons all-purpose flour**
- **⅓ cup milk or half-and-half (light cream)**
- **Thin slices of lemon (optional)**

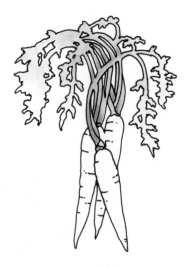

Unwrap both packages of fish and let stand at room temperature for 20 to 30 minutes. Preheat oven to 450°.

Meanwhile, combine carrots, 3 tablespoons of the butter, lemon peel, lemon juice, thyme, and salt. Cut each block of fish into 2 or 3 equal portions. Place each piece in a shallow individual ramekin (about 2-cup size) or place slightly apart in a single layer in a 2 to 3-quart shallow baking pan.

Mound carrot mixture on fish pieces in equal amounts. Cover tightly with foil. Bake in preheated 450° oven until fish flakes readily when prodded in thickest portion with a fork (about 35 to 40 minutes).

Pour cooking liquid off fish into a large measuring cup and add water, if needed, to make 1⅓ cups; set aside. Cover fish and keep warm.

In a pan, melt remaining 3 tablespoons butter over low heat. Stir in flour and cook until bubbly. Remove from heat; using a wire whip, gradually stir in the 1⅓ cups fish liquid as well as milk. Return to heat and cook, stirring, until thickened. Add salt and pepper to taste. Pour sauce over fish and carrots. Garnish each serving with a thin slice of lemon, if desired. Makes 4 to 6 servings.

Poached Fish in Cheese Sauce

Frozen fish simmers alongside peas, onions, and potatoes before the poaching liquid goes into a cheese-laden sauce.

- **1½ tablespoons lemon juice**
- **1 bay leaf**
- **¼ cup dry white wine**
- **3 whole black peppers**
- **2 whole allspice**
- **¼ teaspoon salt**
- **1 package (1 lb.) frozen fish fillets**
- **6 *each* small new potatoes and small white boiling onions (cut in half if larger than 1½ inches in diameter)**
- **1 cup frozen peas**
- **2 tablespoons butter or margarine**
- **1½ tablespoons all-purpose flour**
- **¼ cup milk or half-and-half (light cream)**
- **¼ teaspoon dry mustard**
- **⅔ cup shredded Swiss cheese Dash of ground nutmeg**

In a 10-inch frying pan, mix lemon juice, bay leaf, wine, peppers, allspice, and salt. Add fish (unthawed), potatoes, and onions. Add water just to cover fish. Bring to a boil, cover, reduce heat, and simmer until fish is almost opaque throughout (about 18 minutes).

Add peas (unthawed); cover and simmer until fish flakes readily when prodded in thickest portion with a fork (about 4 to 6 minutes). With a slotted spatula, lift out fish and vegetables; cover and keep warm. (If potatoes are not done, continue cooking them alone until tender.) Boil poaching liquid, uncovered, until reduced to ¾ cup. Strain liquid to remove seasonings; set liquid aside and discard seasonings.

In a pan, melt butter or margarine over low heat. Stir in flour and cook until bubbly. Remove from heat; using a wire whip, gradually stir in reserved poaching liquid, along with milk and mustard. Return to heat and cook, stirring, until thickened. Add Swiss cheese and nutmeg; continue stirring until cheese melts. Pour over fish and vegetables. Makes 2 servings.

over fish and chill 30 minutes, turning fish occasionally to marinate all sides.

Remove fish from marinade and drain briefly. Combine cornmeal and flour on wax paper or in shallow pan. Roll each fish piece in cornmeal mixture to coat all sides evenly; shake off excess.

In a wide frying pan, heat butter and oil (about ⅛ inch deep) until it foams but doesn't brown. Promptly add as many fish pieces as will fit without crowding. Cook, turning once—over medium-high heat if pieces are ⅝ inch thick or less; over medium heat if pieces are thicker than ⅝ inch—until lightly browned. Fish is cooked if it flakes readily when prodded in thickest portion with a fork. For a 1-inch-thick piece of fish (measured in thickest portion), allow 10 minutes total—5 minutes on each side. (Allow same ratio of thickness to time—1 inch:10 minutes—for fish of all thicknesses.)

Remove each piece as it is done; arrange on a warm serving platter and keep warm while you cook remaining fish. Add more butter and oil to pan if necessary.

When all the fish is cooked, serve immediately. Makes 4 to 6 servings.

Catfish Creole

Seasonings borrowed from the Creole cooking of Louisiana add flavor depth to the tomato sauce masking the fish.

 2 tablespoons butter or margarine
 1 large onion
 ½ cup *each* chopped celery and chopped green pepper
 1 clove garlic, minced or pressed
 1 large can (1 lb. 12 oz.) whole tomatoes
 1 lemon, sliced
 1 tablespoon *each* Worcestershire and paprika
 1 bay leaf
 1 teaspoon salt
 ¼ teaspoon *each* thyme leaves and liquid hot pepper seasoning
 2 pounds skinned, dressed catfish, cut in 1½-inch-thick steaks (to skin, see directions in "How to prepare for cooking," preceding)
 Hot cooked rice

Melt butter in wide frying pan over medium heat; add onion, celery, green pepper, and garlic. Cook until soft (about 7 minutes); add tomatoes and their liquid (break up tomatoes with a

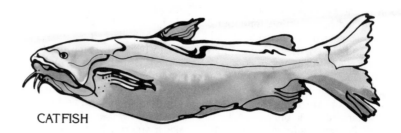

CATFISH

spoon), lemon slices, Worcestershire, paprika, bay leaf, salt, thyme, and liquid hot pepper seasoning. Cook, stirring occasionally, for about 15 minutes or until sauce is slightly thickened.

Press fish pieces down into sauce; spoon some of the sauce over top of fish. Cover pan and simmer gently until fish flakes readily when prodded in thickest portion with a fork. For a 1½-inch-thick piece of fish (measured in thickest portion), allow 15 minutes.

To serve, spoon fish and sauce over hot cooked rice. Makes 4 to 6 servings.

COD, ATLANTIC or PACIFIC

The cod is almost a symbol of New England to many people, and it's not surprising, since most fresh cod comes from the eastern coast. However, some cod is actually western in origin, and these days cod in frozen or dried and salted form is available just about everywhere, even in places where fresh cod never appears. Salt cod must be "refreshed" (simmered repeatedly to remove salt and rehydrate fish) before it can be used in cooking; directions follow.

Choosing your method. The mild flavor and very soft, flaky texture of cod make it ideal for poaching or adding to soups, stews, and casseroles. It is also excellent baked (see directions in "Basic Methods," pages 14–31). You'll find sauce possibilities on page 20 and seasoned butters on page 29.

Refreshing salt cod. Wash fish in running cold water for about 15 minutes. Place in a pan, cover generously with water, and slowly heat to simmering. Drain, add fresh water to cover, and repeat this process until fish is no longer too salty for your taste (this generally

takes 3 or 4 heatings). Now the cod is ready for cooking. (You can do the refreshing process as much as 12 hours ahead; cover and chill refreshed cod until needed.) If *cooked* fish is called for in a recipe, refreshed cod can be flaked into small natural divisions, put in a pan, covered with water, and gently simmered for 15 minutes more. It may then be added to any dish, ready to serve.

Capered Cod & Cabbage

Wedges of green cabbage surround a mound of sauced salt cod; both are garnished with a crumbled topping of hard-cooked egg. You can refresh the fish and prepare sauce and egg ahead, then finish the dish at serving time.

 1 pound boned salt cod, refreshed (see directions in "Refreshing salt cod," preceding)
 Water
 4 hard-cooked eggs
 3 tablespoons butter or margarine
 1 medium-size onion, finely chopped
 3 tablespoons all-purpose flour
 1½ cups regular-strength chicken broth
 1 cup half-and-half (light cream)
 ¼ cup capers and their liquid
 1 small head cabbage
 Boiling salted water
 Parsley sprigs

Flake fish into small natural divisions, place in a pan, cover with water, and simmer gently, covered, for 15 minutes.

Meanwhile, separate yolks and whites of eggs. Rub whites through a fine wire strainer; then, keeping yolks and whites separate, rub yolks through strainer. Set aside (cover and chill, if made ahead).

In a pan, heat butter over medium heat; add onion and cook until soft. Blend in flour; then, using a wire whip gradually stir in chicken broth, cream, 2 tablespoons of the capers and 1 tablespoon of the caper liquid. Bring sauce to boiling and cook, stirring, for about 2 minutes. (Sauce may be made ahead, covered and chilled, then reheated; thin if necessary with a little more cream or broth.)

Meanwhile, cut the cabbage into 6 wedges; do not core. Immerse in boiling salted water and cook, uncovered, for 3 minutes after boil resumes or until cabbage is bright green and tender to bite. Drain thoroughly and arrange wedges in ring around edges of a platter.

Drain cooked fish and blend into sauce; heat through. Pour fish and sauce in center of cabbage ring and top decoratively with sieved egg white and yolk. Garnish with remaining 2 tablespoons capers and parsley sprigs. Serve immediately. Makes 6 servings.

Fresh Creamed Cod Dinner

Chunks of mild white fish, tender little russet potatoes, and bright green peas are bathed in a generous lemony cream sauce to make this whole-meal stew.

1½ **pounds small new potatoes,
    unpeeled
    Boiling salted water**
  2 **pounds fresh skinless cod
    fillets or frozen cod fillets,
    thawed**
  2 **tablespoons butter or
    margarine**
  8 **whole allspice**
1½ **teaspoons salt**
  1 **teaspoon sugar**
  2 **cups water**
  3 **tablespoons all-purpose flour**
  1 **package (10 oz.) frozen peas,
    thawed**
  2 **tablespoons lemon juice**
  1 **egg yolk**
  3 **tablespoons whipping cream**

Cook potatoes in lightly salted boiling water for about 15 to 25 minutes or until tender when pierced.

Meanwhile, wipe fish with damp cloth; cut into 1½-inch cubes. Melt butter in pan with tight-fitting lid; put fish pieces into it. Add allspice, salt, and sugar; mix gently. In a small bowl and using a wire whip, gradually blend water into flour to make a smooth paste; pour over fish. Cover and simmer gently until fish flakes readily when prodded in thickest portion with a fork. For a 1½-inch-thick piece of fish (measured in thickest portion), allow 15 minutes.

When potatoes are done, remove them from water, drain briefly, and arrange in a warm serving bowl; cover and keep warm. Bring potato water to a boil; add peas and simmer just until heated through. Drain and add to potatoes; cover and keep warm. When fish is cooked, remove from poaching liquid with slotted spoon; add to potatoes and mix gently. Cover and keep warm.

Using wire whip, blend lemon juice with egg yolk and cream. Add to fish poaching liquid and cook, stirring, over medium heat until slightly thickened (about 3 minutes). Pour sauce over the fish and vegetables; serve immediately in wide soup plates. Makes 4 to 6 servings.

Fresh Cod Potato Cakes

Under the crispy, thin coating of these classic fish cakes, the centers are meltingly soft and savory, flecked with parsley and lots of green onion. Serve them with chili sauce and maybe a poached egg on top. They make a hearty, warming breakfast, the kind that New England fishermen have been enjoying for centuries.

  2 **medium-size baking potatoes
    (about 1 lb. total), peeled
    Boiling salted water**
  ¼ **cup butter or margarine**
  1 **cup thinly sliced green onion
    (including some tops)**
  2 **tablespoons chopped parsley**
  ¾ **teaspoon *each* garlic salt and
    oregano leaves**
  ¼ **teaspoon pepper**
  2 **eggs**
  1 **pound fresh skinless cod
    fillets, or frozen cod fillets,
    thawed**
  ⅓ **cup all-purpose flour, unsifted**
  2 **tablespoons cornmeal
    Salad oil**

Cut potatoes into quarters. Cook in lightly salted boiling water for 20 to 30 minutes or until tender when pierced. Drain thoroughly; mash potatoes; stir in the butter, onion, parsley, garlic salt, oregano, pepper, and eggs.

Wipe fish with damp cloth; cut in 1-inch cubes. Cook in boiling water to cover until fish flakes readily when prodded in thickest portion with a fork. For 1-inch-thick fish cubes, allow 10 minutes. Drain; flake fish and mix thoroughly with potato mixture. Cool, cover, and chill for at least 1 hour.

Combine flour and cornmeal on wax paper or in shallow pan. Form fish mixture into patties about 3 inches in diameter and ¾ inch thick. Coat both sides of each patty with flour mixture; shake off excess. Arrange in single layer on wax paper within reaching distance of range.

Heat salad oil (about ⅛ inch deep) in a wide frying pan over medium heat until it ripples when pan is tilted. Add as many patties as will fit without crowding; cook until lightly browned (about 6 to 8 minutes), turning once.

When done, remove patties from pan and drain briefly on paper towels. Arrange on warm serving platter; cover and keep warm while you cook remaining patties. When all are cooked, serve immediately. Makes 4 to 6 servings.

COD, ATLANTIC

CROAKER

For a small fish, the croaker is notably noisy—it gets its name from the resonant drumming sound it makes during spawning season. A tasty southeastern fish, croaker is available whole and in fillets, and it can be cooked readily in either form.

(Continued on page 44)

Hot buttered grapes and a mild cream sauce lift delicately
sautéed sole fillets far above the ordinary. Round out this refreshingly light meal
with a butter lettuce and cucumber salad and puffy dinner rolls. The recipe for
Flounder or Sole with Grapes is on page 50.

43

Choosing your method. The croaker is mild-flavored and tender, and takes well to a panful of butter. You can bake it, broil it, butter-sauté it, oven-fry it, or pan-fry it (see directions in "Basic Methods," pages 14–31). You'll find sauce possibilities on page 20 and seasoned butters on page 29.

Deviled Croaker

When the fish has finished frying, you stir white wine, shallots, and mustard into the pan juices to make a richly flavorful sauce.

- ½ cup dry white wine
- 2 teaspoons Dijon mustard
- ½ teaspoon thyme leaves
- ¼ teaspoon rubbed sage
- ¼ teaspoon salt
- 4 whole croakers (*each* about 8 to 12 oz.), cleaned and scaled
   All-purpose flour
   Half butter or margarine and half salad oil (about 2 tablespoons *each*)
- ¼ cup chopped shallots
- 1 large clove garlic, minced or pressed
   Chopped parsley

Combine wine, mustard, thyme, sage, and salt; set aside. Wipe fish with damp cloth, inside cavities and outside. Coat fish with flour; shake off excess. Arrange in single layer on wax paper within reaching distance of range.

In a wide frying pan, heat butter and oil (about ⅛ inch deep) over medium heat until it foams but doesn't brown. Promptly add as many fish as will fit without crowding. Cook, turning once, until lightly browned and fish flakes readily when prodded in thickest portion with a fork. For a 1-inch-thick fish, allow 10 minutes total—5 minutes on each side. (Allow same ratio of thickness to time—1 inch:10 minutes—for fish of all thicknesses.)

Remove fish when they are done; arrange on a warm serving platter and keep warm while you cook remaining fish, adding more butter and oil to pan if necessary. When all fish are cooked, keep warm while you make sauce.

To same frying pan, add shallots and garlic and cook over medium-high heat, stirring, until soft (about 3 minutes). Pour wine mixture over shallots; boil rapidly, stirring, until sauce thickens slightly (about 1 minute). Pour evenly over croaker; garnish with chopped parsley and serve immediately. Makes 4 servings.

Pecan-crusted Croaker

There's a nip of chili seasoning in the crunchy nut coating of these oven-fried fish.

- 4 whole croakers (*each* about 8 to 12 oz.), cleaned and scaled
- ⅔ cup finely chopped pecans
- ⅔ cup fine dry bread crumbs
- 1 tablespoon finely chopped parsley
- 1 teaspoon chili powder
- 2 eggs
   About 2 to 3 tablespoons butter or margarine
   Salt and pepper

Preheat oven to 500°. Put a large, shallow baking pan in oven to preheat. Wipe fish with damp cloth, inside cavities and outside. Combine the pecans, bread crumbs, parsley, and chili powder in shallow pan or on piece of wax paper. In a shallow pan, beat eggs slightly. Dip each fish in egg to coat all over; drain briefly. Then roll in crumb mixture to coat evenly on all sides. Arrange in single layer on wax paper within reaching distance of range.

Remove pan from oven; put butter in pan and swirl until melted (butter should be about ⅛ inch deep).

Lay a fish in pan; turn to coat with melted butter. Repeat with remaining fish, arranging in single layer in pan. Return pan to oven and bake until fish is lightly browned and flakes readily when prodded in thickest portion with a fork. For a 1-inch-thick fish (measured in thickest portion) allow 10 minutes. (Allow same ratio of thickness to time—1 inch : 10 minutes—for fish of all thicknesses.)

When fish is done, transfer to a warm serving platter, salt and pepper to taste, and serve immediately. Makes 4 servings.

DRUM, BLACK

From the southeastern coast and the Gulf comes an attractive silver and black fish, the black drum, so called because of the vibrating, "drumming" sound it makes. Though often quite large, it can be bought in sizes you can use for poaching or baking whole to serve for a family meal or a dinner party. Black drum can also be purchased in steak or chunk form.

Choosing your method. The drum is a very delicately flavored fish; stuff and bake it as recommended for Salmon with Lemon Rice Stuffing (see page 65), or poach or oven-fry it (see directions in "Basic Methods," pages 14-31). You'll find sauce possibilities on page 20 and seasoned butters on page 29.

Classic Drum Stockpot

Out of one pot come a subtle sipping soup, an assortment of vegetables—herb-seasoned potatoes, carrots, and leeks—and a regal chunk of delicately poached fish to be served with a golden mushroom sauce. At the fish market, ask for extra fish scraps to make the stock; also supply yourself with cheesecloth to wrap the fish for poaching.

CROAKER

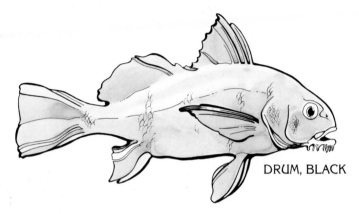

DRUM, BLACK

3 tablespoons butter or margarine
1 medium-size onion, thinly sliced
1 large can (47 oz.) regular-strength chicken broth
1½ pounds fish scraps (heads or tails)
½ teaspoon thyme leaves
1 bay leaf
½ teaspoon dry basil
6 small new potatoes, unpeeled
6 carrots, peeled or scrubbed
3 leeks, split in half lengthwise and washed thoroughly
1 whole dressed drum with head and tail removed (about 4 lb.)
  Golden mushroom sauce (recipe follows)
1 tablespoon lemon juice
1 cup whipping cream

In a kettle (6-qt. size or larger), melt butter over medium-high heat; add onion and cook, stirring frequently, until golden. Pour in broth.

Rinse fish scraps (you can use head and tail of drum as part of scraps) and add to broth, along with thyme, bay leaf, and basil. Simmer together, covered, about 20 minutes. Then add potatoes and carrots; cover and simmer 20 minutes. Add leeks and cook until all vegetables are tender when pierced but still resistant to fork (5 to 10 minutes more).

With a slotted spoon, remove vegetables to serving platter, cover with foil, and keep warm. Strain poaching liquid to remove fish scraps; discard scraps and return liquid to kettle.

Wipe fish with damp cloth, inside cavity and outside; wrap loosely in cheesecloth, folding edges together over top of fish. Bring poaching liquid to a boil and, holding ends of cheesecloth, lower fish gently into liquid. Simmer gently until fish flakes readily when prodded in thickest portion with a fork. (To test, fold back cheesecloth.) For a 2-inch-thick piece of fish, measured in thickest portion, allow 20 minutes. (Allow same ratio of thickness to time—1 inch:10 minutes—for fish of all thicknesses.)

Meanwhile, prepare mushroom sauce. When fish is done, lift from liquid (reserve liquid) and arrange in center of platter with vegetables; remove cheesecloth carefully.

Spoon a little of the butter from mushroom sauce over fish and vegetables to moisten them. Immediately stir lemon juice into reserved poaching liquid; then stir in cream and heat through. Serve in mugs to accompany platter of fish and vegetables. Makes 8 servings.

Golden mushroom sauce. Melt ½ cup (¼ lb.) butter or margarine in frying pan. Add ½ pound sliced mushrooms and cook over medium heat, stirring occasionally, until golden. Stir in 2 tablespoons lemon juice. Pour into serving bowl to pass with platter of fish.

EEL, COMMON

To Americans, eel is not the familiar fish that it is to Europeans; nonetheless, it is available fresh in many fish markets on the eastern coast, and it is deliciously tender and mild.

EEL, COMMON

Choosing your method. Eels can be butter-sautéed, pan-fried, oven-fried, poached, or added to soups, stews, and casseroles (see directions in "Basic Methods," pages 14-31). You'll find sauce possibilities on page 20 and seasoned butters on page 29. Eel is also popular smoked (see directions in "Building a Simple Smoker," page 120).

How to prepare for cooking. When an eel has been dressed and skinned, it is ready to cook. If it is only dressed or is whole, you must skin it before cooking. With a sharp knife or cleaver, cut off the head of the eel and any fins, including those around the tail (kitchen shears are sometimes helpful in removing fins). Make a vertical cut about 2 inches long from the "shoulders" of the fish toward the tail, and free from the flesh a top corner of the skin along the cut. Using a pair of pliers, grasp the loose corner and work the skin downward, toward the tail, using the knife to free the skin from the flesh wherever necessary. Eventually (after some tugging) the skin will just turn inside out and pull right off.

Matelote of Eel

The eel is a delicate fish; it makes a subtle stew when simmered in a white wine broth with tender little onions and slices of carrot.

1½ pounds skinned, dressed eel, cut in 2-inch lengths (to skin, see directions in "How to prepare for cooking," preceding)
1 dozen small boiling onions, peeled
2 medium carrots, scrubbed or peeled and thinly sliced
1½ cups dry white wine
1½ cups regular-strength chicken broth
1 bay leaf
½ teaspoon thyme leaves
1 clove garlic, minced or pressed
2 tablespoons butter or margarine
2 tablespoons all-purpose flour
½ cup half-and-half (light cream)
  Salt and pepper
  Chopped parsley

(Continued on page 47)

Dramatic and different, this golden brown soufflé
contains small wine-poached flounder fillets. The poaching liquid is incorporated
into a smooth, thick sauce. The recipe for Flounder or Sole Fillet Soufflé
starts on the facing page.

Wipe fish with damp cloth. In a large pan, combine onions, carrots, wine, broth, bay leaf, thyme, and garlic. Bring to boiling; reduce heat, cover, and simmer 10 minutes or until onions are tender. Add fish; simmer gently until fish flakes readily when prodded in thickest portion with a fork. For a 2-inch-thick fish (measured in thickest portion), allow 20 minutes.

Carefully lift fish and vegetables from poaching liquid with slotted spoon (reserve poaching liquid). Drain briefly and arrange in deep 3 to 5-quart serving dish; cover and keep warm while you complete sauce.

Melt butter in pan over medium-low heat. Stir in flour and cook until bubbly. Using a wire whip, gradually stir in half-and-half and reserved poaching liquid. Continue cooking, stirring constantly, until slightly thickened (about 10 to 15 minutes). Salt and pepper to taste. Pour over fish and vegetables and sprinkle with parsley. Serve immediately. Makes about 4 servings.

FINNAN HADDIE

"What had he had? Had he had haddie?" queries a famous limerick from the British Isles. Haddie, or finnan haddie as it's properly called, originated in Britain and is a smoked haddock or cod—tender golden fillets with a penetratingly smoky flavor. Though finnan haddie appears occasionally in western markets, it is most often sold on the east coast.

Choosing your method. You can bake, broil, oven-fry, or poach finnan haddie (see directions in "Basic Methods," pages 14–31). You'll find sauce possibilities on page 20 and seasoned

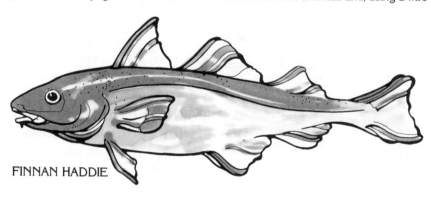

FINNAN HADDIE

butters on page 29. The distinctive flavor of this fish tends to command any dish that features it.

Finnan Haddie Mushroom Casserole

The British serve it for breakfast, but this creamy smoked fish casserole makes an unusual and satisfying meal at any time of day.

1½ **pounds finnan haddie (thawed if frozen)**
   About 2 cups milk
3 **tablespoons butter or margarine**
¼ **cup sliced almonds**
½ **pound mushrooms, sliced**
3 **tablespoons all-purpose flour**
2 **chicken bouillon cubes**
1 **cup hot water**
¾ **cup half-and-half (light cream)**
½ **teaspoon Dijon mustard**
⅛ **teaspoon liquid hot pepper seasoning**
⅓ **cup sliced green onion (including some tops)**
2 **hard-cooked eggs, chopped**
   Salt and pepper

Place fish in a wide frying pan and just cover with milk. Cover pan and simmer over low heat 20 minutes or until fish flakes readily when prodded in thickest portion with a fork. Drain, discarding milk; when fish is cool enough to handle, break into bite-size pieces, discarding bones. Set fish aside.

Melt butter in a 3-quart pan over medium heat; add almonds and cook until lightly browned, stirring often. Lift out almonds with slotted spoon and set aside. Add mushrooms to pan and cook until limp and golden brown. Then stir in flour until well blended.

Dissolve bouillon cubes in hot water; blend with half-and-half and, using a wire

whip, gradually stir into mushroom mixture. Cook, stirring constantly, until bubbly and thickened (about 10 to 15 minutes). Stir in mustard, hot pepper seasoning, onion, eggs, fish, and salt and pepper to taste; heat through. Pour into a serving bowl and garnish with almonds. Makes 4 to 6 servings.

FLOUNDER or SOLE

The different varieties of flounder and sole are all members of the flatfish family; their broad, flat, platterlike bodies yield wide, flat fillets. Unmatched in popularity, they have a uniquely delicate flavor and tender texture which, when cooked, produce dishes of great subtlety.

Most of the so-called "soles" found in American markets are actually varieties of flounder. Despite their different names, though, flounder and sole can be cooked in the same ways (with allowances for size differences), so we offer one set of recipes for use with any flounder or sole.

Easterners will find blackback flounder, yellowtail flounder, fluke, dab, lemon sole, and gray sole in their markets; westerners find petrale, rex, Dover, English, sand, and rock soles and sand dabs. These may appear whole or drawn (and can be cooked that way), but they are sold most often in the familiar fillet form.

Choosing your method. Considering the delicacy of these fish, you will probably not want to choose a cooking method that will overpower the flounder or sole's flavor. We suggest butter-sautéing, oven-frying, pan-frying (try it with small whole flounders or soles), baking, broiling, or poaching (see directions in "Basic Methods," pages 14–31). You'll find sauce possibilities on page 20 and seasoned butters on page 29.

Flounder or Sole Fillet Soufflé

(Pictured on facing page)

Tucked in under the glorious golden cloud of soufflé are little wine-poached fillets; their poaching liquid is whipped into a smooth sauce while the soufflé bakes.

(Continued on page 48)

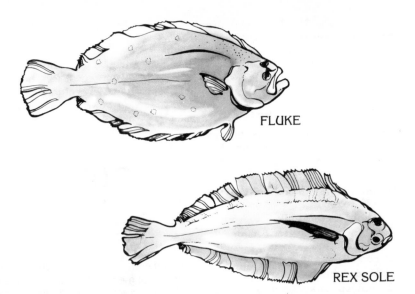

FLUKE

REX SOLE

Baked Flounder or Sole Duxelles

A lacy topping of cheese and crumbs bakes over tender fish on a bed of seasoned mushrooms. Make it ahead, if you like.

- 1 tablespoon olive oil or salad oil
- 1 tablespoon all-purpose flour
- ¼ pound mushrooms, finely chopped
- ⅓ cup finely chopped shallots or white part of green onions
- ¾ teaspoon tarragon leaves, crushed
- ½ cup finely chopped parsley
- ⅓ cup dry white wine or regular-strength chicken broth
- ¼ cup whipping cream
- 1½ to 2 pounds skinless flounder or sole fillets
  Salt, pepper, and paprika
- 3 slices firm white bread
- 2 tablespoons butter or margarine
- 1 cup shredded Swiss cheese

Put olive oil into a bake-and-serve dish (about 9 by 13 inches); stir in flour and spread mixture evenly over bottom of baking dish. Combine mushrooms with shallots, tarragon, and ¼ cup of the parsley; sprinkle evenly over bottom of baking dish. Drizzle evenly with wine and cream.

Wipe fish with damp cloth. Sprinkle lightly with salt, pepper, and paprika and arrange evenly on top of mushroom mixture. Pull bread apart with a fork to make 1 cup fresh crumbs. Melt butter in a pan and stir in crumbs; cook, stirring, over medium heat until lightly browned; set aside. (This much can be done up to 12 hours ahead; cover and chill fish.)

Preheat oven to 350°; mix remaining ¼ cup parsley with buttered crumbs and sprinkle over fish. Bake, uncovered, for about 15 to 20 minutes (about 30 to 40 minutes if chilled) or until fish flakes readily when prodded in thickest portion with a fork. Sprinkle cheese over top and return to oven just until cheese melts. Makes 6 servings.

Poached Flounder or Sole with Spring Vegetables

Little bundles of milk-poached fish share a platter with tender spring vegetables and pink shrimp; they're sauced in a delicate blend of Sherry, dill, and the seasoned milk.

…Flounder or Sole Fillet Soufflé (cont'd.)

- 6 small, skinless flounder or sole fillets (about 1¼ lb. total)
  About ½ cup dry white wine, dry vermouth, or regular-strength chicken broth
- 2 tablespoons finely chopped shallots or white part of green onions
- 1 tablespoon chopped parsley
  Salt and pepper
  Freshly grated nutmeg
- 6 eggs
- 5 tablespoons butter or margarine
- 5 tablespoons all-purpose flour, unsifted
- ¾ cup milk
- ½ cup freshly shredded Parmesan cheese

Preheat oven to 400°. Wipe fish with damp cloth; layer fillets evenly over bottom of a 1½ or 2-quart soufflé dish or other round casserole with straight sides. Pour wine over fish and sprinkle evenly with shallots and parsley, about ½ teaspoon salt, ⅛ teaspoon pepper, and a dash of nutmeg. Cover dish tightly with foil and bake for about 15 minutes or just until fish turns opaque.

Meanwhile separate 4 of the eggs; set aside. In a pan, melt 3 tablespoons of the butter over medium heat. Stir in 3 tablespoons of the flour and ¼ teaspoon salt; cook until bubbly. Remove from heat and, using wire whip, gradually stir in milk; return to heat and cook, stirring, until thick and smooth. Remove from heat and beat in the 4 egg yolks and ¼ cup of the cheese.

In a bowl, beat the 4 egg whites until they hold short, distinct, moist-looking peaks. Fold about half the egg whites thoroughly into yolk mixture, then gently fold in remaining egg whites.

When fish is cooked, remove from oven and, holding fish in dish with a wide spatula, carefully drain all poaching liquid into a bowl or a measuring cup; add wine or chicken broth, if necessary, to make 1 cup; set aside.

Make sure fish is evenly distributed in dish; sprinkle evenly with about 3 tablespoons of the cheese. (If you are using a 1½-quart dish, shape a collar of foil to raise sides about 1 inch; with cord, tie securely to soufflé dish.) Mound soufflé mixture evenly over top of fish; sprinkle with remaining cheese. Put on middle rack of oven; immediately lower heat to 375° and bake for about 25 minutes until soufflé is lightly browned and appears set in center when dish is gently shaken. You can hold it in oven with heat turned off up to about 5 more minutes, if necessary.

While soufflé bakes, melt remaining 2 tablespoons butter in small pan. Stir in remaining 2 tablespoons flour and cook until bubbly. Remove from heat and, using a wire whip, gradually stir in fish poaching liquid. Cook, stirring, until mixture boils and thickens.

Beat remaining 2 eggs slightly. Beat some of the hot sauce into eggs; then stir egg mixture back into pan and cook, stirring, for about 30 seconds—but do not boil. Remove from heat, taste, and add salt and pepper if needed. If sauce is ready before soufflé finishes baking, set it over hot water to keep warm.

When soufflé is done, remove collar (if used). Spoon out and serve immediately; pass a bowl of the sauce at table. Makes about 6 servings.

Spring vegetables (recipe follows)
About 2 cups milk
1 **small onion, sliced**
6 *each* **whole allspice and whole black peppers**
About 1 teaspoon salt
1 **bay leaf**
1½ to 2 **pounds small skinless flounder or sole fillets**
¼ **pound medium-size raw shrimp, shelled and deveined** (see directions on page 116), **or small, cooked shrimp**
3 **tablespoons butter or margarine**
3 **tablespoons all-purpose flour**
2 **tablespoons dry sherry**
1 **teaspoon** *each* **Dijon mustard and dill weed**

Prepare vegetables (directions follow) and arrange on warm serving platter. Cover and keep warm while you prepare fish.

In a wide frying pan, combine milk, onion, allspice, pepper, salt, and bay; heat slowly until scalded (just beginning to bubble at edges).

Meanwhile, wipe fish with damp cloth; loosely roll each fillet and secure with string. Set fish (and shrimp, if raw) in scalding milk; cover and poach until shrimp is pink and fish flakes readily when prodded in thickest portion with a fork. For a ½-inch-thick piece of fish (measured in thickest portion after rolling), allow 5 minutes. (Allow same ratio of thickness to time—1 inch:10 minutes—for fish of all thicknesses.)

Lift fish and shrimp from poaching liquid with slotted spoon; drain briefly (reserve poaching liquid). Carefully remove cords from fish and arrange on platter with vegetables; cover and keep warm while you make sauce. (You can prepare the dish up to this point as much as an hour ahead; cover fish and vegetables tightly and keep warm in a 225° oven.)

Strain poaching liquid thoroughly; discard seasonings. Melt butter in pan over medium-low heat; stir in flour and cook until bubbly. Remove from heat and, using a wire whip, gradually stir in poaching liquid. Return to heat and cook, stirring, until thickened (about 10 minutes).

Blend in sherry, mustard, and dill (if sauce needs thinning, you can add more milk). Spoon some of the sauce over flounder and vegetables; pour the rest into a bowl and pass at table. Makes 6 servings.

Spring vegetables. Scrub and trim about 1½ pounds small new potatoes, 1 bunch small carrots (or cut 4 large carrots lengthwise in quarters, and slice in 2-inch lengths), and 1½ pounds asparagus. Cook vegetables separately in lightly salted boiling water just until tender; drain (or steam vegetables). Melt 2 tablespoons butter or margarine in a pan; stir in 2 tablespoons finely chopped parsley. Turn vegetables in parsley butter until coated and warm.

Marinated Flounder or Sole with Vegetables

A dish of cool, marinated fish and slivered vegetables is refreshing on a hot summer's day. An added advantage is that it's low in calories.

1½ **pounds skinless flounder or sole fillets**
About 2 tablespoons lemon juice
1 **medium-size onion**
2 **small carrots**
2 **small celery stalks**
¼ **cup white wine vinegar**
½ **cup water**
2 **teaspoons thyme leaves**
¼ **teaspoon sugar**
⅛ **teaspoon pepper**
1 **bay leaf**
¾ **teaspoon salt**
½ **teaspoon paprika**
Salad oil
1 **clove garlic, minced or pressed**
Lettuce, chopped parsley, lemon wedges

Wipe fish with damp cloth; cut into serving-size pieces (about 3 by 5 inches), if desired. Sprinkle with lemon juice; set aside.

Cut onion lengthwise into ¼-inch-wide strips; cut carrots and celery into strips ¼ inch wide and 2 inches long. Set aside.

Combine wine vinegar, water, thyme, sugar, pepper, bay leaf, and ½ teaspoon of the salt. Set aside.

Pat fish lightly with paper towels and sprinkle evenly with paprika and remaining ¼ teaspoon salt. In a wide frying pan, heat salad oil, about ⅛ inch deep, over medium heat.

Add fish and cook, turning once, until fish flakes readily if prodded in thickest portion with a fork. For a 1-inch-thick piece of fish (measured in thickest portion), allow 10 minutes total—5 minutes on each side. (Allow same ratio of thick-

ness to time—1 inch:10 minutes—for fish of all other thicknesses.) Remove fish from frying pan and arrange in shallow baking pan.

Add 1 tablespoon salad oil and carrots to frying pan and cook, stirring, for 2 minutes. Add onion, celery, and garlic and cook, stirring, 2 minutes more. Pour in vinegar mixture; cover and simmer 1 minute. Spoon over fish and let cool. Cover and chill at least 4 hours or until next day.

To serve, lift fish from pan and place on lettuce-lined serving platter. Spoon vegetables over fish; garnish platter with parsley and lemon wedges. Makes 4 servings.

Flounder or Sole Florentine au Gratin

Madeira-poached fish, gilded in a sauce thick with golden Swiss cheese, rests on a bed of spinach.

2 **pounds skinless flounder or sole fillets**
½ **cup dry madeira or dry sherry**
2 **tablespoons lemon juice**
Salt and pepper
2 **tablespoons butter or margarine**
2 **tablespoons all-purpose flour**
½ **teaspoon** *each* **chicken stock base and Dijon mustard**
⅓ **cup whipping cream**
About ¾ cup shredded Swiss cheese
2 **packages** (*each* 10 oz.) **frozen chopped spinach, thawed**

Preheat oven to 400°. Wipe fish with damp cloth. Fold fillets in half and arrange side by side in large, shallow baking pan. Mix madeira and lemon juice and pour over fish. Sprinkle lightly with salt and pepper; cover tightly and bake until fish flakes readily when prodded in thickest portion with a fork. For a 1-inch-thick piece of fish (measured in thickest portion when folded), allow 10 minutes. (Allow same ratio of thickness to time—1 inch:10 minutes—for fish of all thicknesses.)

Remove from oven; holding fish in pan with a wide spatula or pan lid, drain off all liquid into a measuring cup. Add enough water to poaching liquid to make 1 cup; set aside. Cover fish.

Melt butter in a pan over medium heat and stir in flour, chicken stock base, and mustard; cook until bubbly. Using a wire whip, gradually add reserved poaching liquid and whipping cream. Cook, stirring, until bubbling and thickened (about 8 to 10 minutes). Stir in ½ cup of the Swiss cheese. (Cover sauce and chill until next day if made ahead.)

Squeeze all moisture possible from spinach and distribute spinach evenly in bottom of a shallow 1½-quart casserole; arrange cooked fish evenly on top —do not unfold. (Cover and chill until next day, if made ahead.)

Just before serving time, preheat oven to 450°; in a pan, reheat sauce until bubbling and spoon evenly over fish. Sprinkle with remaining Swiss cheese. Bake for 7 to 8 minutes (15 to 18 minutes if chilled) or until bubbling slightly; then broil briefly, if necessary, to brown top. Makes 6 servings.

Flounder or Sole with Grapes

(Pictured on cover and page 43)

Under a glaze of cream and a tumble of hot buttered grapes are fillets sautéed to a tender golden brown.

1½ **pounds skinless flounder or sole fillets**
Freshly grated nutmeg
Salt
All-purpose flour
Half butter or margarine and half salad oil (about 2 tablespoons *each*)
1 **cup seedless green grapes**
½ **cup whipping cream**
Lemon slices
Watercress

Wipe fish with damp cloth; cut into serving-size pieces (3 by 5 inches), if desired. Lightly sprinkle fish pieces with nutmeg and salt. Coat with flour; shake off excess. Arrange fish in single layer on wax paper within reaching distance of range.

In a wide frying pan, heat butter and oil (about ⅛ inch deep) until it foams but doesn't brown. Promptly add as many fish pieces as will fit without crowding. Cook, turning once—over medium-high heat if pieces are ⅝ inch

thick or less; over medium heat if pieces are thicker than ⅝ inch—until fish is lightly browned and flakes readily when prodded in thickest portion with a fork. For a 1-inch-thick piece of fish (measured in thickest portion) allow 10 minutes total—5 minutes each side. (Allow same ratio of thickness to time—1 inch:10 minutes—for fish of all thicknesses.)

Remove each piece as it is done; arrange on a warm serving platter and keep warm until all fish is cooked. Add more butter and oil to pan, if necessary, and repeat process with remaining fish.

When last fish is removed from pan, add grapes to pan and swirl over high heat just until grapes are warm and their color is a brighter green. Pour over fish.

Add cream to pan and boil over high heat, stirring and scraping to blend with pan drippings, until cream is a shiny, light golden color; drizzle sauce evenly over fish and grapes. Garnish with lemon slices and watercress and serve immediately. Makes 4 servings.

SANDWICH SMÖRGÅSBORD

Herring fillets and anchovies lend character and lively flavor to these open-faced, knife-and-fork sandwiches. Stacked with onion, herbs, and cucumbers on bread slices or muffin halves, they make a delicious light entrée or snack.

The sandwiches not only go together with a minimum of effort, but also are exceptionally attractive. And with a favorite beverage, they make an easy meal to serve. Depending on appetites, one or two sandwiches can make a generous serving.

Bacon-Tomato-Herring Sandwich

Blend 1 cup large or small curd cottage cheese with 1½ teaspoons prepared horseradish (or to taste). Split and toast 2 plain or whole wheat English muffins.

For each sandwich, spread an equal amount of cottage cheese mixture on each muffin half and top with 1 or 2

thin slices of tomato. Divide 1 large can (8 oz.) kippered herring fillets evenly among muffins and cover each with a strip of crisply cooked and drained bacon. Garnish with lettuce leaves. Makes 4 sandwiches.

Matjes Herring Sandwich

(Pictured on facing page)

Thinly slice ½ cucumber (peeled, if desired) and 1 small onion. Combine in a bowl with 2 tablespoons salad oil or olive oil, 1 tablespoon *each* vinegar and water, and ¼ teaspoon *each* oregano

leaves, dry basil, and salt; mix well. Chill at least 20 minutes.

Spread 4 to 6 slices of pumpernickel bread with sour cream or mayonnaise. Arrange a butter lettuce leaf on each. Divide 1 large can (8 oz.) matjes herring or kippered herring fillets evenly among bread slices; drain the marinated cucumbers and onions and arrange them over the herring. Garnish with a sprig of fresh dill and a cherry tomato half. Makes 4 to 6 servings.

Anchovy & Onion Sandwich

(Pictured on facing page)

Thinly slice 4 or 5 green onions with tops. Spread 4 to 6 slices of rye bread with mayonnaise or butter. Top each with a mound of green onions; cross 2 flat anchovy fillets (drained) over green onions and sprinkle with a small spoonful of finely chopped, hard-cooked egg yolk. Makes 4 to 6 sandwiches.

A delight for the eyes as well as the palate, a sandwich smörgåsbord
presents herring fillets and anchovies for a delectable, Scandinavian-inspired entrée or snack.
The recipes are on the facing page.

GROUPER

Grouper is so similar to the more widely known sea bass that it is often mistaken for it. Like the sea bass, grouper is a mild, white-fleshed fish; it appears in south-eastern markets, drawn or dressed and in steaks and fillets.

Choosing your method. The versatile grouper can be cooked any number of ways—try baking, broiling, deep-frying, oven-frying, pan-frying, or poaching it (see directions in "Basic Methods," pages 14–31). You'll find sauce possibilities on page 20 and seasoned butters on page 29.

GROUPER

Grouper Baked in Lemon Cream

A hot oven melds lemon, onion, and cream together into a rich sauce as it cooks the chunk of fish.

- 1 **skinless grouper fillet (about 2 lb.)**
- 1 **cup whipping cream**
- 5 **teaspoons lemon juice**
- 2 **tablespoons instant minced onion**
- ⅛ **teaspoon salt**
- 1 **egg yolk**

Preheat oven to 400°. Wipe fish with damp cloth; arrange in a greased, large, shallow baking pan.

In a bowl, combine cream, lemon juice, onion, and salt and mix well. Pour evenly over fish. Bake, uncovered, until fish flakes readily when prodded in thickest portion with a fork. For a 1-inch-thick piece of fish (measured in thickest portion), allow 10 minutes. (Allow same ratio of thickness to time—1 inch:10 minutes—for fish of all thicknesses.)

When done, remove pan from oven.

With a wide spatula, lift fish from hot cream mixture; drain briefly and transfer to a warm serving platter. Cover and keep warm.

In a small pan, beat egg yolk slightly. Using a wire whip, beat a little of the hot cream mixture into egg. Then pour remaining hot cream mixture into egg mixture, beating constantly. Cook egg and cream mixture, stirring, over low heat until slightly thickened (about 5 to 10 minutes)—do not boil. Pour evenly over fish and serve immediately. Makes 4 to 6 servings.

HADDOCK

From New England comes a fine-flavored, all-purpose fish—haddock—with a history that goes back to the 13 colonies. It is mild and slightly chewy and comes in drawn or fillet form; small haddock is also available under the name "scrod" and is very tender. Haddock, like cod, can be bought frozen almost anywhere in the United States.

HADDOCK

Choosing your method. Haddock is very adaptable; bake, broil, deep-fry, oven-fry, or poach it (see directions in "Basic Methods," pages 14–31). You'll find sauce possibilities on page 20 and seasoned butters on page 29. Haddock is even good smoked—then it's like the famous finnan haddie. (To smoke fish, see directions in "Building a Simple Smoker," page 120; for information on finnan haddie, see page 47.)

Golden Haddock Fillet

Simple is the word for this crunchy mayonnaise-coated fish; serve it sizzling hot from the oven.

- 1½ **pounds skinless haddock fillet**
  All-purpose flour
- ¾ **cup mayonnaise**
- ¾ **cup coarsely crushed unseasoned croutons**
- 1 **teaspoon garlic salt**
  Butter or margarine
  Lemon wedges and parsley sprigs

Preheat oven to 425°; place large, shallow baking pan in oven. Wipe fish with damp cloth. Coat with flour; shake off excess. Lay on wax paper.

With a small spatula, spread half the mayonnaise over top and sides of fish. Combine crushed croutons and garlic salt. Sprinkle half the crouton mixture evenly over mayonnaise coating and pat lightly.

Remove pan from oven. Put butter in pan and swirl until melted (butter should be about ⅛ inch deep). Lay fish, mayonnaise side down, in pan. Spread top with remaining mayonnaise and sprinkle evenly with remaining crumbs, patting lightly.

Return pan to oven and bake until fish flakes readily when prodded in thickest portion with a fork. For a 1-inch-thick piece of fish (measured in thickest portion), allow 10 minutes. (Allow same ratio of thickness to time—1 inch:10 minutes—for fish of all thicknesses.) Serve immediately, garnished with lemon wedges and parsley. Makes 4 servings.

HALIBUT, PACIFIC

The halibut is an all-time favorite of many cooks. It is sold fresh in season in the West; off season and in areas outside the West, you can buy it frozen. Most halibuts are very large fish and are available only in steak form, but in the West it is occasionally possible to buy a whole 6 to 10-pound "chicken" (or small) halibut if you order in advance from your market.

Choosing your method. Halibut can be baked, broiled, butter-sautéed, deep-fried (if fresh), oven-fried, pan-fried, or poached (see directions in "Basic Methods," pages 14 – 31). You'll find sauce possibilities on page 20 and seasoned butters on page 29.

Halibut Salad Avgolemono

For a festive occasion, serve a stunning platter of chilled poached halibut steaks lavished with a lemony sour cream sauce and topped with shrimp and olives.

- **4 halibut steaks (*each* about 1 inch thick), thawed if frozen**
- **2 cups water**
- **4 *each* whole cloves and whole black peppers**
- **2 slices lemon**
- **1 carrot, cut in large chunks**
- **1 medium-size onion, cut in large chunks**
- **½ teaspoon salt**
- **Avgolemono/sour cream dressing (recipe follows)**
- **1 cucumber**
- **1 bunch radishes**
- **2 tomatoes**
- **Parsley sprigs**
- **Pitted ripe olives**
- **8 large shrimp, cooked, shelled, deveined, and chilled (see directions on page 116)**

Wipe fish with damp cloth and place in a wide frying pan. Pour in water and tuck cloves, peppers, lemon slices, carrots, and onion around fish; sprinkle evenly with salt. Bring to a boil, reduce heat, cover, and simmer gently until fish flakes readily when prodded in thickest portion with a fork. For a 1-inch-thick piece of fish (measured in thickest portion), allow 10 minutes.

With a wide spatula, transfer fish to a large serving platter, arranging in a single layer; cover and chill. Reserve poaching liquid for avgolemono/sour cream dressing.

To serve, arrange fish steaks crosswise in single layer down center of platter. Peel and slice cucumber thinly and arrange along one side of fish. Trim and slice radishes thinly and scatter over cucumber slices. Cut tomatoes in wedges and arrange along other side of fish; sprinkle tomatoes with a few parsley sprigs. Spoon avgolemono/sour cream dressing evenly over fish and garnish each steak with a few olives and 2 of the shrimp. Makes 4 to 6 servings.

Avgolemono/sour cream dressing. Strain reserved poaching liquid. In top of a double boiler, directly over high heat, boil rapidly until reduced to ¾ cup. Beat 3 egg yolks until light yellow; then beat in 1½ tablespoons lemon juice. Using wire whisk, gradually stir hot poaching liquid into egg mixture.

Return mixture to top of double boiler and place over hot (not boiling) water. Stirring constantly, heat gently just until sauce is thickened (about 5 to 10 minutes). Let cool; then cover and chill. When thoroughly chilled (about 1 hour), blend sauce into 1 cup sour cream and chill again until ready to use. Makes 1½ cups.

Halibut with Rosemary

From the Greek tavernas comes this recipe for pan-fried fish in a piquant marinade, redolent of garlic and rosemary.

- **1½ to 2 pounds halibut steaks (*each* about 1 inch thick), thawed if frozen**
- **Salt and pepper**
- **All-purpose flour**
- **⅓ cup olive oil**
- **¼ cup white wine vinegar**
- **2 tablespoons water**
- **3 cloves garlic**
- **½ teaspoon fresh or dry rosemary**

Wipe fish with damp cloth; cut into serving-size pieces (3 by 5 inches), if desired. Sprinkle with salt and pepper; coat with flour, shaking off excess. Arrange in single layer on wax paper within reaching distance of range.

Heat oil in a wide frying pan over medium heat until oil ripples when pan is tilted. Add as many fish as will fit in pan without crowding and cook, turning once, until fish is browned and flakes readily when prodded in thickest portion with a fork. For a 1-inch-thick piece of fish (measured in thickest portion), allow 10 minutes total—5 minutes on each side. When fish is done, transfer to a warm serving platter and keep warm; repeat process with remaining fish.

When last fish is removed from pan, add vinegar and water to pan drippings. When sizzling stops, add garlic and rosemary; boil rapidly until reduced by half, stirring and scraping occasionally to blend with drippings. Remove garlic with slotted spoon and discard; spoon vinegar mixture over fish. Serves 4 to 6.

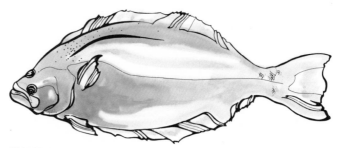

HALIBUT, PACIFIC

Bursting with smoked salmon, rice, and vegetables tossed
in a curry-lemon-yogurt dressing, juicy tomatoes make a refreshing main-dish salad.
The recipe is on page 68.

KINGFISH

"Kingfish" is a suitably aristocratic name for this distinguished (and largest) member of the mackerel family. Long, lithe, and silver-skinned, the kingfish comes from the southeastern coast and the Gulf and is sold in the markets of those regions in whole and drawn form and as steaks or fillets.

Choosing your method. Like other mackerels, kingfish has a pronounced flavor; the methods that suit it best are baking, barbecuing, broiling, oven-frying, and poaching (see directions in "Basic Methods," pages 14–31). You'll find sauce possibilities on page 20 and seasoned butters on page 29.

KINGFISH

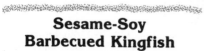

Sesame-Soy Barbecued Kingfish

Large kingfish fillets make a dramatic entrée when barbecued whole, basted to a deep mahogany with a soy-and-sherry sauce, and spangled with toasted sesame seed.

> 2 **large kingfish fillets** (*each about 2 lb.*), **skin on**
> ¼ **cup butter or margarine**
> 3 **tablespoons soy sauce**
> 2 **tablespoons** *each* **lemon juice and dry sherry**
> 2 **to 3 teaspoons sesame seed, toasted**

About 30 to 45 minutes before you plan to begin cooking, ignite coals (you'll need about 30 long-burning briquets). Wipe fish with damp cloth. Cover skin side of each fillet with heavy-duty foil; press smoothly to fit.

In a pan, melt butter; stir in soy sauce, lemon juice, and sherry.

When coals are covered with gray ash, arrange in a single solid layer to underlie entire area to be used on grill. Knock ash off coals and let burn down until moderately hot (about 5 to 10 minutes longer). Adjust grill height to 6 inches above coals.

Lay fish on grill, foil side down, to fit over coals; baste thoroughly with soy mixture. Cover barbecue with lid or heavy-duty foil (see directions in "Barbecuing a Large Whole Fish," page 17). Lifting lid often to baste fish with soy mixture, cook, without turning, until fish flakes readily when prodded in thickest portion with a fork. For a 1-inch-thick piece of fish (measured in thickest portion), allow 10 minutes. (Allow same ratio of thickness to time—1 inch:10 minutes—for fish of all thicknesses.)

When done, transfer fish on foil to a warm serving platter and sprinkle evenly with sesame seed. To serve, cut down to skin and lift fish off foil with wide spatula (be careful not to catch the foil). Makes 8 to 10 servings.

LINGCOD

The native western lingcod is not a true cod at all; it's actually a rather odd-looking kind of fish known as a "greenling" (and often its raw flesh has a greenish tint). But behind the lingcod's unusual appearance lurks one of the finest eating fish of the West, its tender flesh distinctively delicate and white when cooked. Available whole and in steaks or fillets, the lingcod is a versatile and graceful addition to any cook's repertoire.

Choosing your method. From simple family dishes to fancy, festive ones, the lingcod adapts easily; bake, broil, butter-sauté, deep-fry, oven-fry, pan-fry, or poach it (see directions in "Basic Methods," pages 14–31). You'll find sauce possibilities on page 20 and seasoned butters on page 29. You might also try lingcod in any of the recipes given for other lean, mild, tender fish. (To identify other lean fish discussed in this book, see buying guide charts, pages 8–11.)

Basque Chilled Lingcod Platter

Typical Basque seasonings—onion, garlic, celery, thyme—flavor a hearty vegetable sauce in which you poach the lingcod.

> ½ **cup olive oil or salad oil**
> 4 **large onions, thinly sliced**
> 4 **cloves garlic, minced or pressed**
> 2 **cups thinly sliced celery**
> ¾ **teaspoon thyme leaves, crumbled**
> **Salt**
> ½ **teaspoon pepper**
> **About 3 pounds skinless lingcod fillets**
> ½ **cup finely chopped parsley**
> 2 **large tomatoes, seeded and coarsely chopped**
> 1 **can (3½ oz.) large pitted ripe olives, drained**

In a wide frying pan, heat oil over medium-high heat; add onions and sauté until soft (about 10 minutes). Stir in garlic, celery, thyme, 1 teaspoon salt, and pepper. Push mixture to sides of pan, leaving center clear.

(Continued on page 56)

LINGCOD

Meanwhile, wipe fish with damp cloth and cut into serving-size pieces (about 3 by 5 inches). Salt lightly and arrange in single layer in center of pan, spooning some of the vegetable mixture over fish.

Heat to simmering, cover tightly, reduce heat to low, and cook until fish flakes readily when prodded in thickest portion with a fork. For a 1-inch-thick piece of fish (measured in thickest portion), allow 10 minutes. (Allow same ratio of thickness to time—1 inch:10 minutes—for fish of all thicknesses.) With a wide spatula, lift fish from pan and arrange on a serving platter; cover and chill thoroughly (at least 2 hours).

Boil vegetable mixture, stirring occasionally, for 7 to 10 more minutes or until it becomes a thick sauce. Pour into a small bowl; cover and chill thoroughly (at least 2 hours).

Shortly before serving, stir parsley into vegetable mixture; pour evenly over fish. Garnish platter with tomatoes and olives; serve immediately. Serves 6.

Stuffed Layered Lingcod

Quantities of butter-sautéed almonds and onions add a savory crunch to the stuffing mounded between layers of lingcod fillets.

6 tablespoons butter or margarine
1 small onion, chopped
1 cup sliced almonds
1 cup coarsely crushed unseasoned croutons
¾ teaspoon salt
½ teaspoon ground sage
⅛ teaspoon pepper
About 3 to 4 pounds skinless lingcod fillets (at least 4 fillets)
2 tablespoons butter or margarine, melted
2 tablespoons fine dry bread crumbs

Preheat oven to 375°. In a pan, melt the 6 tablespoons butter over medium-high heat. Add onion and almonds and sauté for about 5 minutes, stirring frequently. Remove from heat; add croutons, salt, sage, and pepper and mix well.

Wipe fish with damp cloth. Arrange half the fillets to cover bottom of a greased shallow baking pan. Spread stuffing evenly over layer of fish; cover evenly with remaining fillets. Brush top of fish with the 2 tablespoons melted butter and sprinkle evenly with bread crumbs.

Bake, uncovered, for about 35 minutes or until fish flakes readily when prodded in thickest portion with a fork. To serve, slice through all 3 layers and include both layers of fish as well as stuffing in each serving. Makes 6 to 8 servings.

MACKEREL

In almost any coastal area, you'll find fresh mackerel for sale, but the varieties differ from region to region. New England has the small Atlantic mackerel, with iridescent, midnight blue markings. Farther south along the eastern coast appears the Spanish mackerel, larger and spotted with yellow. And on the west coast, you'll find the Pacific mackerel, similar to the Atlantic mackerel. These fish are generally sold whole or in fillets. Served whole, especially, they make dramatic entrées.

Choosing your method. The pronounced flavor of the mackerel makes it a particularly good candidate for baking, barbecuing, broiling, and oven-frying (see directions in "Basic Methods," pages 14–31). You'll find sauce possibilities on page 20 and seasoned butters on page 29.

Mackerel with Ham & Green Onion Sauce

Borrowed from Oriental cooking, the flavorings for this baked whole fish are fresh ginger, soy sauce, and plenty of green onions (you'll need a supply of cheesecloth, too).

1 can (about 14 oz.) regular-strength chicken broth
2 tablespoons soy sauce
3 thin slices fresh ginger root, *each* about 3 inches long by 1 inch wide, or ¼ teaspoon ground ginger
2 whole mackerel (*each* about 1½ lb.) or 1 large whole mackerel (about 2½ lb.), cleaned and scaled
¼ pound cooked ham
2 tablespoons salad oil
1 tablespoon *each* cornstarch and water
½ cup thinly sliced green onion (including some tops)
Hot cooked rice

Preheat oven to 375°. In a small pan, combine chicken broth, soy, and ginger; bring to boiling. Reduce heat and simmer for about 5 minutes to blend flavors.

Meanwhile, wipe fish with damp cloth, inside cavities and outside. Moisten and wring dry a piece of cheesecloth for each fish. Wrap each fish in cheesecloth, folding edges together on top of fish, and set in a large, shallow baking pan (tail can turn up, if necessary).

Pour hot sauce over fish and cover pan tightly with foil. Bake until fish flakes readily when prodded in thickest portion with a fork (to test, fold back cheesecloth). For a 1-inch-thick fish (measured in thickest portion), allow 10 minutes. (Allow same ratio of thickness to time—1 inch:10 minutes—for fish of all thicknesses.)

Meanwhile, cut ham in slivers. In pan that contained sauce, heat salad oil over medium-high heat until it ripples when pan is tilted. Add ham and sauté until lightly browned. Set ham and drippings aside.

When fish is done, lift from sauce,

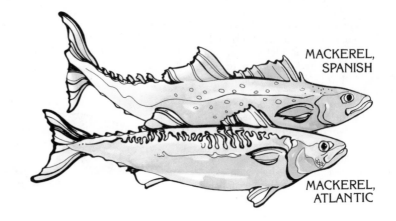

MACKEREL, SPANISH

MACKEREL, ATLANTIC

supporting with cheesecloth, and transfer to warm serving platter. Carefully remove cheesecloth; cover fish and keep warm.

Pour sauce through wire strainer into small pan; discard ginger. Boil sauce rapidly, if necessary, to reduce to 1½ cups. Blend cornstarch into water until smooth and add to pan. Stir until boil resumes; then stir in ham and drippings, and green onions. Remove from heat.

With slotted spoon, lift some of the ham and onions from sauce and distribute evenly over top of fish as a garnish. Pour remaining sauce into a serving bowl; pass at table to spoon over portions of fish and hot cooked rice.

To serve fish, cut directly to bone, then slide a wide spatula between flesh and ribs and lift off each serving. When top half has been served, lift and remove backbone (sever from head, if necessary) before serving bottom half. Makes 4 servings.

Parmesan Barbecued Mackerel

A tangy cheese crust and smoky flavor complement the sturdy mackerel. When you buy the fish, have it boned at the market.

- 4 whole mackerels (*each* about 1¼ lb.), cleaned and scaled; or 2 mackerels (*each* about 2½ lb.), boned and filleted; or 3 pounds mackerel fillets, skin on
- ½ cup *each* salad oil and lemon juice
- 2 tablespoons chopped parsley
- 1 teaspoon dry basil
- 1 cup grated Parmesan cheese
- ½ teaspoon garlic salt

Wipe fish with damp cloth. If using fillets, cut them into pieces about 4 inches long. Combine oil, lemon juice, parsley, and basil, and pour over fish. Cover and chill for 1 hour, turning once or twice.

About 30 to 45 minutes before you plan to begin cooking, ignite coals (for a 1½ to 2½-lb. fish, you need about 35 long-burning briquets). When coals are covered with gray ash, arrange in single, solid layer to underlie entire area to be used on grill. Knock ash off coals and let burn down until moderately hot (about 5 to 10 minutes longer). Adjust grill height to 4 to 6 inches above coals.

Remove fish from marinade (reserve marinade). On wax paper or in a shallow pan, combine Parmesan and garlic salt. Thickly coat fish in cheese mixture; pat

lightly. Arrange in single layer on wax paper until ready to cook.

Grease grill. Arrange fish on grill to fit over coals; drizzle with reserved marinade. Cook, turning once and drizzling frequently with marinade, until fish is browned and flakes readily when prodded in thickest portion with a fork.

For a 1-inch-thick piece of fish (measured in thickest portion), allow 10 minutes. (Allow same ratio of thickness to time—1 inch:10 minutes—for fish of all thicknesses.) When fish is done, transfer to a warm serving platter and serve immediately. Makes 4 to 6 servings.

MULLET

The mullet is an ancient fish—thousands of years ago, it was cultivated for food in the deltas of the Nile River and was much admired and sought-after by the Romans. In the United States today, it is found primarily on the southeastern coast and in the Gulf.

Choosing your method. A number of cooking methods work well with mullet; among them are baking, barbecuing, broiling, oven-frying, and pan-frying (see directions in "Basic Methods" pages 14−31). You'll find sauce possibilities on page 20 and seasoned butters on page 29. Mullet is also delicious when smoked (see directions in "Building a Simple Smoker," page 120).

Barbecued Mullets with Basil-Garlic Baste

Mild mullets are roasted whole over the coals, cloaked in a pungent herb baste that brings out their flavor.

- 4 whole mullets (*each* about 1 lb.), cleaned and scaled
- 1 cup *each* salad oil and white wine vinegar
- 1 small clove garlic, minced or pressed
- 1 tablespoon chopped parsley
- 1 teaspoon salt
- ½ teaspoon dry basil
- ⅛ teaspoon pepper

About 30 to 45 minutes before you plan to begin cooking, ignite coals (you'll need about 50 to 60 long-burning briquets).

Wipe fish with damp cloth, inside cavities and outside. With a sharp knife, cut 3 or 4 shallow, diagonal slashes in both sides of each fish. Arrange in single layer in a wide, shallow baking pan.

Combine oil, vinegar, garlic, parsley, salt, basil, and pepper. Pour over fish in pan; turn fish to coat thoroughly with herb mixture. Marinate at room temperature 10 minutes, turning occasionally.

When coals are covered with gray ash, arrange in a single solid layer to underlie entire area to be used on grill. Knock ash off coals and let burn down until moderately hot (about 5 to 10 minutes longer). Adjust grill height to 6 inches above coals.

Grease grill. Remove fish from marinade (reserve marinade) and arrange on grill to fit over coals. Cook, turning once and basting frequently with reserved marinade, until fish is browned and flakes readily when prodded in thickest portion with a fork. For 1-inch-thick fish (measured in thickest portion), allow 10 minutes. (Allow same ratio of thickness to time—1 inch:10 minutes—for fish of all thicknesses.)

When done, transfer fish to a warm serving platter and serve immediately. Makes 4 servings.

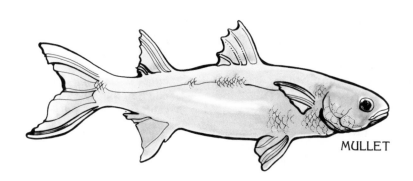

MULLET

OCEAN PERCH

The tender, rosy little fish known as ocean perch are caught off the New England coast and sometimes sold whole and fresh in eastern markets. More common, however, are the frozen ocean perch fillets found in markets across the United States.

OCEAN PERCH, ATLANTIC

Choosing your method. Ocean perch's delicate, flaky flesh is well suited to baking, broiling, butter-sautéing, oven-frying, pan-frying, and poaching (see directions in "Basic Methods," pages 14–31). You'll find sauce possibilities on page 20 and seasoned butters on page 29. These little fillets can also be used in the recipes given for "Flounder or Sole" (see pages 47–50).

Ocean Perch Salad in Wine Aspic

A tangy horseradish sauce accompanies this cool main-dish salad of perch fillets and shrimp suspended in a molded wine gelatin.

- 2 **envelopes unflavored gelatin**
  About 1½ cups cold water
- 1 **pound small ocean perch fillets (preferably skinless)**
- 1 **cup dry white wine**
- ¼ **cup lemon juice**
- ¾ **teaspoon salt**
- ¼ **teaspoon liquid hot pepper seasoning**
- 2 **egg whites, beaten until frothy**
- ⅓ **cup each finely chopped celery and green pepper**
- 2 **tablespoons chopped chives**
- ¼ **pound small cooked shrimp**
  Horseradish sauce (recipe follows)
  Watercress

Sprinkle gelatin over ½ cup of the water to soften; set aside. Wipe fish with damp cloth; roll each fillet and tie with string. Combine 1 cup of the water, wine, lemon juice, salt, and hot pepper seasoning in a frying pan; bring mixture to a boil.

Place fish rolls in liquid and simmer gently, covered for about 2½ minutes. Lift cover and carefully turn rolls over in poaching liquid. Replace cover and simmer for another 2½ minutes or until fish flakes readily when prodded in thickest portion with a fork. Remove fish from liquid (reserve liquid); cover and chill while you prepare aspic.

To clarify reserved poaching liquid, stir in egg whites; bring liquid to a boil and cook for about 1 minute without stirring. Strain through damp cloth. Stir in reserved gelatin mixture until dissolved; add water to make 2¾ cups. Chill until syrupy.

Gently blend celery, green pepper, chives, and shrimp into gelatin mixture. Pour into a 4½-cup (8-inch) ring mold. Remove strings from fish rolls and arrange rolls in gelatin, spaced evenly. Chill until set (at least 3 hours). Meanwhile, prepare horseradish sauce.

To serve, unmold gelatin salad onto a large round serving platter; garnish with watercress. Pass horseradish sauce at table with salad. Makes 4 to 6 servings.

Horseradish sauce. Blend ½ cup *each* sour cream and mayonnaise, 2 tablespoons *each* prepared horseradish and drained capers (reserve caper liquid), and 1 teaspoon *each* sugar and liquid from capers. Pour into serving bowl; cover and chill.

Ocean Perch & Crab Mousse

Crusty gold on top, delicately fragile beneath, these individual baked ramekins are party fare, served with a wine sauce full of shrimp.

- ¾ **pound skinless perch fillets**
- ¼ **pound crab meat**
- 2 **egg yolks**
- 2 **eggs, separated**
- ¾ **cup half-and-half (light cream)**
- 3 **tablespoons all-purpose flour**
- 1 **teaspoon salt**
- ⅛ **teaspoon freshly grated nutmeg**
- 1 **tablespoon lemon juice**
- 1 **tablespoon brandy**
- 1 **cup whipping cream**
  Shrimp sauce (recipe follows)

Preheat oven to 350°. In a blender, combine fish and crab; whirl until ground to a paste. Turn into a bowl; add the 4 egg yolks, one at a time, beating until smooth after each addition. Beat in half-and-half, flour, salt, nutmeg, lemon juice, and brandy. Whip cream until stiff and fold gently into fish mixture. Beat egg whites until they hold stiff, moist peaks; fold gently into fish mixture.

Butter 6 individual ramekins (*each* about 2-cup capacity); distribute fish mixture evenly among them. Place ramekins in 2 shallow baking pans; fill pans halfway with hot water. Bake, uncovered, for 25 minutes or until mousse is puffed and set in center, appearing firm when dishes are gently shaken.

Meanwhile, prepare shrimp sauce. When mousse is done, remove ramekins from hot water and let cool 10 minutes. Then serve, accompanied by shrimp sauce. Makes 6 servings.

Shrimp sauce. In a pan, combine 1½ cups regular-strength chicken broth, ½ cup dry white wine, and 2 tablespoons lemon juice; boil, uncovered, until reduced to 1 cup liquid.

Beat 2 egg yolks until light yellow; blend in 2 teaspoons cornstarch and ½ cup half-and-half (light cream). Using a wire whip, gradually blend hot broth mixture into egg mixture. Return to pan and cook over low heat, stirring constantly, until thickened (about 5 to 10 minutes). Stir in 1 tablespoon dry sherry and ½ cup (¼ lb.) small cooked shrimp. Heat through (do not boil) and pour into a serving bowl.

PIKE

The name "pike" is used for a number of different fresh-water fish. They range from the huge muskellunge and moderately large pickerel (both mainly midwestern sport fish) to the pike perches:

(Continued on page 60)

Start the festivities! Line the cavity of a sleek and regal whole salmon
with sliver-thin lemon and onion slices; then barbecue it for a rich, smoky flavor.
Barbecuing instructions are on pages 16–18.

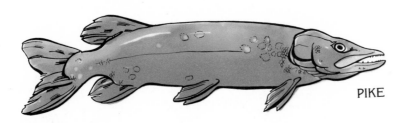

PIKE

...Pike (cont'd.)

the yellow pike perch and walleyed pike, available commercially and relatively small (weighing 1 to 1½ pounds each). Most pike is lean, white, and firm-fleshed. The small pike perches are most likely to be available whole, drawn, or in fresh or frozen fillets.

Choosing your method. A large whole pickerel can be stuffed and baked or barbecued. The smaller whole pike perches adapt well to butter-sautéing or pan-frying; they are also good oven-fried. Pike perch fillets and pickerel fillets or steaks can be prepared by any of the basic methods (see directions in "Basic Methods," pages 14–31). When broiling or barbecuing these lean fish, baste them with plenty of butter or oil to keep them from drying out.

Cheese-crusted Pike Perch

Oven-fry these plump fish in a crusty coating of Parmesan cheese, then serve them sizzling hot with a spicy chili sauce.

- **2 whole pike perches (*each* about 1 to 1½ pounds), cleaned and scaled**
- **½ cup fine dry bread crumbs**
- **¼ cup grated Parmesan cheese**
- **¼ cup finely chopped parsley Salt and pepper**
- **1 egg About 2 to 3 tablespoons butter or margarine**
- **1 can (8 oz.) tomato sauce**
- **1 teaspoon *each* onion salt and chili powder**
- **¾ teaspoon sugar**

Preheat oven to 450°. Put a large, shallow baking pan in oven. Wipe fish with damp cloth, inside cavities and outside.

Combine bread crumbs, cheese, parsley, and salt and pepper to taste on a piece of wax paper. In a shallow bowl, beat egg slightly. Dip each fish in egg to coat all over; drain briefly. Then roll in

crumb mixture to coat evenly on all sides; shake off excess. Lay in single layer on wax paper.

Remove pan from oven; put butter in pan and swirl until melted (butter should be about ⅛ inch deep).

Lay a fish in pan; turn to coat with butter. Repeat with other fish. Return pan to oven and bake until fish is browned and flakes readily when prodded in thickest portion with a fork. For a 2-inch-thick fish (measured in thickest portion), allow 20 minutes total. (Allow same ratio of thickness to time—1 inch: 10 minutes—for fish of all thicknesses.)

Meanwhile, in a small pan over medium heat, combine tomato sauce, onion salt, chili powder, and sugar; cook, stirring, until bubbly; keep warm.

When fish is done, remove pan from oven. Pour sauce evenly over fish; return pan to oven and bake just until sauce is heated through and bubbly. Serve immediately. Makes 4 servings.

Pike & Shrimp Casserole

For a quick family meal or a company dinner, present this easy pike and shrimp combination—just layer the ingredients and bake it.

- **1 pound skinless pike perch fillets, thawed if frozen**
- **¼ pound small cooked shrimp**
- **3 tablespoons fine dry bread crumbs**
- **¼ teaspoon pepper**
- **2 tablespoons lemon juice**
- **¼ pound mushrooms, thinly sliced**
- **2 tablespoons quick tartare sauce (see recipe on page 21) or mayonnaise**
- **2 tablespoons thinly sliced green onion**
- **1 clove garlic, minced or pressed**
- **1½ tablespoons butter or margarine, softened**
- **¼ cup dry vermouth**

Preheat oven to 425°. Generously butter a shallow 1½-quart baking dish. Arrange half the fillets in an even layer over bottom of dish. Sprinkle evenly with half the shrimp, 1½ tablespoons of the bread crumbs, ⅛ teaspoon of the pepper, 1 tablespoon of the lemon juice, and half the mushrooms. Beginning with remaining fish fillets, repeat layering.

Mix together tartare sauce, green onion, garlic, and butter; dot mixture over top of casserole. Drizzle vermouth evenly over casserole.

Bake, covered, for 20 minutes or until fish flakes readily when prodded in thickest portion with a fork. Makes 4 servings.

POMPANO

From the warm waters of the Gulf of Mexico comes a beautiful, silvery, round fish, revered among seafood gourmets as one of the most delicious of marine fish. This is the pompano, richly flavored and firm in flesh. It is usually sold whole or drawn because its handsome appearance encourages whole presentation. However, if fillets are called for, as they are in the classic dish, "Pompano en Papillote," you will find the pompano relatively easy to bone (see directions on page 7).

Choosing your method. The pompano is adaptable; bake, barbecue, broil, butter-sauté, oven-fry, pan-fry, or poach it (see directions in "Basic Methods," pages 14–31). You'll find sauce possibilities on page 20 and seasoned butters on page 29.

Madeira-broiled Pompano

These handsome fish are broiled whole, seasoned with a mellow baste of tarragon-scented butter and madeira, then garnished with a few sprigs of fresh watercress.

- **2 whole pompano (*each* about 2 lb.), cleaned and scaled**
- **2 teaspoons salt**
- **½ teaspoon pepper**
- **2 tablespoons chopped parsley**
- **½ cup (¼ lb.) butter or margarine, melted**
- **3 tablespoons dry madeira**
- **½ teaspoon tarragon leaves Watercress**

Turn on broiler and preheat broiler pan. Wipe fish with damp cloth, inside cav-

(Continued on page 63)

FISH IN THE RAW

Raw fish: is it food for barbarians? Not at all! Venerable and sophisticated cuisines such as the Italian, the Mexican, and the Japanese rank certain raw fish dishes as subtle delicacies.

The trick to serving delicious raw fish is to choose the very freshest fish possible (preferably right out of the water)—clams and oysters still alive in their shells, fish fillets or steaks with no odor at all and no hint of brown around their edges—in order to get the characteristically mild, fresh, delicate flavor. Contrary to popular conception, a great raw fish will never taste strong and fishy; if it does, the fish isn't fresh enough!

Raw Oyster or Clam Cocktail

(Pictured on page 110)

To serve raw oysters or clams on the half shell in their own liquid, follow directions in "Cleaning and opening clams," page 88, or "Cleaning and opening oysters," page 106. Pull off top shell of either oyster or clam, cut shellfish free, and serve it from bottom shell or in a dish. Take care, in all cases, to preserve as much of the juices as possible. Chill oysters and clams until ready to serve.

Serve raw clams and oysters plain, swimming in their own juices. If you like, you can top each half shell with a teaspoon of spicy cocktail sauce.

Spicy cocktail sauce. In a bowl, combine ½ cup catsup, 1 tablespoon lemon juice, ¼ teaspoon liquid hot pepper seasoning, and 1½ teaspoons *each* prepared horseradish, Worcestershire, and sugar; stir until blended. Chill until serving time. Makes about ⅔ cup.

Sashimi

Classic sashimi is a striking presentation: extra-thin slivers of rosy raw tuna (resembles uncooked lamb in color), pale sea bass, halibut, or albacore arranged atop shredded carrot and daikon radish and accompanied by a dish of piquant wasabi (horseradish) paste. (You can also use more common seasonings and vegetables to make it American-style.)

- **1 large daikon (about 1 lb.), peeled; or 1 head iceberg lettuce (about 1 lb.)**
- **⅓ small carrot, peeled**
- **1 pound boneless, skinless, fresh bluefin or yellowfin tuna, Pacific albacore, white sea bass, or halibut**
  Wasabi paste or alternate seasoning (directions follow)
  Parsley sprigs
  Soy sauce

Shred daikon into long, fine strands (if your grater doesn't make long strands, use a vegetable peeler to slice daikon lengthwise into paper-thin strips; then cut strips into slivers with a very sharp knife). You should have about 3 cups. (If using lettuce, slice very thinly and tear into shreds—enough to make 3 cups.) Shred carrot the same way; mix with daikon or lettuce. Immerse mixture in ice water.

Wipe fish quickly with damp cloth; pat dry with paper towels. Cut away and discard any dark portions of flesh (in red-fleshed fish, these will be almost black). If fish is wide, cut lengthwise, with the grain, into 2 or 3 strips (1 to 2 inches wide). Place strips on cutting board. Using a very sharp, thin-bladed knife, cut strips across the grain into ⅛ to ¼-inch slices (as thin as possible). To keep flavor fresh, handle fish no more than necessary.

Drain daikon or lettuce mixture. Arrange evenly on a chilled serving platter. Transfer fish slices to serving platter with spatula, one row at a time, and arrange over daikon mixture in rows, leaving about ⅓ of the daikon exposed on one end of platter (Japanese custom is to arrange fish in rows with uneven numbers of slices—such as 9, 11, or 13).

Place wasabi paste or alternate seasoning on platter at one side of sliced fish; cluster parsley sprigs at other. To serve, provide each individual with a small dish of soy sauce and suggest that he or she mix a small amount of wasabi paste into soy sauce to use as a dipping sauce for fish and vegetables. Makes 4 servings (6 appetizer servings).

Wasabi paste. To 4 teaspoons wasabi powder (available in most Oriental markets), gradually add 4 teaspoons water, blending into a smooth paste. Cover and let stand for about 5 minutes. Makes about 2½ tablespoons.

Alternate seasonings. You can make a paste by blending 4 teaspoons dry mustard with 3 teaspoons water until smooth. Or use about 2 tablespoons prepared horseradish, drained slightly, or grated fresh ginger root.

Scallop Seviche

A summer evening appetizer, Mexican-style, is a marinated raw scallop salad served ice-cold in nests of lettuce.

- **1 pound raw scallops, coarsely chopped, thawed if frozen**
  Lemon or lime juice
- **2 ripe tomatoes, peeled, seeded, and diced**
- **1 cup finely chopped green onion (including some tops)**
- **1 firm but ripe avocado, peeled and diced**
  Salt
  Fresh coriander (cilantro), minced (optional)
  Canned California green chiles, seeded and minced (optional)
  Lettuce leaves

Place scallops in a deep bowl; barely cover with fresh lemon or lime juice. Cover bowl and let stand in refrigerator for about 2 hours or until scallops lose their translucence and become opaque and white. Drain well and mix with tomatoes, onion, and avocado; season to taste with salt. Add coriander and/or green chiles to taste, if desired. Line 8 small plates with lettuce and top with scallop mixture, divided evenly. Makes 8 appetizer servings.

Parchment heart reveals a dazzling display of pompano,
shrimp, and crab topped with a mushroom-shallot sauce. The recipe for this elegant entrée—
Pompano en Papillote—is on the facing page.

POMPANO

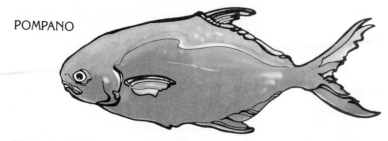

...Madeira-broiled Pompano (cont'd.)

ities and outside. With a sharp knife, cut 4 or 5 shallow, diagonal slashes in both sides of each fish. Combine salt, pepper, and parsley; sprinkle evenly on both sides of each fish.

Remove pan from broiler; brush with some of the melted butter. Combine remaining butter with madeira and tarragon. Arrange fish side by side on pan and baste generously with butter mixture. Return pan to broiler (adjust pan to proper distance from heat source: 4 inches for fish up to 1½ inches thick, 6 inches for thicker fish). Broil, turning once and basting frequently with butter mixture, until fish is browned and flakes readily when prodded in thickest portion with a fork. For a 1-inch-thick fish (measured in thickest portion), allow 10 minutes total—5 minutes on each side. (Allow same ratio of thickness to time—1 inch:10 minutes—for fish of all thicknesses.)

When done, transfer fish to a warm serving platter; pour any remaining baste evenly over fish and garnish with watercress. Makes 4 to 6 servings.

Pompano en Papillote

(Pictured on facing page)

Nestled inside the heart-shaped packets of parchment is a savory New Orleans classic: fillet of pompano smothered in shrimp, crab, and à creamy, shallot-flavored sauce. The dish can be made ahead. Look for the parchment near the other paper products in your market.

Basic poaching liquid (see recipe on page 28; omit lemon juice or vinegar)
6 skinless pompano fillets (*each about 8 oz.*)
Water
Dry white wine
About ½ cup (¼ lb.) butter or margarine
½ pound mushrooms, sliced
⅓ cup finely chopped shallots
⅓ cup all-purpose flour, unsifted
¼ cup whipping cream
¼ pound *each* small cooked shrimp and crabmeat

Strain poaching liquid, pour into a wide frying pan, and bring to simmering. Wipe fish with damp cloth; arrange fillets in single layer in simmering poaching liquid. If necessary, add equal parts water and wine to pan until liquid barely covers fish. Simmer gently, covered, until fish feels firm and is almost done (about 5 to 6 minutes for a ¾-inch-thick fillet, measured in thickest portion). With a wide spatula, carefully lift fish from pan; drain briefly and set aside (do *not* unfold). Boil poaching liquid rapidly until reduced to 2½ cups; pour into a bowl and reserve. Rinse out pan.

Preheat oven to 450°. (If you are making the dish ahead, wait until 40 minutes before serving time; then preheat oven to 400°.) In frying pan, melt 2 tablespoons butter over medium heat. Add mushrooms and cook, stirring frequently, until golden brown. With a slotted spoon, remove mushrooms from pan and set aside. Reduce heat to low and add 4 more tablespoons butter to pan. Add shallots and cook, stirring, until soft. Add flour and cook, stirring, until bubbly. Remove from heat and, using a wire whip, gradually stir in reserved poaching liquid. Cook, stirring, until sauce thickens. Stir in cream and mushrooms until well blended. Let cool to room temperature.

Fold 6 pieces of parchment paper (about 15 by 15 inches) in half and cut each into a heart shape about 11 inches at crease and 14 inches wide.

Melt about 2 more tablespoons butter; open each parchment heart and brush inside lightly with melted butter. Place a fish fillet in each heart, fitting fold of fillet against center crease.

Distribute shrimp and crab equally among fillets, tucking shellfish into fold of each fillet (reserve 6 shrimp to serve as garnish, if desired). Then top each fillet with sauce, dividing it equally among them (top with reserved shrimp, if desired). Fold other half of heart over fish. Starting at rounded top, roll and crimp edges tightly together; twist end of heart to seal. Place on cooky sheets. Brush tops of hearts lightly with any remaining melted butter.

Bake in 450° oven, uncovered, until paper browns (about 8 to 10 minutes). If made ahead, chill as long as 24 hours; then bake in 400° oven for about 20 minutes.

To serve, cut a cross in top of each packet with a sharp knife. Pull back paper to reveal fish. Makes 6 servings.

PORGY/SCUP

In the coastal waters that stretch from Cape Cod, Massachusetts, to Cape Hatteras, North Carolina, are found schools of porgies (also known as "scup"). These little fish, sold whole or drawn in eastern markets, are called "salt-water panfish" because they can be sautéed whole in your frying pan. Like many fresh-water trout and other panfish, one porgy makes a hearty serving.

Choosing your method. Porgies are usually cooked whole, rather than in fillets or steaks. You can barbecue, broil, oven-fry, or pan-fry them (see directions in "Basic Methods," pages 14 – 31). You'll find sauce possibilities on page 20 and seasoned butters on page 29.

Barbecued Stuffed Porgy

Tucked into these little whole fish are crisp bits of celery and onion flecked with parsley and chervil; bacon wraps the outside to roast over the coals.

4 whole porgies (*each* about 10 to 12 oz.), cleaned and scaled
½ cup finely chopped onion
½ cup finely chopped celery
¼ cup chopped parsley
1 teaspoon dry chervil
½ teaspoon salt
¼ teaspoon pepper
4 to 8 slices bacon
1 lemon, thinly sliced

About 30 to 45 minutes before you plan to begin cooking, ignite coals (you'll need about 35 to 45 long-burning briquets).

Wipe fish with damp cloth, inside cavities and outside. Combine onion, celery, parsley, chervil, salt, and pepper; mix well. Divide stuffing evenly into 4 parts and tuck 1 part into cavity of each fish. Wrap 1 or 2 bacon slices around each fish crosswise and secure with wooden picks (bacon will help to hold stuffing in fish).

(Continued on page 64)

PORGY/SCUP

When coals are covered with gray ash, arrange in a single, solid layer to underlie entire area to be used on grill. Knock ash off coals and let burn down until moderately hot (about 5 to 10 minutes longer). Adjust grill height 4 to 6 inches above coals.

Grease grill. Arrange fish on grill to fit over coals; cook, turning once, until fish is well browned and flakes readily when prodded in thickest portion with a fork. For a 1-inch-thick fish (measured in thickest portion), allow 10 minutes total—5 minutes on each side. (Allow same ratio of thickness to time—1 inch: 10 minutes—for fish of all thicknesses.)

When done, transfer fish to a warm serving platter. Arrange lemon slices on fish and serve immediately. Makes 4 servings.

ROCKFISH

Rows of brightly colored fish grace the western markets, stout, sturdy-looking, and spiny-finned. These are the rockfish; they may be any one of 50 varieties, available in whole form or in fillets. One of the more popular varieties of rockfish is called "red snapper," not to be confused with the Florida fish (see page 73). All rockfish have the same lean, mild, white flesh and texture, so they can all be cooked the same way. Many rockfish make attractive entrées when cooked whole.

Choosing your method. Rockfish is a great all-purpose fish; bake, barbecue, broil, butter-sauté, deep-fry, oven-fry, pan-fry, or poach it (see directions in "Basic Methods," pages 14 – 31). You'll find sauce possibilities on page 20 and seasoned butters on page 29. If you're feeling adventurous, try rockfish in one of the recipes given for another lean, mild fish. (To identify other lean fish, see buying guide charts, pages 8 – 11.)

Rockfish with Italian Tomato & Olive Sauce

Robust herbed tomato sauce, studded with ripe olives, bakes over a whole rockfish to make this handsome Italian presentation. (A supply of cheesecloth is necessary.)

¼ **cup olive oil or salad oil**
1 **medium-size onion, finely chopped**
2 **stalks celery, finely chopped**
3 **cloves garlic, minced or pressed**
½ **cup chopped parsley, lightly packed**
1 **can (1 lb.) whole tomatoes**
1 **can (8 oz.) tomato sauce**
1 **can (about 14 oz.) regular-strength beef or chicken broth**
2 **teaspoons basil, crumbled**
¼ **teaspoon thyme leaves**
1 **can (6 or 7 oz.) pitted ripe olives, drained**
1 **whole dressed rockfish (3 to 6 lb.—allow ¾ lb. per serving)**
   Lemon slices and chopped parsley
   Hot cooked rice

Preheat oven to 375°. In a frying pan, combine oil, onion, celery, garlic, and parsley. Cook over medium heat, stirring occasionally, until vegetables have softened; then add tomatoes and their liquid, tomato sauce, broth, basil, and thyme leaves. Break up tomatoes with a spoon; then add olives. Boil, stirring frequently, until sauce is reduced to 3½ cups.

Meanwhile, wipe fish with damp cloth, inside cavity and outside. Moisten and wring dry a piece of cheesecloth. Wrap fish in cloth, folding edges together on top of fish, and set in a shallow baking pan large enough to contain fish. (If fish is too long for pan, simply turn up its tail.)

Spoon hot sauce around fish, then cover pan tightly with lid or foil. Bake until fish flakes readily when prodded in thickest portion with a fork (to test, fold back cheesecloth). For a 3-inch-thick fish (measured in thickest portion), allow about 30 minutes cooking time. (Allow same ratio of thickness to time—1 inch:10 minutes—for fish of all thicknesses.)

When fish is done, lift from sauce, supporting with cheesecloth, and transfer to warm serving platter. Carefully remove cheesecloth; cover fish and keep warm.

Pour sauce back into frying pan and boil rapidly to reduce again to 3½ cups. Garnish fish with lemon slices, parsley, and some of the olives from the sauce; serve immediately. Serve sauce in a separate bowl to spoon over portions of fish and hot rice.

To serve fish, cut directly to bone, then slide a wide spatula between flesh and ribs and lift off each serving. When top half has been served, lift and remove backbone (sever from head, if necessary) before serving bottom half. Makes 4 to 8 servings.

ROCKFISH

SABLEFISH

The sablefish fisheries are among the oldest on the west coast. Ever since 1890, these buttery, mild fish have been sold in western markets whole and in fillets or steaks. Sablefish are also smoked commercially and sold across the country, often under the name "Alaska smoked cod." The sablefish's unusual velvet-soft texture is due to its relatively high fat content; its name comes from its sable-black skin.

Choosing your method. The cooking methods best suited to sablefish are barbecuing, broiling, oven-frying, and poaching (see directions in "Basic Methods," pages 14-31). You'll find sauce possibilities on page 20 and seasoned butters on page 29. Sablefish can also be smoked, with excellent results (see directions in "Building a Simple Smoker," page 120).

Sablefish Poached in Tart Broth

A refreshingly tart and spicy poaching liquid complements the soft, mild flesh of fresh sablefish. Cheesecloth is required to hold the fragile fish together as it cooks.

1 **quart water**
1 **cup white wine vinegar**
1 **tablespoon salt**
½ **teaspoon sugar**
4 *each* **whole black peppers and whole allspice**
1 **bay leaf**
½ **medium-size onion, sliced**
About 3 pounds skinless sablefish steaks or fillets
Melted butter and chopped parsley

In a wide frying pan, combine water, wine vinegar, salt, sugar, peppers, all-

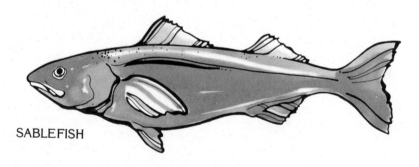

SABLEFISH

spice, bay leaf, and onion. Bring to a boil.

Meanwhile, wipe fish with damp cloth. Moisten and wring dry a piece of cheesecloth for each piece of fish; wrap each piece, folding edges together on top of fish, and carefully set into broth, one piece at a time. Let broth return to a simmer after each addition. When simmering resumes after last addition, remove pan from heat; let stand 5 minutes or until fish flakes readily when prodded in thickest portion with a fork (to test, fold back cheesecloth).

Transfer fish to warm serving platter, supporting with cheesecloth. Carefully remove cheesecloth and serve fish immediately, topped with plenty of melted butter and chopped parsley. Serves 6.

SALMON

For distinguished richness and elegance, the salmon is among the highest-ranking of fish. A sleek, regal form, a silver skin contrasting with the unique red blush of the flesh, a distinctive yet delicate flavor—all contribute to its reputation. It is hard to resist, for example, a gently poached whole salmon bathed in an ethereally light hollandaise. (If you'd like to make one, see poaching directions on page 27 and sauce directions on page 20.)

Among the Pacific salmon, there are five main varieties—king, coho, sockeye, pink, and chum—all of which may be bought whole, drawn, and in steaks or fillets. (To serve whole, the king and the coho varieties are the most majestic choices.)

On the west coast, salmon is available fresh in season and frozen out of season; elsewhere in the United States, it is available frozen. The flesh colors differ according to the variety, from the sock-

eye's deep salmon through the paler color of the coho and pink salmon, to the lightest pink of the chum. The king ranges from deep red to almost white.

Choosing your method. It is hard to go wrong with salmon; you can bake, barbecue, broil, butter-sauté, deep-fry, oven-fry, pan-fry, or poach it successfully (see directions in "Basic Methods," pages 14–31). You'll find sauce possibilities on page 20 and seasoned butters on page 29. Leftover cold poached salmon is very good added to salads and sandwiches or gently reheated in a soup or stew. Salmon is delicious, too, when smoked (see directions in "Building a Simple Smoker," page 120).

Smoked salmon. (See smoked salmon recipe on page 68.) There are several kinds of smoked salmon on the market. One is called lox, which is actually "cooked" in a salt cure, then very lightly smoked so that it's ready to eat. It can be sliced wafer-thin for use in sandwiches or hors d'oeuvres—it has a buttery richness, a subtle, salty smoke flavor, and bright salmon color.

Other types of smoked salmon are drier than lox; they're called kippered, mild cure, or Indian-type cure salmon (perishability varies with the type of smoking done—check at the market when you buy the fish). They may need steaming to make them ready to use in salads or casseroles.

How to Steam Smoked Salmon. Set piece of fish to be steamed on a rack over boiling water; cover and steam just until heated through. A 1-pound piece of fish takes about 10 to 15 minutes. Add hot fish immediately to a hot entrée. Or let steamed fish cool; then flake and chill it for cold dishes.

Barbecued Salmon with Lemon Rice Stuffing

A feast for eyes and palate, this dramatic whole salmon is lined with sliver-thin slices of grapefruit and stuffed with a lemony pilaf of mushrooms and rice. If you don't have a barbecue, bake it instead with bacon strips atop.

1 **whole salmon (3 to 8 lb.), cleaned and scaled**
Lemon rice stuffing (recipe follows)
1 **small thin-skinned grapefruit (if barbecuing) or 4 strips bacon (if baking)**
Melted butter

Ignite coals about 45 minutes before you intend to begin cooking. (You'll

SALMON, KING

need about 25 to 50 long-burning briquets for a 3 to 8-lb. fish.)

Prepare lemon rice stuffing (for a 3 to 5-lb. fish, use only half the recipe).

Wipe fish with damp cloth, inside cavity and outside. Lightly pack stuffing into cavity; sew opening with heavy thread (wrap any leftover stuffing in foil and heat on grill while fish cooks).

Cut a piece of heavy-duty foil to fit one side of fish; grease foil generously. Slice grapefruit as thinly as possible; lay half the slices, overlapping slightly, on greased foil. Lay fish on foil and press foil smoothly to fit fish. Arrange remaining grapefruit slices evenly on top of fish. If desired, insert a thermometer into fish in thickest portion (next to, but not touching, dorsal fin).

When coals are covered with gray ash, divide them in half and arrange one half in one long row, 2 briquets wide, that spans length of fish. Arrange remaining coals in same manner parallel to first row, leaving an empty channel, equal to width of fish, down center of barbecue. Adjust grill height to 6 inches above coals.

When the coals are moderately hot (about 5 to 10 minutes longer), place fish, foil side down, on center of grill between rows of coals. Arrange a wad of foil under tail to support it and protect it slightly from heat. Drizzle fish with melted butter. Cover entire surface of barbecue, either with a lid or with foil (tuck foil over edges of barbecue to seal in heat and smoke).

Cook fish, basting occasionally with melted butter, until fish flakes readily when prodded in thickest portion with a fork or until thermometer registers 120°. For a 3-inch-thick fish (measured in thickest portion after stuffing), allow at least 30 minutes. (Allow same ratio of thickness to time—1 inch:10 minutes —for fish of all thicknesses.) If, when slit with sharp knife, flesh is still dark or translucent near backbone, continue cooking, cutting a new slit every 5 minutes to check for doneness.

When fish is done, hold a warm serving platter near fish on grill; slide a wide metal spatula under foil at each end of fish and lift fish carefully onto platter.

Serve immediately, cutting directly to bone, crosswise, then sliding wide metal spatula between meat and ribs and lifting off each serving. Spoon out some of the stuffing to accompany each serving. When top half has been served, lift and remove backbone (sever from head, if necessary) and cut down to skin to serve bottom half (be careful not to catch foil). A 4-pound salmon makes about 8 servings.

Lemon rice stuffing. In a pan, melt 3 tablespoons butter or margarine over medium-high heat. Add 1 cup sliced celery and 1 small onion (chopped); sauté, stirring, until vegetables are soft (about 5 minutes). Add ¼ teaspoon thyme leaves, 2 teaspoons grated lemon peel, ¼ cup lemon juice, and 2½ cups water. Bring to a boil. Mix in 1¼ cups long-grain white rice and cover, reduce heat to low and cook for 20 minutes or until all liquid is absorbed.

Meanwhile, melt 3 tablespoons butter or margarine over medium-high heat in a frying pan; add 1 to 2 cups sliced mushrooms and sauté, stirring, until soft (about 5 minutes). When rice is done, stir in mushrooms, along with 1½ teaspoons salt and ⅛ teaspoon pepper. Makes enough for an 8-pound fish.

To bake whole salmon. If you intend to bake your salmon, preheat oven to 450° when you start to make stuffing (recipe precedes).

If your salmon is 6 pounds or larger, make sure your oven will contain it. If not, omit stuffing and cut fish in half through backbone; bake halves according to directions that follow, side by side in oven.

Wipe and stuff fish as directed for barbecuing. Cut a piece of heavy-duty foil to fit one side of fish. Coat entire fish well with melted butter; lay on foil and press foil smoothly to fit fish. Lay fish, foil side down, in shallow, well-greased baking pan large enough to contain fish (tail may turn up, if necessary). Arrange

bacon strips evenly, crosswise, on top of fish. If desired, insert a thermometer as directed for barbecuing fish.

Bake, uncovered, until fish flakes readily when prodded in thickest portion with a fork or until thermometer registers 120° (for cooking time, see directions for barbecuing, preceding).

When fish is done, remove pan from oven. Hold a warm serving platter close to fish. Slide a wide metal spatula under foil at each end of fish and lift fish carefully onto platter. Serve as directed for barbecued fish.

Avocado-masked Spring Salmon

Lavishly splendid is this oven-poached whole salmon, chilled and thickly masked in a hollandaise blended smoothly with avocados. Make it the centerpiece of a buffet dinner. (You'll need cheesecloth to poach the fish.)

 1 whole salmon (about 6 or 7 lb.), cleaned and scaled, head and tail removed
   Salt
 1 medium-size onion, thinly sliced
 ½ lemon, thinly sliced
 2 cups dry white wine
 1 bay leaf
 1 teaspoon tarragon leaves
10 whole black peppers
   Boiling water
   Avocado mask (recipe follows)
   Lemon slices and chopped parsley

Preheat oven to 425°. Wipe fish with damp cloth, inside cavity and outside. Sprinkle inside of cavity lightly with salt. Moisten and wring dry enough cheesecloth to wrap fish; place fish on cloth and fold edges together on top of fish. Arrange fish in a greased, wide baking pan, poaching pan, or roasting pan deeper than thickness of fish and long enough to contain it (tail can turn up, if necessary).

Distribute onion and lemon slices evenly around fish. To pan add wine, bay leaf, tarragon, 1 teaspoon salt, and peppers. Pour enough boiling water over fish just to cover it (about 2 to 3 quarts). Cover tightly and bake until fish flakes when prodded in thickest portion with a fork (to test, fold back cheesecloth). For a 3-inch-thick fish (measured in thickest portion), allow 30 min-

(Continued on page 68)

Bountiful! What other word so aptly describes Provençal Sea Bass,
oven baked and blanketed with shrimp, tomatoes, mushrooms, and black olives?
The recipe is on page 69.

utes. (Allow same ratio of thickness to time—1 inch:10 minutes—for fish of all thicknesses.)

Remove pan from oven; supporting with cheesecloth, lift fish from liquid. Drain and let cool on rack.

When fish is still slightly warm, transfer to warm serving platter; carefully remove cheesecloth, gently pull off skin, and remove fins. Cover and chill at least 2½ hours. Just before serving, spread fish thickly with avocado mask and arrange lemon slices on top of avocado mixture. Then sprinkle with chopped parsley.

To serve, cut directly to bone, then slide a wide spatula between flesh and ribs and lift off each serving. When top half has been served, lift and remove backbone (sever from head, if necessary) before serving bottom half. Accompany each serving with some of the avocado mask. Makes 12 servings.

Avocado mask. In a blender or bowl, combine 2 medium-size ripe avocados (peeled), 1 can (6 oz.) hollandaise sauce, ½ teaspoon tarragon leaves, and 3 tablespoons lemon or lime juice. Whirl to blend, or beat with a rotary beater until well blended. If you prefer, you can make your own hollandaise sauce (see recipe on page 24); use ¾ cup in avocado mask (reserve remainder for other uses).

Salmon Steaks with Spinach

Scandinavian tastes inspired these dill-seasoned salmon steaks. They are broiled, then served atop a bed of spinach.

- **2 pounds fresh spinach**
- **4 salmon steaks (*each* about 1 inch thick)**
- **Salt and pepper**
- **1 teaspoon dill weed**
- **¼ cup butter or margarine**
- **1 large onion, chopped**
- **1 clove garlic, minced or pressed**
- **Lemon wedges**

Wash spinach and shake off water. Cut into 1-inch-wide strips and set aside. Turn on broiler and preheat broiler pan.

Wipe fish with damp cloth. Remove broiler pan and grease lightly; arrange fish in single layer on pan. Broil about 4 inches from heat for 5 minutes. Remove pan from broiler; turn fish and season to taste with salt and pepper. Sprinkle

evenly with dill weed and dot with about 1 tablespoon of the butter. Return pan to broiler and broil fish for about 5 minutes more or until it flakes readily when prodded in thickest portion with a fork.

Meanwhile, in a wide frying pan, melt remaining 3 tablespoons butter over medium-high heat and sauté onion and garlic until soft. Stir in spinach (with water that clings to leaves). Cover pan and cook, stirring occasionally, over high heat for about 3 minutes or until wilted and bright green.

To serve, spoon spinach onto warm rimmed platter. Lay salmon steaks on top. Garnish with lemon wedges. Makes 4 servings.

Poached Salmon Steaks with Broccoli

Broccoli flowerets and thick, pink salmon steaks poach flavorfully in the same liquid. Serve them, hot or cold, with freshly made mayonnaise sauce, green and herb-scented.

- **About 1 quart water**
- **1 medium-size onion, sliced**
- **6 whole black peppers**
- **1 bay leaf**
- **1 teaspoon salt**
- **1 bunch broccoli (about 1¾ lb.)**
- **4 salmon steaks (*each* about 1 inch thick)**
- **Green sauce (recipe follows)**

In a wide frying pan, combine and bring to a boil 1 quart of the water, onion, peppers, bay leaf, and salt. Simmer for 15 minutes.

Meanwhile, trim tough ends from broccoli and cut flower ends lengthwise into pieces of uniform size. Add broccoli to pan of poaching liquid and simmer, uncovered, stirring occasionally, just until stems are tender when pierced (about 5 to 10 minutes). Remove broccoli with a slotted spoon and drain briefly; arrange on a large, warm serving platter and keep warm. (If you plan to serve dish cold, place broccoli on a cold serving platter and let cool.)

Wipe fish with damp cloth. Set in single layer in poaching liquid (add water just to cover fish, if necessary); cover and simmer gently about 10 minutes (measured from the moment simmering resumes) or until fish flakes readily when prodded in thickest portion with a fork. Remove each piece with slotted spatula; let drain briefly and arrange on platter with broccoli. Serve hot with green sauce. Or cover, chill

thoroughly, (at least 2 hours), and serve with chilled green sauce. Makes 4 servings.

Green sauce. First assemble ⅔ cup tightly packed chopped fresh spinach, 2 tablespoons chopped parsley, and ½ teaspoon tarragon leaves. Over low heat, melt ⅓ cup butter or margarine. Measure ¼ cup salad oil; set aside.

In a blender, combine 2 egg yolks, ¼ teaspoon salt, and 1 tablespoon lemon juice; cover and whirl until well blended. When butter is melted and bubbling hot, turn blender on high speed and add butter in a thin, steady stream about 1/16 inch wide. When all butter is incorporated, start adding the salad oil in a thin, steady stream. (If sauce becomes too thick before all the oil has been added, turn off blender. Add some of the spinach and whirl to blend; then, with blender running on high speed, add remaining oil according to preceding directions.)

Turn off blender and add remaining spinach, parsley, and tarragon; whirl until greens are finely chopped and thoroughly blended into sauce. Serve at room temperature with hot fish, or cover and chill (at least 1 hour) to serve with cold fish. Makes 1 cup sauce.

Smoked Salmon Salad in Tomatoes
(Pictured on page 54)

Tomato tulips sprout a lively combination of salmon chunks, eggs, rice, and an assortment of cool vegetables in this main-dish salad. A curry-lemon-yogurt dressing served at the table piques the flavors.

- **3 cups cooked long-grain rice, cooled**
- **About 8 ounces kippered salmon, steamed, cooled, and flaked (see "Smoked salmon," page 65)**
- **1 cup sliced celery**
- **1 package (10 oz.) frozen green peas, thawed**
- **4 large tomatoes**
- **½ cup sliced green onion (including some tops)**
- **¼ cup diced red bell pepper**
- **3 hard-cooked eggs**
- **Fresh mint (optional)**
- **Small cooked shrimp (optional)**
- **Curry dressing (recipe follows)**

In a large bowl, combine rice, flaked fish, celery, peas, green onion, and red pepper. Chop eggs coarsely and add to salad. Mix together lightly. Cover and chill up to 3 hours if made ahead.

Remove tomato stems. Without slicing through, cut each tomato into 4 to 6 wedges. Carefully spread tomatoes open and spoon salad evenly into center of each.

To serve, garnish with shrimp and mint, if desired. Pass curry dressing at the table. Makes 4 servings.

Curry dressing. In a bowl, combine ½ cup *each* mayonnaise and unflavored yogurt, 2 tablespoons finely chopped fresh mint, 1 tablespoon lemon juice, 1 teaspoon curry powder, ½ teaspoon *each* salt and dry basil, and a dash of cayenne; stir to blend. Cover and chill up to 3 hours if made ahead. Makes about 1 cup.

SEA BASS

Sea basses come in various shapes and sizes from both ends of the country. The black sea bass and the white sea bass are southwestern fish; the common sea bass is from the east coast.

Black sea bass ranges from 50 to 600 pounds in weight (which accounts for one of its nicknames: giant sea bass), so it is available only in steaks, chunks, and fillets. The white sea bass, available in steaks, chunks, and fillets, may range up to 50 pounds. But the common sea bass (also commonly known as "black," though it's a different fish from the western black sea bass) weighs between ½ and 4 pounds and can be bought whole, drawn, dressed, or filleted.

Choosing your method. All three of the sea basses are lean, mild-flavored, adaptable fish; try baking, broiling, butter-sautéing, oven-frying, pan-frying, or poaching them (see directions in "Basic Methods," pages 14–31). You'll find sauce possibilities on page 20 and seasoned butters on page 29.

Provençal Sea Bass
(Pictured on page 67)

The fish bakes in the oven in a flavorful blanket of tomatoes, mushrooms and shrimp; olives and lemon wedges are the garnish.

> 3 tablespoons butter or margarine
> ¼ pound mushrooms, thinly sliced
> 2 small tomatoes, peeled and coarsely chopped
> 2 cloves garlic, minced or pressed
>   Salt and pepper
> 2 pounds sea bass steaks
> ½ pound medium-size raw shrimp, shelled and deveined (see directions in "Shelling and deveining shrimp," page 116)
>   Tomato wedges, ripe olives, parsley sprigs, and lemon wedges

Preheat oven to 400°. In a frying pan over medium heat, melt butter; add mushrooms and cook just until limp; then stir in tomatoes and garlic; heat through. Season to taste with salt and pepper.

Wipe fish with damp cloth; cut into serving-size pieces (about 3 by 5 inches), if desired. Arrange pieces in single layer, without crowding, in greased large, shallow baking pan. Sprinkle lightly with salt and pepper and spoon mushroom mixture evenly over fish; arrange shrimp evenly over fish.

Bake, uncovered, until fish flakes readily when prodded in thickest portion with a fork and shrimp are pink. For a 1-inch-thick piece of fish (measured in thickest portion), allow 10 minutes. (Allow same ratio of thickness to time—1 inch: 10 minutes—for fish of all thicknesses.)

Remove fish from oven; transfer to a warm serving platter, along with vegetable mixture (discard pan juices).

To serve, tilt platter slightly and spoon off juices that have accumulated; discard. Garnish platter with tomato wedges, olives, parsley sprigs and lemon wedges. Makes 4 to 6 servings.

Tomato-Orange Sea Bass

There's a tart-sweet tang to the tomato sauce that blankets these baked fish steaks—the seasoning is the reason: orange juice and peel.

> 2 tablespoons olive oil or salad oil
> 1 medium-size onion, finely chopped
> 2 cloves garlic, minced or pressed
> 1 can (1 lb.) whole tomatoes
> 1½ teaspoons chili powder
> ½ teaspoon *each* salt and dry basil
> ⅛ teaspoon ground cumin
> 4 large sea bass steaks (*each* about 1 inch thick)
> 1 large, juicy orange
> 1½ teaspoons cornstarch
>   Chopped parsley

In a frying pan, heat oil over medium-high heat; add onion and garlic and sauté until soft but not browned. Stir in tomatoes and their liquid (break them up with a spoon), chili powder, salt, basil, and cumin. Simmer, uncovered, stirring occasionally, for 25 to 30 minutes or until sauce is thick and reduced to about 1¾ cups.

Meanwhile, preheat oven to 350°. Wipe fish with damp cloth; sprinkle lightly with salt and pepper. Arrange in single layer in a greased, large, shallow, flameproof baking pan.

Using a vegetable peeler, cut thin strips from outer peel of orange, then cut in slivers to make 1 teaspoon slivered peel; set aside. Ream orange and measure ⅓ cup juice (reserve remainder for other uses); add juice to tomato sauce and blend well. Spread sauce evenly over fish and bake, uncovered, for about 20 minutes or until fish flakes readily when prodded in thickest portion with a fork.

When done, lift fish from sauce with slotted spatula; arrange on warm serving platter; keep warm. Blend a little liquid from baking pan into cornstarch, then blend cornstarch mixture into remaining pan liquid. Cook over high heat, stirring, until thickened; pour over fish. Sprinkle with reserved orange peel and parsley. Makes 4 servings.

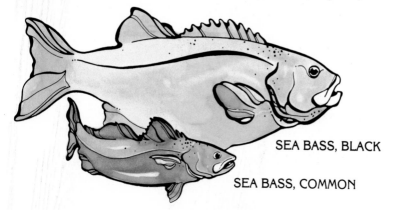

SEA BASS, BLACK

SEA BASS, COMMON

Chervil-flavored butter enhances the richness of Butter-broiled Shad Roe.
Serve it with toast, crisp bacon, and champagne for a delectable and elegant brunch.
The recipe is on page 72.

SEA TROUT, GRAY & SPOTTED

Sea trouts are reminiscent of some fresh-water trouts, both in looks and flavor, but they're actually salt-water fish caught in mid and southeastern coastal waters. These long, slender fish (often called "weakfish" because of the softness of their raw flesh) are mild in flavor with a moist, tender-firm texture. They can be bought whole, drawn, and in fillets. Though the gray variety tends to be a little larger than the spotted one, they are equally delicious cooked the same way.

Choosing your method. Whole or filleted sea trout turn out well if baked, barbecued, broiled, butter-sautéed, or pan-fried (see directions in "Basic Methods," pages 14–31). You'll find sauce possibilities on page 20 and seasoned butters on page 29. Sea trout can also be used in recipes given for freshwater trout (see page 79).

Sea Trout Stuffed with Ham & Olives

A simple stuffing of minced ham, green onions, and olives, and a quick bake in a hot oven set whole sea trouts off to perfection.

- ½ cup (¼ lb.) butter or margarine, softened
- 1 cup finely chopped ham
- 1 cup thinly sliced green onion (including some tops)
- ½ cup finely chopped pimento-stuffed green olives
- 4 whole sea trout (*each* about 1 lb.) or 2 whole sea trout (*each* about 2 lb.), cleaned and scaled
  All-purpose flour
  Butter or margarine
  Salt and pepper

Preheat oven to 500°. Wipe fish with damp cloth, inside cavities and outside. Put a wide, shallow baking pan in oven to preheat.

Combine softened butter, ham, onion, and olives; mix well. Divide evenly among fish, tucking stuffing into each fish cavity. Coat fish with flour; shake off excess. Arrange fish in single layer on wax paper within reaching distance of range.

Remove pan from oven. Put butter in pan and swirl until melted (butter should be about ⅛ inch deep).

Lay a fish in pan; turn to coat with melted butter. Repeat with rest of fish, arranging in single layer in pan.

Return pan to oven and bake, uncovered, until fish flakes readily when prodded in thickest portion with a fork. For a 1-inch-thick fish (measured in thickest portion after stuffing), allow 10 minutes. (Allow same ratio of thickness to time—1 inch:10 minutes—for fish of all thicknesses.)

When done, transfer fish to a warm serving platter; add salt and pepper to taste and serve immediately. Makes 4 servings.

SHAD & ROE

A favorite springtime fish, the shad has been popular since the colonial days of the early Dutch settlers. It is even rumored that shad was George Washington's favorite fish.

These days it is a rarer fish, but is still sold, along with the treasured delicacy "shad roe" (the eggs of the shad), in the East and the Northwest during the spring season, March through May. It is a bony fish and consequently sold only whole or drawn; its flesh is deliciously meatlike and juicy. The roe is often served either as a stuffing for the shad or by itself as a breakfast or lunch dish, light and delicate, yet rich in flavor. Roe requires some special preparation before it is cooked—directions follow.

Choosing your method. Washington is said to have liked his shad ovenfried; you might also like it baked, barbecued, or poached (see directions in "Basic Methods," pages 14–31). You'll find sauce possibilities on page 20 and seasoned butters on page 29.

How to prepare shad roe for cooking. The roe of shad is contained in two separate pouches, loosely joined by a thin membrane; they are sold as a set. A fairly large set, weighing about ¾ pound, divides nicely into 2 servings.

Before cooking shad roe, wash the set gently, being careful not to break the membrane covering. Pat dry with paper towels. Do not separate the set until after you have cooked it.

SEA TROUT, GRAY

SEA TROUT, SPOTTED

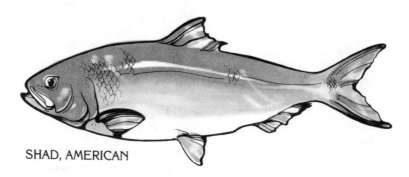

SHAD, AMERICAN

Butter-broiled Shad Roe

(Pictured on page 70)

Herbed lemon butter enhances the shad roe's rich flavor as it broils; serve the roe on toast with crisp bacon for a pleasant brunch.

- **2 large sets shad roe** (*each about ¾ lb.*)
- **6 tablespoons butter or margarine**
- **3 tablespoons lemon juice**
- **½ teaspoon dry chervil**
- **4 slices warm buttered toast, cut in half diagonally**
- **2 teaspoons** *each* **chopped chives and chopped parsley**
- **Salt and pepper**
- **Crisp, cooked bacon strips**
- **Lemon wedges**

Remove broiler pan and turn on broiler. Prepare roe for cooking (see preceding directions). Arrange roe in single layer on well-greased rack of broiler pan. In small pan, melt butter; stir in lemon juice and chervil. Baste roe generously with butter mixture and broil about 4 inches from heat for about 5 minutes on each side, turning once and basting several times with butter mixture. Roe is done when it is opaque throughout; to test, prod in thickest portion with a knife.

Remove roe to a warm serving platter and surround with buttered toast pieces. Stir chives and parsley into remaining butter mixture and pour over roe. Salt and pepper to taste. Serve with crisp bacon and lemon wedges to squeeze over roe. Makes 4 servings.

Bacon-baked Shad

If you're lucky enough to have a roe shad, you can use the roe to make a tasty stuffing for the fish when you bake it.

- **1 whole dressed shad (about 5 to 6 lb.)**
- **Salt and pepper**
- **1 set shad roe (optional)**
- **8 strips bacon**

Preheat oven to 375°. Wipe fish with damp cloth, inside cavity and outside. Sprinkle cavity with salt and pepper.

If you are stuffing fish with roe, prepare roe for cooking (see preceding directions); then tuck set of roe into cavity of fish. Lay 4 strips bacon side by side, crosswise, on a broiler pan. Lay fish on bacon and arrange remaining bacon,

SHARK, LEOPARD

crosswise, on top of fish.

Bake, uncovered, until fish flakes readily when prodded in thickest portion with a fork. For a 4-inch-thick fish (measured in thickest portion after stuffing), allow 40 minutes. (Allow same ratio of thickness to time—1 inch:10 minutes—for fish of all thicknesses.)

To serve, slice fish into steaks, sawing through bone. Makes about 6 servings.

SHARK

Say "shark" to someone and the chances are that person will picture a huge, open-mouthed monster with rows of menacing teeth. This image of shark makes it hard for people to imagine eating such a fish, and yet shark meat is as tasty, moist, and tempting as swordfish.

Shark has the firm, meatlike texture associated with swordfish, and it can be cooked any number of different ways. Moreover, it has the added advantage of possessing only one "bone"—a long spinal column of cartilage—so it's virtually boneless. A number of shark varieties can be bought in steaks, chunks, or fillets on the west coast, among them grayfish, soupfin, thresher, and leopard. On the east coast, dogfish is the main variety of shark available, also in steaks and fillets.

Choosing your method. Once you've decided to try shark, you'll get such delicious results from baking, barbecuing, broiling, and poaching (see directions in "Basic Methods," pages 14 – 31) that you'll be a lifelong fan. Sauce possibilities are on page 20 and seasoned butters on page 29. If you like, try substituting shark in swordfish recipes (see page 79).

Shark on Skewers

With Mediterranean flair, these shark kebabs are threaded with aromatic bay leaves, grilled over coals, and served in a piquant sauce.

- **2 pounds skinless shark steaks or fillets**
- **½ cup lemon juice**
- **½ cup salad oil or olive oil**
- **2 tablespoons chopped parsley**
- **1 teaspoon dry mustard**
- **1 clove garlic, minced or pressed**
- **½ teaspoon salt**
- **¼ teaspoon pepper**
- **About 20 bay leaves**

About 30 to 45 minutes before you plan to begin cooking, ignite coals (you'll need about 25 long-burning briquets).

Wipe fish with damp cloth; cut into 1½-inch cubes. In a bowl, combine lemon juice, oil, parsley, mustard, garlic, salt, and pepper; stir until blended. Pour ⅔ of lemon marinade over fish cubes; turn fish to coat with marinade; then cover and chill for 30 minutes. Pour remaining marinade into serving bowl and reserve to serve as lemon sauce for the cooked kebabs.

When coals are covered with gray ash, arrange in a single layer to underlie entire area to be used on grill. Knock ash off coals and let burn down until moderately hot (about 5 to 10 minutes longer). Adjust grill height to 6 inches above coals and grease grill.

With slotted spoon, lift fish from lemon marinade and drain briefly; reserve marinade for basting purposes. Thread fish on skewers, alternating every piece with a bay leaf. Arrange on grill to fit over coals and baste generously with marinade. Cook, turning once and basting frequently with marinade, until fish is browned and flakes readily when prodded in thickest portion with a fork (allow 5 to 10 minutes on each side).

When done, serve immediately, accompanied by reserved lemon sauce to spoon over individual servings. Makes 4 servings.

SMELT

These small, quicksilver fish take their name from the Anglo-Saxon word "smoelt," meaning smooth and shining. American Indians have been eating smelt for untold centuries, as have Europeans. Smelt are very tasty fish, being delicately sweet and tender. A pound of them, on the average, contains 8 to 12 fish. They are caught and sold fresh and whole on the west coast and the northeastern coast, but are also sold in 1-pound bags, frozen whole or drawn, throughout the United States.

Should you notice that some smelt are labeled as fresh-water or lake fish, don't be surprised; some of these little fish adapted themselves to fresh instead of salt water, so they're caught in inland waters as well.

Choosing your method. Smelts served simply are a special treat; try baking, barbecuing, broiling, butter-sautéing, deep-frying, oven-frying, or pan-frying them (see directions in "Basic Methods," pages 14–31). You'll find sauce possibilities on page 20 and seasoned butters on page 29.

Finnish Smelt Rooster
(Pictured on page 75)

Slowly bake a stack of smelts and bacon in a thick rye crust until the bones are soft enough to eat and the crust grows crispy.

- **1 package active dry yeast**
- **1 cup warm water (about 110°)**
- **2 teaspoons salt**
- **About ¾ cup butter or margarine, melted**
- **1¾ cups dark rye flour**
- **About 1½ cups all-purpose flour**
- **1 pound cleaned, dressed frozen smelt or 2 pounds fresh smelt**
- **Dash pepper**
- **4 strips thickly sliced bacon**
- **Melted butter and lemon wedges**
- **Radishes (optional)**

In a large bowl, combine yeast and water; let stand for 5 minutes. Add 1 teaspoon of the salt and ¼ cup of the butter (cooled to lukewarm). Stir in 1½ cups of the rye flour, then gradually stir in as much of the all-purpose flour as needed to make a stiff dough.

Turn out on a floured board and knead just until well blended (dough shouldn't be elastic). Place in a greased bowl, turn over to grease top, cover, and let rise in a warm place until almost doubled (about 1 hour).

Meanwhile, thaw frozen smelt (or clean and dress fresh smelt, removing heads and tails). Sprinkle fish with remaining 1 teaspoon salt and a light sprinkling of pepper; then dust all over, using up remaining ¼ cup rye flour. Also cut bacon into about ½-inch-long pieces.

Preheat oven to 300°. Punch down dough and roll out on a lightly floured board to an oval shape, about 12 by 16 inches. Arrange half the bacon in center of dough to cover an area about 6 inches square. Stack half the fish like firewood on top of bacon, placing each succeeding layer of fish at right angles to the preceding layer and keeping stack about 6 inches square. Top with remaining bacon, then with remaining fish stacked in same manner.

Bring sides of dough carefully up and over fish, overlapping layers on top. Place, seam side down, on a well-greased 9-inch pie or cake pan, shaping fish-filled dough like a round loaf of bread, but handling gently so that fish inside does not poke holes in dough. Prick top with a pick in several places. Brush with some of the remaining melted butter. Bake for 4 hours; after 1 hour, brush again with melted butter.

After 4 hours, remove from oven, cover with a piece of foil, and allow to stand for about 15 minutes to soften crust slightly.

To serve, slice off top of crust; spoon out fish and some of soft inside crust. Break off chunks of crunchy outside crust to eat with fish. Pass melted butter to drizzle on fish, and lemon to squeeze over. Garnish with radishes, if desired. Makes 5 or 6 servings.

SNAPPER, RED

The red snapper more than lives up to its name—it is the most vividly, brilliantly red fish in the markets, with the same shimmering color on head, back, fins, and tail. Its striking color, plus a well-formed body, a pure white, moist flesh, and a distinctively delicate flavor make the red snapper a star performer in any meal, especially when served whole.

Appropriately, considering its exotic color, the red snapper comes from the Gulf of Mexico; it is sold in the East in whole or drawn form, or in steaks or fillets. Don't confuse it with the common rockfish called "red snapper" that is sold in the West.

Choosing your method. For a dinner party, stun your guests with a whole poached red snapper served with a sauce. In steak or fillet form, red snapper is also delicious baked, broiled, butter-sautéed, oven-fried, pan-fried, or poached. (See directions in "Basic Methods," pages 14–31.) You'll find sauce possibilities on page 20 and seasoned butters on page 29.

Ginger-steamed Red Snapper

Utterly simple yet superbly beautiful, a whole red snapper steams over hot water, seasoned only with slivers of fresh ginger and green onion plus a hint of soy and sherry.

- **1 whole red snapper (about 3 to 4 lb.), cleaned and scaled**
- **2 slices fresh ginger root (each about 2 inches long and ¼ inch thick), peeled and cut in slivers**
- **¼ teaspoon salt**
- **2 teaspoons each soy sauce, salad oil, and dry sherry**
- **2 green onions, cut in 2-inch lengths, then in slivers**

Wipe fish with damp cloth, inside cavity and outside. Lay on a buttered, rimmed, heatproof serving dish large enough to contain fish (tail can turn up, if necessary). Distribute ginger slivers evenly over top of fish.

Stir together salt, soy, oil, and sherry; pour evenly over fish. Cover serving dish completely with a double thickness of wax paper.

(Continued on page 74)

SMELT

...Ginger-steamed Red Snapper (cont'd.)

In a large wok, wide frying pan, or deep roasting pan, large enough to contain serving dish, bring 1 or 2 inches of water to a boil. Set dish with fish on a rack over water and cover pan tightly with lid or foil.

Simmer rapidly until fish flakes readily when prodded in thickest portion with a fork. For a 3-inch-thick fish (measured in thickest portion), allow 30 minutes. (Allow same ratio of thickness to time—1 inch:10 minutes—for fish of all thicknesses.) To test fish, remove wok or pan from heat, lift lid carefully —opening away from you to release steam—and fold back a corner of wax paper; prod in thickest portion of fish with a fork. Be sure to re-cover fish and pan well for any additional cooking.

When fish is done, lift hot dish from steamer (protecting hands); discard wax paper and dry base of dish with towel. Spoon a little of the liquid from bottom of dish over fish and sprinkle onion slivers evenly over top.

Serve immediately, cutting directly to the bone, then sliding a wide spatula between flesh and ribs and lifting off each serving. When top half has been served, lift and remove backbone (sever from head, if necessary) before serving bottom half. Makes 6 to 8 servings.

Red Snapper, Brazilian-style

Firm, white-fleshed red snapper steaks and abundant shrimp poach in a sauce of tomatoes robustly seasoned with green chiles and garlic.

> 3 tablespoons olive oil or salad oil
> 1 medium-size onion, chopped
> ¼ cup seeded and chopped green pepper
> 2 cloves garlic, minced or pressed
> ¼ cup seeded and chopped canned California green chiles
> 1 can (1 lb. 12 oz.) pear-shaped tomatoes, drained
> ¾ teaspoon salt
> ¼ teaspoon pepper
> 1½ pounds red snapper steaks (*each* about ½ inch thick)
> ¾ pound medium-size raw shrimp, shelled and deveined (see directions in "Shelling and deveining shrimp," page 116)
> 3 tablespoons lemon juice
> 2 tablespoons chopped parsley
> Hot cooked rice

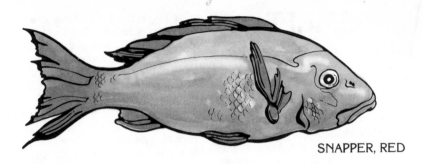

SNAPPER, RED

Heat 2 tablespoons of the oil in a wide frying pan over medium heat; add onion, green pepper, and garlic, and cook until onion is soft. Add chiles, tomatoes (break them up with a spoon), salt, and pepper. Simmer, uncovered, for 30 minutes or until thick enough to hold shape in spoon.

Arrange fish steaks in single layer in sauce; distribute shrimp evenly over top. Drizzle with remaining tablespoon oil and the lemon juice. Simmer, covered, for about 15 minutes or until fish flakes readily when prodded in thickest portion with a fork. With a slotted spatula, transfer fish to serving dish.

Boil sauce, uncovered, stirring, until thickened (about 5 to 10 minutes). Pour sauce over fish. Sprinkle with parsley and serve, spooning sauce over rice. Makes about 6 servings.

SPOT

These plump little fish derive their simple name from the black mark they have on their flanks, just behind the gills. A member of the croaker family (see page 42), the spot is a mild, tender panfish, available whole or drawn on the mid and southeastern coasts; one or two of them make a serving.

Choosing your method. The cooking methods that are most successful with spot are baking, broiling, butter-sautéing, oven-frying, and pan-frying (see directions in "Basic Methods," pages 14–31). You'll find sauce possibilities on page 20 and seasoned butters on page 29. Spot can also be used in recipes calling for whole croaker (see page 42).

Spot à la Provençale

A kind of hot salade Niçoise, this dish offers small, oven-toasted fish atop layers of sautéed vegetables.

> 8 whole spot (*each* about 6 oz.), cleaned and scaled, heads removed
> All-purpose flour
> Olive oil
> 1 large green pepper, seeded and cut in thin strips
> 1 large clove garlic, minced or pressed
> 3 large cooked new potatoes (about 1 lb. total), unpeeled, sliced ¼ inch thick
> About 2 to 3 tablespoons butter or margarine
> 1 large onion, thinly sliced
> 3 large tomatoes, sliced ½ inch thick
> 3 tablespoons chopped parsley
> ½ teaspoon tarragon leaves
> 1 small can (2 oz.) anchovy fillets (optional)
> Pitted ripe olives

Preheat oven to 500°. Wipe fish with damp cloth. Coat fish with flour; shake

(Continued on page 77)

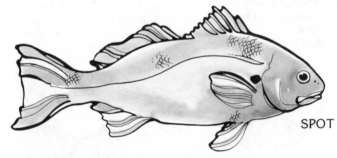

SPOT

Hoist in a net full of shiny, diminutive smelts,
and you've got the makings of Finnish Smelt Rooster! Stack them with thickly sliced bacon
and bake them slowly in a thick rye crust, according to the recipe on page 73.
The raw vegetables can be eaten out of hand.

THE JOYS OF CAVIAR

For centuries, caviar has delighted the epicure with its uncommon texture and salty pungency. The connoisseur eats it chilled by the spoonful or spreads it generously over toast (see photo on page 78), savoring its rich flavor. The inventive cook soon discovers that caviar lends distinction to appetizers, dips, salads, and other dishes.

Mention caviar and the next word that usually comes to mind is "expensive." It's true that the cost of some imported caviars is prohibitive; but other excellent domestic and foreign caviars are both widely available and reasonably priced.

Caviar, the salted eggs—roe—of sturgeon or other fish, is available black or red. For our recipes, you can choose fresh dark sturgeon caviar, preserved sturgeon caviar, or preserved red caviar of salmon. Lumpfish and whitefish caviars are found both in their natural light shades and colored to resemble the gray-to-black hues of sturgeon caviar. Usually, the name of the fish is on the label; when it's not, it's sturgeon caviar.

Each caviar has unique qualities: fresh sturgeon caviar is usually less salty than the others; preserved sturgeon caviar has a more liquid consistency; lumpfish caviar has an interesting crunchy texture; whitefish caviar is tiny and tender; and salmon caviar is the most pungent.

When you're serving a very salty caviar, avoid using silver dishes—the salt can damage the metal.

If you've never used caviar before, make a small investment in a jar of it and add dazzle to your next party with one of our recipes. If you're already a caviar devotee, add these recipes to your repertoire.

Caviar-studded Cheese Round

A little caviar goes a long way when you spread it over a round of this luscious spiced cream cheese. Easy and elegant, it can be made ahead and frozen, if you like.

2 **large packages (each 8 oz.) cream cheese (softened)**
2 **tablespoons grated onion**
1 **tablespoon lemon juice**
2 **tablespoons mayonnaise**
1 **teaspoon liquid hot pepper seasoning**
3 **ounces caviar**
   Lemon slices, cut in halves
   Unsalted sesame rounds or celery stalks

In a bowl, combine cream cheese, onion, lemon juice, mayonnaise, and hot pepper seasoning; beat until well blended. Shape into a mound, lightly cover, and chill 1 hour or until firm. Unwrap and gently spread top and sides with caviar. Lightly cover and chill at least 2 hours, or freeze for longer storage. Garnish with lemon slices. Serve with unsalted sesame rounds or celery stalks. Makes 10 appetizer servings.

Caviar Mousse

For very special finger food appetizers, cut this mousse into small cubes and serve on small lettuce leaves.

1 **envelope (1 tablespoon) unflavored gelatin**
2 **tablespoons cold water**
½ **cup boiling water**
2 **tablespoons lemon juice**
2 **tablespoons mayonnaise**
   Dash of liquid hot pepper seasoning
1 **jar (about 3½ oz.) caviar**
2 **cups sour cream**
   Lettuce leaves, torn into small pieces

Sprinkle gelatin over cold water; let stand 5 minutes to soften. Add boiling water and stir until dissolved. Let cool slightly. Stir in lemon juice, mayonnaise, hot pepper seasoning, caviar, and sour cream. Pour into a shallow dish about 8 inches square. Chill until set (about 2 to 3 hours). Cut into cubes and serve on lettuce leaves. Makes 6 to 8 appetizer servings.

New Potato Salad with Caviar

A delightful blending of mild and pungent flavor gives this salad special status.

   About 4 large thin-skinned new potatoes (2½ lbs. total)
   Boiling salted water
   Oil and vinegar dressing (recipe follows)
½ **teaspoon dill weed**
½ **cup chopped green onion**
1 **jar (about 4 oz.) lumpfish caviar**
   Parsley sprigs

Cook potatoes in boiling salted water for about 30 minutes or until tender when pierced. Drain and let cool completely. Cut potatoes into ¼-inch-thick slices and arrange in shallow rimmed dish. Prepare oil and vinegar dressing; stir in dill weed and ¼ cup of the green onion. Pour over potato slices. Cover and chill at least 4 hours or overnight.

Spoon caviar into a strainer and rinse with cool water; drain for several minutes. Place in a small container and set in middle of a large platter. Arrange potato slices in slightly overlapping rows on platter. Spoon dressing over potatoes to moisten; sprinkle with remaining ¼ cup green onion. Garnish with parsley. Top individual servings with a dollop of caviar. Makes 8 servings.

Oil and vinegar dressing. Combine ⅔ cup salad oil, ⅓ cup white wine vinegar, ½ teaspoon *each* dry mustard and sugar, 1 teaspoon salt, and ¼ teaspoon pepper. Stir until well blended. Makes about 1 cup.

off excess. Arrange in single layer on wax paper. Put a large, shallow baking pan in oven to preheat.

In a wide frying pan, heat 2 tablespoons olive oil over medium-high heat. Add pepper strips and sauté, stirring often, just until soft but still bright green (about 3 minutes). Remove from pan, drain briefly, and set aside. Add 1 tablespoon oil and sprinkle garlic evenly in pan. Arrange about half the potato slices in single layer in pan; sauté, turning once, until lightly browned on both sides (about 6 minutes); arrange on a large warm serving platter and keep warm. Repeat with remaining potatoes, adding oil if necessary.

While potatoes brown, remove baking pan from oven. Put butter in pan and swirl until melted (butter should be about ⅛ inch deep). Lay a fish in pan; turn to coat with butter. Repeat with remaining fish, arranging in single layer. Return pan to oven and bake until fish is lightly browned and flakes readily when prodded in thickest portion with a fork. For 1-inch-thick fish (measured in thickest portion), allow 10 minutes. (Allow same ratio of thickness to time—1 inch:10 minutes—for fish of all thicknesses.) When done, remove from oven; cover and keep warm until you have finished sautéing vegetables.

When all potatoes are browned and arranged on serving platter, lower heat to medium. Add onion and more oil, if needed, to pan and cook until soft and golden (about 8 minutes). Remove from pan and arrange evenly on top of potatoes. Raise heat to medium-high and add tomato slices to pan. Sprinkle evenly with parsley and tarragon; sauté briefly, turning once carefully, just until heated through. Arrange on top of onion.

Arrange cooked fish on top of tomatoes; garnish each fish with a strip of anchovy, if desired. Decorate platter with ripe olives and reserved green pepper strips. Serve immediately. Serves 4.

STRIPED BASS

The striped bass is an eastern market fish, distinguished both in looks and in flavor. If bought and cooked whole, it makes an attractive dinner presentation, but it is also sold in fillets for less dramatic dishes. Because of its mild, slightly

STRIPED BASS

sweet flavor and its firm white flesh, the striped bass is very adaptable; try it in some of the recipes for other lean, mild fish given in this book. (To identify other lean fish discussed in this book, see buying guide charts, pages 8-11.)

Choosing your method. Striped bass will respond well to any of these cooking methods: baking, barbecuing, broiling, butter-sautéing, oven-frying, pan-frying, poaching (see directions in "Basic Methods," pages 14–31). You'll find sauce possibilities on page 20 and and seasoned butters on page 29.

Stuffed Striped Bass with Mushroom Sauce

Tender vegetables make the stuffing for this striped bass, which is baked whole and coated in a smooth, wine-flavored mushroom sauce.

1 whole striped bass (about 4 lb.), cleaned and scaled
Salad oil
2 medium-size carrots, coarsely shredded
¼ cup finely chopped celery
3 tablespoons chopped parsley
Mushroom sauce (recipe follows)

Preheat oven to 450°. Wipe fish with damp cloth, inside cavity and outside. Rub oil over outside of fish until completely coated. Combine carrots, celery, and parsley and tuck mixture into cavity of fish; skewer closed or sew with heavy thread.

Lay fish in a greased, shallow baking pan large enough to contain fish (tail can turn up, if necessary). Bake until fish flakes readily when prodded in thickest portion with a fork. For a 3-inch-thick fish (measured in thickest portion), allow 30 minutes. (Allow same ratio of thickness to time—1 inch:10 minutes—for fish of all thicknesses.)

Meanwhile, about 10 minutes before fish is done, prepare mushroom sauce. When fish is cooked, remove pan from oven and transfer fish to a warm serving

platter. Pour any remaining juices from pan into mushroom sauce and blend well.

Pour some of the sauce over fish and serve immediately, cutting directly to bone, then sliding a wide spatula between flesh and ribs and lifting off each serving. When top half has been served, lift and remove backbone (sever from head, if necessary) before serving bottom half. Pass remaining sauce in a serving bowl at table. Makes 6 servings.

Mushroom sauce. In a pan, heat 2 tablespoons butter or margarine over medium-high heat until bubbly. Add ¼ cup chopped onion and sauté until golden. Add ¾ pound sliced mushrooms and cook, stirring occasionally, until limp; stir in 1½ cups whipping cream, ⅓ cup dry white wine, and a pinch of thyme leaves. Continue to cook, stirring constantly, for about 2 minutes. (Sauce can be kept warm, if necessary, over gently simmering water; stir occasionally.) Makes about 4 cups.

Tomato-barbecued Striped Bass

The firm, sweet flesh of the striped bass grills well, drenched in a pungent, onion-laden barbecue sauce.

1 whole, dressed striped bass (about 7 to 8 lb.), skinned and filleted, or about 4 to 5 pounds large skinless striped bass fillets
½ cup salad oil
¾ cup *each* chopped onion and catsup
⅓ cup lemon juice
3 tablespoons *each* sugar and Worcestershire
2 tablespoons prepared mustard
½ teaspoon pepper
Salt

About 30 to 45 minutes before you plan to begin cooking, ignite coals (you'll need about 30 to 40 long-burning briquets). Meanwhile, wipe fillets with damp cloth. Line one side of each fillet

(Continued on page 79)

Opulent and distinctive, black sturgeon, salmon, and whitefish caviars
are chilled in chopped ice and served with crunchy Melba toast and dry champagne.
Recipe ideas for caviar are on page 76.

78

SWORDFISH

...Tomato-barbecued Striped Bass (cont'd.)
with heavy-duty foil; press smoothly to fit; cover and chill.

In a pan, heat oil over medium heat; add onion and cook until soft. Add catsup, lemon juice, sugar, Worcestershire, mustard, pepper, and salt to taste. Simmer, uncovered, for 15 minutes or until thickened.

When coals are covered with gray ash, arrange in a single, solid layer to underlie entire area to be used on grill. Knock ash off coals and let burn down until moderately hot (about 5 to 10 minutes longer). Adjust grill height to 6 inches above coals.

Lay fish on grill, foil side down, to fit over coals; baste generously with onion mixture. Cover barbecue with lid or heavy-duty foil as directed in "Barbecuing a Large Whole Fish," page 17. Lifting lid or foil to baste frequently with onion mixture, cook, without turning, until fish flakes readily when prodded in thickest portion with a fork. For a 2-inch-thick piece of fish (measured in thickest portion), allow 20 minutes. (Allow same ratio of thickness to time—1 inch: 10 minutes—for fish of all thicknesses.)

Transfer fish to a warm serving platter. To serve, cut down to foil and lift fish off with a wide spatula (be careful not to catch foil). Pour remaining onion mixture into serving bowl and pass at table. Makes 8 to 10 servings.

SWORDFISH

Swashbuckling pirate of the undersea world, the swordfish is a dramatic fish. Weighing from 200 to 600 pounds and possessing a long, swordlike bill for hunting purposes, it swaggers about the mid to northeastern and the western coastal waters. Swordfish's popularity as an eating fish comes from its pronounced meatlike flavor and texture. Long a favorite of many seafood lovers, swordfish is available—fresh in the summer season and frozen off-season—in steaks and chunks.

Choosing your method. The swordfish is a sturdy fish; it stands up best to baking, barbecuing, broiling, and oven-frying (see directions in "Basic Methods," pages 14–31). You'll find sauce possibilities on page 20 and seasoned butters on page 29. Similar to shark, swordfish can be used in shark recipes (see page 72).

Broiled Swordfish, Sinaloa

Swordfish steaks, broiled Mexican-style with a garlic-butter baste and a sprinkling of dry mustard and chopped anchovies, are sure to rouse cries of "Olé!"

2 **tablespoons butter or margarine**
2 **tablespoons lemon juice**
1 **clove garlic, minced or pressed**
4 **swordfish steaks (each about ¾ inch thick)**
1 **teaspoon dry mustard**
6 **flat anchovy fillets, drained and chopped**

Turn on broiler and preheat broiler pan. In a small pan, heat butter together with lemon juice and garlic until butter is melted; set aside. Wipe fish with damp cloth.

Remove broiler pan from broiler and grease well. Arrange fish on pan in single layer; baste well with garlic-butter mixture and broil about 4 inches from heat until lightly browned (about 4 minutes). Turn fish and sprinkle evenly with mustard and chopped anchovies. Continue broiling until second side is lightly browned and fish flakes readily when prodded with a fork (about 4 more minutes). Serve fish immediately. Makes 4 servings.

Swordfish Stroganoff

A zany stroganoff is concocted from sautéed swordfish strips mingled with mushrooms in a tangy sour cream sauce, then served over green noodles. Delicious!

3 **swordfish steaks (each about ½ lb.)**
¼ **cup butter or margarine**
1 **large onion, thinly sliced**
¼ **pound mushrooms, sliced**
¼ **cup dry white wine**
2 **teaspoons lemon juice**
1 **teaspoon each salt and Worcestershire**
½ **teaspoon Dijon mustard**
  Dash pepper
1½ **cups sour cream**
  Hot cooked green noodles, buttered
  Paprika and chopped parsley

Wipe fish with damp cloth; cut away and discard skin and cut fish into strips about ½ by 2 inches. In a wide frying pan, melt butter over medium heat. Add onion and cook until soft, then add mushrooms and cook, stirring, until limp. Remove onion and mushrooms from pan with slotted spoon; set aside. Raise heat to medium-high; add fish strips and cook, stirring frequently, until white and firm, and fish flakes readily when prodded with a fork (about 4 or 5 minutes).

Meanwhile, blend wine, lemon juice, salt, Worcestershire, mustard, and pepper with sour cream until smooth. When fish is done, return mushrooms and onion to pan along with sour cream mixture. Stir gently to blend. Lower heat slightly and cook, stirring, just until sour cream is heated through (do not boil). Serve over green noodles, sprinkled with paprika and parsley. Makes 4 servings.

TROUT

The varieties of fresh-water trout are many and they differ from region to region, but any of them will suit the most demanding connoisseur. Served whole (as trout almost always are), their lovely, graceful shapes appeal to the eye. Their firm flesh and distinctive, though mild, flavor whet the appetite of even the most hesitant eaters of fish, and to a fish lover, a taste of fresh trout, no matter how simply prepared, is ecstasy.

Varieties of trout are sold drawn and dressed (often frozen) all across the country. They can all be cooked using the same recipes.

TROUT, RAINBOW

Choosing your method. The versatility of the trout lends itself to all techniques of preparation—bake, barbecue, broil, butter-sauté, deep-fry, oven-fry, pan-fry and poach it (see directions in "Basic Methods," pages 14–31). You'll find sauce possibilities on page 20 and seasoned butters on page 29. The flavor of trout is also enhanced by smoking (see directions in "Building a Simple Smoker," page 120). If you have a very large trout to cook, try a recipe given for sea trout (page 71) or for salmon (pages 65–69).

Fried Trout with Pork Sauce

Gingery pork and mushroom sauce smothers deep-fried trout and lightly cooked spinach to make this unusual Oriental dish for two.

> 6 medium-size Oriental dried mushrooms
> Hot water
> 1 bunch (about 1 lb.) fresh spinach
> ½ pound lean boneless pork
> Cornstarch
> Salt
> ⅛ teaspoon pepper
> 1 tablespoon *each* soy sauce and dry sherry
> ¾ cup regular-strength chicken broth
> Salad oil
> 2 whole cleaned trout (*each* about ½ lb.)
> 2 cloves garlic, minced or pressed
> 1 teaspoon finely chopped fresh ginger root
> ¼ cup thinly sliced green onion (including some tops)

Rinse mushrooms; cover with hot water and soak until soft and pliable (about 20 minutes). Drain mushrooms (discard water); trim off and discard stems. Cut mushrooms into thin strips; set aside.

While mushrooms soak, trim stalks off spinach; wash leaves and drain. Thinly slice pork into ¼-inch-thick strips about 1 by 2 inches. Stir together 1 tablespoon cornstarch, ¼ teaspoon salt, pepper, soy, sherry, and chicken broth; set aside.

Into a wide frying pan, pour salad oil to a depth of ½ inch; heat to 400° on a deep-frying thermometer. Meanwhile, wipe fish with damp cloth, inside cavities and outside. Sprinkle lightly with salt and coat each fish with cornstarch; shake off excess. Add fish to pan and cook, turning once, until fish flakes readily when prodded in thickest portion with a fork (about 2½ minutes on each side). Drain on paper towels; keep warm.

Drain oil from pan and discard. With paper towels, wipe any browned bits from pan. Add 1 tablespoon oil and place over high heat. Add spinach and half of garlic; cook, turning spinach constantly, just until wilted (about 30 seconds). Arrange evenly in a shallow serving dish; keep warm.

To same frying pan, add another 2 tablespoons salad oil. Place over high heat and add remaining garlic, the pork slices, and ginger; cook, stirring, until pork is lightly browned (about 4 minutes). Add broth mixture and mushrooms; cook, stirring, until sauce boils and thickens (about 5 minutes).

Arrange fish on spinach; pour pork sauce over and sprinkle with green onion. Serve fish immediately. Makes 2 servings.

Hemingway's Trout
(Pictured on page 83)

"A pan of fried trout can't be bettered," Ernest Hemingway wrote. "But there is a good and bad way of frying them."

The good way, according to the novelist, is to coat fresh trout with cornmeal, then cook them slowly in bacon drippings until crispy outside but still moist inside. We've done that—and added some special touches of our own.

> 3 green onions, chopped (or ¼ cup freeze-dried chives)
> 1 tablespoon chopped parsley or dried parsley flakes
> 2 tablespoons lemon juice
> ¼ teaspoon pepper
> 6 whole cleaned trout (*each* about 8 oz.)
> Seasoned salt
> 6 strips bacon
> ½ cup baking mix (biscuit mix)
> 2 tablespoons yellow cornmeal
> Lemon wedges (optional)

Combine green onions, parsley, lemon juice, and pepper. Sprinkle trout cavities with salt, then spread each with onion mixture.

In a wide frying pan over medium heat, cook bacon until crisp. Remove bacon from pan and drain. Leave 2 or 3 tablespoons of the drippings in pan and reserve remaining drippings.

Combine baking mix and cornmeal on a piece of wax paper. Coat trout on both sides with mixture. Arrange half the trout in pan. Cook, turning once, until fish is lightly browned and flakes readily when prodded in thickest portion with a fork. For a 1-inch-thick fish (measured in thickest portion), allow 10 minutes total—5 minutes on each side. (Allow same ratio of thickness to time—1 inch: 10 minutes—for fish of all thicknesses.)

Cook remaining fish in reserved drippings. Slip a bacon strip into cavity of each fish. Garnish with lemon wedges, if desired. Serves 6.

Chilled Trout in Dill Sauce

For an elegantly refreshing dinner presentation, offer a platter of chilled whole trout with a bowl of dill and lemon-flavored sour cream.

> 4 whole cleaned trout (*each* about ½ lb.)
> Basic poaching liquid (see directions on page 28)
> Parsley sprigs and lemon wedges
> 1 cup sour cream
> 4 teaspoons lemon juice
> ¾ teaspoon salt
> ½ teaspoon dill weed

About 3 to 4 hours before you intend to serve, poach trout according to directions in "How to Poach," page 27. When fish are done, transfer to a serving platter and let cool; then cover and chill.

About 10 minutes before serving time, remove cover from fish and, holding fish in place with wide spatula, drain off and discard any juices that may have collected on platter. Wipe platter and garnish with parsley sprigs and lemon wedges.

In a bowl, combine sour cream, lemon juice, salt, and dill weed; mix thoroughly. Serve sauce in small serving bowl to spoon over fish. Makes 4 servings.

Trout & Mushrooms in Cream

Whole trout and a quantity of small mushrooms sauté to buttery tenderness; cream-enriched pan drippings make the satiny sauce for an appealingly simple dish.

- ⅓ **cup butter or margarine**
- ½ **pound small whole mushrooms (or large mushrooms, sliced)**
- 2 **tablespoons finely chopped parsley**
- 4 **whole dressed trout (each about ½ lb.)**
  All-purpose flour
- ¼ **teaspoon salt**
- 2 **tablespoons lemon juice**
- ⅓ **cup whipping cream**

In a wide frying pan, melt butter over medium-high heat; add mushrooms and sauté, stirring frequently, until golden brown (about 5 minutes). Stir in parsley, then remove pan from heat and lift mushrooms from pan with slotted spoon. Arrange evenly to cover bottom of a large warm serving platter; keep warm. Set pan aside.

Wipe fish with damp cloth, inside cavities and outside. Coat fish with flour; shake off excess. Arrange in single layer on wax paper within reaching distance of range. Return pan to medium heat; add salt to remaining butter.

Place in pan as many fish as will fit without crowding. Cook, turning once, until fish is lightly browned and flakes readily when prodded in thickest portion with a fork. For a 1-inch-thick fish (measured in thickest portion), allow 10 minutes total—5 minutes on each side. (Allow same ratio of thickness to time—1 inch:10 minutes—for fish of all thicknesses.)

When fish is done, remove from pan

and arrange on top of mushrooms; keep warm. Repeat process with remaining fish.

After removing last fish, add lemon juice and cream to pan; bring to a boil, stirring and scraping to blend with pan drippings. Spoon immediately over fish and mushrooms, and serve. Makes 4 servings.

Sourdough-stuffed Trout

The tangy crunch of sourdough stuffing, flecked with morsels of green pepper and green onion, transforms these baked trout into an exciting entrée.

- **About 1 small loaf sourdough or crusty Italian bread**
- 2 **tablespoons finely chopped parsley**
- ½ **teaspoon salt**
- ⅛ **teaspoon pepper**
- ½ **cup thinly sliced green onion (including some tops)**
- 1 **medium-size green pepper, finely chopped**
- 3 **tablespoons dry white wine**
- ¼ **cup butter or margarine, melted**
- 6 **whole cleaned trout (each about 12 inches long)**
  Salt and pepper

Preheat oven to 400°. Cut enough bread into ½-inch cubes to make 2 cups (reserve remainder for other uses). Spread bread cubes in single layer on baking sheet and bake, stirring occasionally, until cubes are dry and crisp (about 10 minutes). Remove from oven and pour into a bowl; combine with parsley, the ½ teaspoon salt, pepper, green onion, and green pepper. Drizzle wine and 2 tablespoons of the butter over bread; mix lightly.

Wipe fish with damp cloth, inside cavities and outside. Brush cavities with some of the remaining butter; sprinkle lightly with salt and pepper. Stuff cavities loosely with bread mixture, dividing mix-

ture evenly among fish; skewer edges together or sew with heavy thread. Arrange fish side by side in a greased shallow baking pan (use 2 pans, if necessary, to hold all fish at once). Drizzle any remaining butter evenly over tops of fish.

Bake fish, uncovered, until it flakes readily when prodded in thickest portion with a fork. For a 1-inch-thick fish (measured in thickest portion), allow 10 minutes. (Allow same ratio of thickness to time—1 inch:10 minutes—for fish of all thicknesses.) Makes 6 servings.

TURBOT, GREENLAND

The Greenland turbot is a flatfish; like the halibut or the flounder, it has a broad, flat, platterlike body. But this fish never appears whole and fresh in U.S. markets; instead, it is boned and frozen when caught, and sold from east to west in frozen, filleted form. Greenland turbot has a very white, soft, and flaky flesh, with a texture so remarkably similar to crab that it can be used alongside crab in soups, stews, or salads. Its fat content is low and its flavor is very mild.

Choosing your method. Gentle cooking benefits the lean Greenland turbot; bake, butter-sauté, oven-fry, pan-fry, or poach it (see directions in "Basic Methods," pages 14–31). You'll find sauce possibilities on page 20 and seasoned butters on page 29.

Turbot & Crab Salad, Louis-style

Chunks of snowy turbot and crab team up with lightly cooked broccoli and marinated artichokes in this colorful

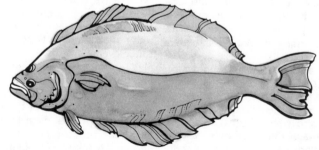

TURBOT, GREENLAND

main-dish salad. The Louis-style dressing is a San Francisco classic—tangy-sweet and creamy.

About 1 pound Greenland turbot fillets, thawed
Water
2 lemon slices
1 pound broccoli
Boiling salted water
Ice water
1 large head butter lettuce
½ pound crabmeat
1 jar (6 oz.) marinated artichoke hearts, drained
2 or 3 hard-cooked eggs, shelled and quartered
Louis-style dressing (recipe follows)
Cherry tomatoes and cucumber slices
Salt and pepper

At least 2 hours before you intend to serve, arrange fillets in single layer in a large frying pan; add ½ cup water and the lemon slices. Bring to a boil; reduce heat, cover, and simmer gently until fish flakes readily when prodded in thickest portion with a fork. For a 1-inch-thick piece of fish (measured in thickest portion), allow 10 minutes. (Allow same ratio of thickness to time—1 inch:10 minutes—for fish of all thicknesses.) Chill fish, covered, in stock, until serving time.

Trim tough ends from broccoli and discard. Cut flower ends lengthwise into pieces of uniform size, with stems no thicker than ½ inch. Drop into boiling salted water to cover; return to a boil and cook, uncovered, for about 3 minutes or just until stems are tender when pierced. Drain at once and immerse broccoli in ice water to cool quickly. When cold, drain well, cover, and chill until serving time.

Just before serving time, wash lettuce; pat dry and arrange some of the large outer leaves around edge of a large platter or tray. Shred remaining lettuce and arrange to cover center portion of platter evenly. Drain fish, discarding liquid. Flake fish with a fork into segments approximately same size as crabmeat. Arrange turbot on shredded lettuce and top with crab.

Cluster artichokes in one corner of platter; arrange eggs in another. Pour about half the Louis-style dressing over fish; pour remainder into a bowl to pass at table with fish. Garnish tray with cherry tomatoes and cucumber slices; season salad with salt and pepper to taste. Makes 4 to 6 servings.

Louis-style dressing. Stir together ¾ cup sour cream, ⅓ cup *each* mayonnaise and tomato-based chili sauce, and 3 tablespoons minced green onion (including some tops). Cover and chill until serving time.

Turbot in Cheese Sauce

Under the crunchy croutons bakes a casserole layered with fish, crumbled bacon, and slivers of egg in a clinging cheese sauce.

Basic poaching liquid (see directions on page 28)
1½ pounds Greenland turbot fillets, thawed
6 tablespoons butter or margarine
3 tablespoons all-purpose flour
1 cup milk
Salt and pepper
Dash of nutmeg
½ teaspoon dry mustard
1 cup shredded Cheddar or Swiss cheese
3 hard-cooked eggs, sliced
6 strips cooked bacon, crumbled
½ cup coarsely crushed croutons

Prepare poaching liquid, omitting allspice and lemon or vinegar; strain liquid and discard vegetables. Wipe fish with damp cloth; cut into ½-inch chunks. Bring liquid to a boil; add fish, return to boil, reduce heat, and simmer, covered, until fish flakes readily when prodded in thickest portion with a fork (about 5 minutes after boil resumes). Lift fish from poaching liquid and set aside. Reserve ½ cup of the liquid.

In a pan, melt ¼ cup butter over medium heat; stir in flour and cook until bubbly. Using a wire whip, gradually add reserved poaching liquid and the milk; cook, stirring, until thickened (about 5 minutes). Add salt and pepper to taste and nutmeg; stir in mustard and cheese until cheese is blended with sauce.

Arrange half of the poached fish evenly in a shallow 1½-quart baking dish. Layer eggs evenly over fish; then sprinkle with half of the bacon. Cover with remaining half of fish; pour cheese sauce evenly over fish.

Melt remaining 2 tablespoons butter in a pan over medium-high heat. Add croutons and remaining bacon; turn to coat with butter. Sprinkle over casserole.

To bake, preheat oven to 400°. Bake casserole, uncovered, until browned and bubbly (about 10 minutes). Makes 4 to 6 servings.

WHITEFISH

A midwestern favorite, whitefish is a freshwater fish from the Great Lakes. It has a delicate flavor and a very white, mild flesh with a moderately high fat content. It is sold whole, drawn, or in fillets; a whole whitefish can range from 2 to 6 pounds. It can also be obtained in smoked form, sometimes called "chub."

Choosing your method. Highly adaptable, whitefish responds well to any of the preparation methods given under "Basic Methods," pages 14–31. Delicate seasonings suit it best. If you can't find it in smoked form, try smoking it yourself (see directions in "Building a Simple Smoker," page 120).

Curried Whitefish Salad

Mounded on lettuce leaves and crowned with a sprinkling of toasted almonds, this salad is an inviting entrée for a warm summer day. Offer a dish of tangy chutney alongside.

⅓ cup slivered almonds
About 1 lb. skinless whitefish fillets, poached, chilled, and cut in chunks (see poaching directions on page 27)
1 medium cucumber, peeled and cut in ½-inch chunks
1 green onion, chopped (including some of the top)
2 hard-cooked eggs, chopped
⅓ cup mayonnaise
2 tablespoons lemon juice
½ teaspoon curry powder
¼ teaspoon salt
Dash of pepper
1 tablespoon chopped Major Grey's chutney
Butter and romaine lettuce leaves
Major Grey's chutney

Spread almonds in a single layer in shallow baking pan. Bake in a 350° oven, shaking occasionally, for 10 minutes or until golden; set aside.

In a bowl, combine fish, cucumber, green onion, and eggs. In another bowl, stir together mayonnaise, lemon juice, curry powder, salt, pepper, chopped chutney, and 2 tablespoons of the almonds; pour over fish mixture. Turn gently to coat with mayonnaise mixture.

Line a serving bowl with lettuce leaves; mound fish mixture over lettuce. Sprinkle evenly with remaining almonds. Pass a small bowl of chutney at table. Makes 4 servings.

A flash in the pan and out come trout
that Hemingway said "can't be bettered." These are stuffed with a lemon-flavored onion
and parsley mixture, then coated and fried in bacon drippings until golden.
The recipe for Hemingway's Trout is on page 80.

83

Whitefish in Lemon Cream Sauce

A sour cream sauce with a hint of lemon adds zest to the mild flavor of whitefish fillets. The sauce is laden with sautéed mushrooms.

- **6 tablespoons butter or margarine**
- **2½ pounds skinless whitefish fillets**
- **¼ teaspoon garlic powder**
- **¼ pound mushrooms, sliced**
- **2 teaspoons all-purpose flour**
- **1 cup sour cream**
- **2 tablespoons lemon juice**
- **1 teaspoon soy sauce**
- **1 teaspoon instant minced onion**
- **¼ teaspoon thyme leaves or dry basil**
- **Salt and pepper**
- **Chopped parsley**

Preheat oven to 450°. In a small pan, melt 4 tablespoons of the butter and spread half the melted butter over bottom of a large, shallow baking pan. Arrange fish in single layer in pan. Pour remaining melted butter evenly over them and sprinkle with garlic powder.

Bake, uncovered, just until fish flakes readily when prodded in thickest portion with a fork. For a 1-inch-thick piece of fish (measured in thickest portion), allow 10 minutes. (Allow same ratio of thickness to time—1 inch: 10 minutes—for fish of all thicknesses.)

Meanwhile, in a pan over medium heat, melt remaining 2 tablespoons butter. Add mushrooms and cook until limp. Stir in flour and cook until bubbly. Remove from heat and blend in sour cream, lemon juice, soy, onion, thyme or basil, and salt and pepper to taste.

When fish is done, remove pan from oven. Reduce oven to 350°. Spoon any liquid out of pan and discard. Pour sour cream mixture evenly over fish. Return to oven and bake 5 to 7 minutes or until sauce is heated through.

Sprinkle with parsley and serve immediately. Makes 6 servings.

Savory Whitefish Bake

Delicate whitefish fillets luxuriate in a creamy wine sauce laden with shredded carrot.

- **2 pounds skinless whitefish fillets**
- **1 small onion, thinly sliced**
- **¾ cup shredded carrot**
- **1 can (10¾ oz.) cream of celery soup**
- **2 tablespoons dry white wine**
- **1 tablespoon lemon juice**
- **½ teaspoon marjoram or thyme leaves**
- **¼ teaspoon garlic powder**
- **¼ cup grated Parmesan cheese**
- **Ground nutmeg**

Preheat oven to 450°. Butter a large, shallow baking pan; arrange fish in single layer in pan, overlapping thin edges. Distribute onion slices over fish; sprinkle evenly with carrot.

In a bowl, stir together soup, wine, lemon juice, marjoram, and garlic powder. Pour mixture evenly over fish and vegetables. Sprinkle with Parmesan cheese and lightly dust with nutmeg.

Bake, uncovered, until fish flakes readily when prodded in thickest portion with a fork. For a 1-inch-thick piece of fish (measured in thickest portion), allow 10 minutes; add 5 to 10 more minutes because of sauce. (Allow same ratio of thickness to time—1 inch: 10 minutes—for fillets of all thicknesses.) Makes 4 to 6 servings.

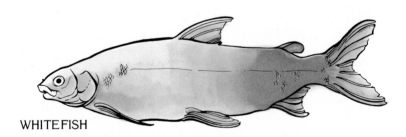

WHITEFISH

WHITING

It wasn't until the 1920s that whiting's potential as a versatile food fish first became known, in the fish-fry shops of St. Louis. Since then, it has become a mainstay of the eastern fish markets, prized for its delicate flavor and soft, tender flesh. Whitings range widely in size from ¾ pound to 18 pounds; they are sold drawn, dressed, and in steak or fillet form.

Choosing your method. Whiting is a very adaptable fish—bake, broil, butter-sauté, deep-fry, oven-fry, pan-fry, or poach it (see directions in "Basic Methods," pages 14–31). You'll find sauce possibilities on page 20 and seasoned butters on page 29.

Whiting with Curried Rice & Papaya

There's a touch of the exotic in this elegant dish; golden, butter-sautéed fish and thick slices of hot, ginger-glazed fruit top a curried pilaf. You can use peaches if papayas aren't available.

- **1 bunch green onions**
- **2 tablespoons butter or margarine**
- **2 to 3 teaspoons curry powder**
- **1½ cups long-grain rice**
- **2 cans (each 14 oz.) regular-strength chicken broth**
- **Water**
- **1½ to 2 pounds skinless whiting fillets**
- **Salt, pepper, paprika, and all-purpose flour**
- **Half butter or margarine and half salad oil (about 2 tablespoons each)**
- **1 teaspoon each sugar and ground ginger**
- **1 large or 2 small papayas (or 2 large peaches), peeled, seeded (or pitted), and cut into thick slices**
- **2 tablespoons lime juice**
- **2 limes, cut in wedges**

Preheat oven to 350°. Slice white part of green onions (slice green tops and reserve). Put 1 tablespoon butter in a large, shallow baking pan and melt in oven. Remove pan and stir in curry powder, rice, and white onion slices until blended. Combine chicken broth with water to make 4 cups liquid; heat to boiling and pour over rice in baking dish. Cover tightly with foil and bake until rice is tender and liquid is absorbed (about 30 minutes).

Meanwhile, wipe fish with damp cloth; cut into serving-size pieces (about 3 by 5 inches), if desired. Season flour with salt, pepper, and paprika; then coat fish with flour and shake off excess. Arrange fish in single layer on wax paper within reaching distance of range.

In a wide frying pan, heat butter and oil (about ⅛ inch deep) until it foams but doesn't brown. Promptly add as many fish pieces as will fit without crowding.

Cook, turning once—over medium-high heat if fillets are ⅝ inch thick or less; over medium if thicker than ⅝ inch—until fish is lightly browned and flakes readily when prodded in thickest portion with a fork. For a ½-inch-thick piece of fish (measured in thickest portion), allow 5 minutes total—2½ minutes on each side. (Allow same ratio of thickness to time—1 inch:10 minutes —for fish of all thicknesses.)

When fish is done, transfer to warm platter. Repeat process with remaining fish. When last fish are transferred to platter, keep warm as you cook fruit.

About 5 minutes before rice is done, melt remaining 1 tablespoon butter in frying pan. Stir in sugar and ginger; then add papaya slices and drizzle with lime juice. Cook until just heated through and glazed, turning carefully once or twice.

Remove rice pilaf from oven and arrange fruit and fish over pilaf. Serve, garnished with lime wedges and reserved tops of green onions. Makes 4 to 6 servings.

Whiting with Avocado

Buttery crescents of avocado add the finishing touch to this elegant dish.

2 tablespoons butter or margarine
¼ cup coarsely chopped slivered almonds
1½ pounds skinless whiting fillets
Salt and pepper
3 tablespoons lime juice
All-purpose flour
Half butter or margarine and half salad oil (about 2 tablespoons *each*)
½ cup whipping cream
1 large avocado
Lime wedges

In a pan, melt the 2 tablespoons butter over medium heat and add nuts. Cook, stirring occasionally, until nuts are

WHITING

lightly browned. Remove from heat and set aside.

Wipe fish with damp cloth; cut into serving-size pieces (about 3 by 5 inches), if desired. Sprinkle evenly with salt, pepper, and 2 tablespoons of the lime juice; let stand for 10 minutes. Coat fish with flour and shake off excess. Arrange in single layer on wax paper within reaching distance of range.

In a wide frying pan, heat butter and oil (about ⅛ inch deep) until butter foams but doesn't brown. Promptly add as many fish pieces as will fit without crowding. Cook, turning once, until fish is lightly browned and flakes readily when prodded in thickest portion with a fork—over medium-high heat if pieces are ⅝ inch thick or less; over medium heat if pieces are thicker than ⅝ inch. For a 1-inch-thick piece of fish (measured in thickest portion), allow 10 minutes total—5 minutes on each side. (Allow same ratio of thickness to time—1 inch:10 minutes—for fish of all thicknesses.)

When done, remove fish to a warm serving platter, cover, and keep warm; repeat process with remaining fish.

When all the fish has been transferred to platter, sprinkle evenly with remaining 1 tablespoon lime juice, cover, and keep warm. Drain any butter from nuts and add butter to pan along with cream. Bring to a boil over high heat, stirring and scraping up any browned particles until blended. Pour cream sauce evenly over fish; cover and keep warm.

Peel, pit, and slice avocado in lengthwise slices; arrange slices evenly on top of fish, then sprinkle evenly with nuts. Serve immediately, garnished with lime wedges to squeeze over fish and avocado. Makes 4 to 6 servings.

Fillet of Whiting Bonne Femme

A French *bonne femme* (good housewife) knows how to poach mild fillets, then use the resulting stock to make this creamy mushroom-wine sauce.

1½ pounds skinless whiting fillets
2 tablespoons finely chopped shallots or ¼ cup thinly sliced green onion (including some tops)
2 lemons, thinly sliced
½ cup dry white wine
Water
½ cup (¼ lb.) butter or margarine
½ pound mushrooms, sliced
2 tablespoons all-purpose flour
2 egg yolks
2 tablespoons whipping cream
Chopped parsley
Lemon wedges

Preheat oven to 400°. Wipe fish with damp cloth. Fold fillets in half crosswise and arrange in a greased large, shallow baking pan. Top with shallots and lemon slices; pour wine over fish. Cover and bake until fish flakes readily when prodded in thickest portion with a fork. For a 1-inch-thick piece of fish (measured in thickest portion after folding), allow 10 minutes. (Allow same ratio of thickness to time—1 inch:10 minutes —for fish of all thicknesses.)

Remove from oven; discard lemon slices. Lift fish from pan with a slotted spatula and arrange on warm serving platter; cover and keep warm. Pour pan liquid into measuring cup; add water, if necessary, to make 1 cup; reserve.

In a pan, melt butter over medium-high heat and sauté mushrooms, stirring frequently, until golden brown. Stir in flour; cook until bubbly. Turn heat to medium-low and, using a wire whip, gradually stir in reserved pan liquid; cook, stirring constantly, until slightly thickened.

Beat egg yolks with cream until well blended; beat in a little of the hot mushroom mixture. Return egg mixture to remaining mushroom mixture in pan and cook, stirring constantly, until thickened (about 5 to 10 minutes—do not boil).

Spoon mushroom sauce evenly over fish and serve immediately, garnished with chopped parsley and lemon wedges. Makes 4 to 6 servings.

For an award-winning streamside picnic,
unpack crusty French bread, a bottle of wine, a crimson mound of crayfish
poached in wine and herbs, and a pot of mayonnaise for dipping.
The recipe for Crayfish in Court Bouillon is on page 100.

A COOK'S CATALOG OF COMMON SHELLFISH

HOW TO SELECT, PREPARE & COOK TO PERFECTION

Proving themselves great lovers of shellfish, Americans will spend hours happily digging clams, and will take sides over whose style of clam chowder is the best. With nutcrackers and picks, they will labor over whole cracked crabs and lobsters, patiently extracting the tender meat and enjoying every succulent bite. They even set up entire restaurants devoted to oysters or crab cakes, shrimp Louis or lobster rolls. Shellfish enthusiasts will find this chapter a mine of valuable information and precious recipe ideas. A selection of the most popular shellfish, sold coast to coast across the U.S., is gathered here and arranged in alphabetical order, from abalone to squid. Each shellfish is accompanied by information on where it is sold, how many varieties are sold and in what form, how to store it, and how to prepare it for cooking and serving—techniques such as opening clams and oysters, cracking crabs, and cleaning squid are included.

ABALONE

Among the most prized of shellfish on the west coast is the abalone, whose sweet and tender flesh comes from the footlike muscle that holds the shell to rocks along the California coast.

Skin divers can dive for fresh abalone, but to cook it, they must know how to pry the whole foot muscle from its single shell, then trim, slice, and pound it into steaks. Frozen abalone, on the other hand, can be bought, already sliced and pounded, in markets throughout the West. These prepared steaks are ready to cook as soon as they have thawed. (Frozen abalone, outside the state of California, is imported from Mexico or Japan —abalone from California waters is prohibited by conservation laws from being shipped out-of-state.)

Storage. Abalone should be cooked and eaten the same day it is purchased. Frozen abalone can be kept at 0° for up to 3 months, wrapped airtight. Thaw only in the refrigerator; do not thaw at room temperature and do not refreeze.

Quick cooking is the key to delicious abalone—a moment too long on the heat, and instead of being tender, it can be as tough and tasteless as leather.

Abalone Amandine

Barely a moment in the pan, and these delicate abalone steaks are done; lavish them with butter-toasted almonds.

½ cup (¼ lb.) butter or
   margarine
½ cup sliced almonds
4 abalone steaks (about 1 lb.
   total), thawed if frozen
   All-purpose flour
¼ teaspoon salt
⅛ teaspoon pepper
1 tablespoon lemon juice

In a wide frying pan, melt butter over medium heat. Add almonds and cook until butter foams and nuts are lightly browned (5 to 10 minutes). Remove from heat; lift almonds from butter with slotted spoon and set aside. Also set aside pan with remaining butter.

Gently pat steaks dry with paper towels. Combine flour, salt, and pepper on wax paper or in a shallow pan. Coat steaks with flour mixture; shake off excess. Arrange in single layer on wax paper within reaching distance of range.

Return pan with butter to medium-high heat; stir in lemon juice and heat until butter begins to foam. Promptly add abalone steaks and cook quickly, turning once, until browned (about 30 to 60 seconds on each side).

When steaks are done, transfer to a warm serving platter. Stir almonds into remaining lemon-butter and pour evenly over steaks; serve immediately. Makes 4 servings.

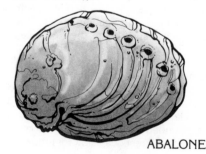

ABALONE

CLAMS

Clams are an American institution; all across the country, traditions have risen around them. In New England, clam chowder lovers battle over the authenticity of Boston's creamy-style chowder versus Manhattan's tomato-based chowder. A day at Coney Island, New York, isn't complete unless you enjoy a roll bursting with plump fried clams. Clam digging is a local pastime on the northwestern shores of Washington; the reward it offers is a potful of fresh clams, steamed in their shells and swimming in butter and parsley.

Clamming is popular at low or minus tides on almost any stretch of American shoreline, but different regions have different regulations regarding daily bag limits, seasons, and approved methods of digging. The best sources of information on clamming—including quarantines and use of tide tables—are the various state fish and game departments around the country. For directions on cleaning fresh clams, see "Cleaning and opening clams," following.

Luckily for those who prefer shopping carts to buckets and shovels, American markets are rich in clams of all descriptions, available both live in the shell and shucked (removed from the shell). On the east coast are the little hard clams, picturesquely called littlenecks, cherrystones, or quahogs (coe-hogs), as the early Indians named them. From the East also come the famous soft-shell clams (so-called because of their thin, brittle shells) and masses of sturdy surf clams. On the west coast are found delicious butter and razor clams, large Pismo clams, and even larger geoduck (goo-ee-duck) clams. (The small butter clams of the West are hard-shell clams equivalent to the hard clams of the East.)

Some varieties of clams, such as soft-shell clams and eastern and western hard-shell clams, are particularly good when bought live, then cooked and served in the shell (or even served raw on the half shell—open as directed in "Cleaning and opening clams;" then see recipe in "Fish in the Raw," page 61). These clams are also occasionally sold in shucked form, ready to cook. Other clams, such as the razor, Pismo, and geoduck, require some preparation for cooking; though they are often sold shucked, trimmed and minced, ground, or pounded into steaks, ready to cook, you'll find directions below for preparing each type of clam in case you buy them live in the shell.

Storage. Clams in shell can be covered with a damp cloth and kept in a cool place for up to 24 hours; check for dead ones before cooking (to check, see "Cleaning and opening clams"). Shucked clams should be used the same day you buy or remove them from shell, or they should be frozen in an airtight container at 0° and kept up to 4 months. Thaw only in the refrigerator; do not thaw at room temperature and do not refreeze.

Cleaning and opening clams. If you have a bucketful of freshly dug clams, you will need to clean them before cooking. Most clams will release the sand and mud in their stomachs if you let them stand for 15 to 20 minutes in clear sea water (or use ⅓ cup salt to 1 gallon tap water—salt content is necessary to keep clams alive); change water and repeat soaking process 2 or 3 times. Scrub shells thoroughly with a stiff-bristled brush under cold running water.

Clams bought in the market in shell have already been cleaned; all they need is the scrubbing just described.

Whether freshly dug or store bought, clams must be checked and any dead ones discarded. With hard clams, gaping shells that do not close when touched mean that the clams are dead. Soft-shell clams are alive if there is some constriction of the siphon, or neck, when touched.

To remove a clam from its shell, you can use one of two methods: steaming and cutting. To steam clams, pour a little boiling water over live clams and let stand a few minutes until shells open; remove clams by cutting hinge or adductor muscles; then plunge into cold water to prevent them from cooking.

To open clams by cutting, insert a strong, thin-bladed knife between the shell halves near the thick end; run knife blade around between shell halves until muscles holding them together are cut (keep a bowl underneath clams to catch nectar). When shell is open, cut hinge or adductor muscles from shell and remove clam. Clams with long necks, like soft-shell and geoduck clams, are easiest to open because they do not have tight-fitting shells.

Once removed from shells, clam meat is ready to be cooked in whole form or served raw on the half shell (as in the case of the little hard-shell clams—see "Fish in the Raw," page 61), or prepared for cooking (as in the case of large clams—see directions following).

How to prepare clams for cooking. Hard clams, butter clams, and soft-shell clams are ready to cook when cleaned and, if desired, shucked. However, razor, Pismo, and geoduck clams, once removed from shell, require further preparation before they can be cooked.

Razor clams. Remove clams from shells either by steaming or cutting (see "Cleaning and opening clams"). Snip off tip of neck with scissors or a sharp knife. Cut open clam lengthwise from base of foot to tip of neck. Remove gills and digestive tract (dark parts of clam) and discard. You may then fry the whole clam, grind it, or mince it.

Pismo clams. Cut clams from shells (see "Cleaning and opening clams"). Rinse in cold running water to remove any sand. Hinge or adductor muscles are tender and may be eaten raw (see "Fish in the Raw," page 61). Cut out stomach and discard; pound remaining firm parts of clam, which may then be fried.

Geoduck clams. Remove clams from shells by steaming (see "Cleaning and opening clams"). Remove skin and stomach; discard. Rinse clams thoroughly, first in hot, then cold water. You can cut 3 steaks from the geoduck: 1 from the breast or internal portion of the clam, and 2 from the neck. These steaks can be fried; the remainder of the meat can be ground or minced.

CLAMS

CLAMBAKE ON THE BEACH

Nothing could be better than a day at the beach: building sand castles, sailing, running on the sand, splashing in the surf, sunning to a golden glow...and then tucking into a hearty, old-fashioned feast of shellfish and corn on the cob, steamed in a firepit filled with hot stones and seaweed, or roasted on a grill over a charcoal fire. It's a great beach picnic for a hungry crowd, and it's easy to do with a minimum of gear and a lot of time.

The rocky beaches of the Northwest and Northeast are well suited to pit cooking. There you can find the smooth, flat stones necessary to line the pit and hold the heat for cooking. Farther south, where sandy beaches are the norm, it makes more sense to barbecue your shellfish treasures over a deep open trench.

In either case, your selection of shellfish (in the shell) should include some or all of the following: live clams; live oysters; cooked, cracked crab (but not soft-shell crab); or cooked, split lobster. And don't forget to bring lots of fresh and succulent corn on the cob. Leave the corn in its husk to protect it while cooking.

The firepit picnic

Essential equipment for a firepit picnic includes a shovel, a rake, an oyster knife, plastic buckets for carrying seaweed, a gunny sack or some burlap, heat-resistant gloves, a large open basket for serving shellfish, a 4½-foot length of flexible hardware cloth about 1 yard wide (available in most hardware stores), firewood or long-burning briquets, butter pot, a basting brush, and serving utensils (including *lots* of napkins).

For each individual, plan to allow about 10 clams, 5 or 6 medium oysters, 1 or 2 ears of corn, and a fourth of a cooked, cracked, large Dungeness crab (or half a cooked, cracked, large blue crab, or half a cooked, split, medium-size lobster).

On an open, rocky beach, select a spot that will still be above the high-tide line for at least another 4 hours. (Do *not*

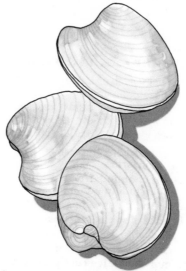

choose a spot under overhanging trees or shrubs; brush fires could result.)

Dig a pit about 4 feet long, 2½ feet wide, and 18 inches deep. Line bottom and sides with large, smooth, flat rocks. (Don't use jagged rocks or ones with definite layers, as they could explode.) With wood or long-burning briquets, build a blazing hot fire in the pit; let fire blaze for 1½ hours, then let it die down. Rake or shovel out coals; douse them thoroughly with sea water, then dispose of them.

Cover hot rocks with a ½-inch layer of freshly gathered wet seaweed. Fold up edges of hardware cloth so it will fit into pit, and place cloth on top of seaweed.

Arrange oysters in single layer over hardware cloth; arrange clams in layer atop oysters, then crabs or lobsters atop clams. Dip corn ears (still in husks) in sea water and place on top of shellfish. Soak burlap with sea water; cover shellfish and corn with damp sack, and anchor sack with rocks. Let steam for 40 minutes.

Using heat-resistant gloves, lift off anchor rocks and burlap; check corn for doneness. If corn kernels are steaming hot and tender when pierced, shellfish is ready for eating. If not, replace sack and rocks and cook for 5 to 10 minutes longer or until done. Then lift out hardware-cloth tray; transfer shellfish and corn to a serving basket or tray.

Serve immediately, accompanied by a pot of melted butter and a brush for swabbing butter on both shellfish and corn. Offer an abundance of crusty French bread, cherry tomatoes and carrot sticks, wedges of watermelon, and white wine or apple cider along with the seafood.

To prevent fires or accidents, be sure to refill the pit with stones, sand, or gravel, before leaving the picnic site.

The barbecue picnic

On a sandy beach, an open-trench barbecue is a better cooking method for your clambake. You'll need the same equipment as you would for a firepit (see preceding directions), but substitute a roll of heavy-duty foil for the burlap, and add a 20-inch length of pipe or stack of bricks.

Choose an appropriate spot on the beach (see preceding directions for firepit). In the sand, dig a trench about 16 inches deep, 18 inches wide, and 4 feet long. Line sides with foil, allowing a 6-inch rim of foil to extend out around top of trench. (Foil reflects heat and also prevents sand from caving in.) To provide support for hardware-cloth grill, poke length of pipe vertically into sand in center of trench, or make a vertical stack of bricks. Top of pipe or bricks should be even with top of trench.

Build a large fire in trench with briquets; when coals are covered with gray ash, rake them into a single solid layer to cover bottom of trench. Lay hardware cloth flat over trench, with pipe or bricks supporting cloth; weight corners with rocks or sand.

Use same amounts of shellfish and corn as for firepit picnic. Dampen corn ears, still in husks, with sea water and arrange in single layer on hardware cloth. Cook, turning corn often, just until clams and oysters open and corn ears start to char (5 to 8 minutes). Serve immediately with accompaniments as suggested for firepit picnic.

Be sure to extinguish the fire with sea water and refill the trench with sand before leaving the picnic site.

Steamed Clams
(Pictured on page 91)

Clams in the shell steam open in a flavorful rice and fresh tomato broth.

- ¼ cup olive oil or salad oil
- 1 large onion, chopped
- 2 cloves garlic, minced or pressed
- 1 teaspoon *each* dry basil and oregano leaves
- ¼ teaspoon fennel seeds, crushed (optional)
- 3 tablespoons chopped parsley
- 1 cup dry white wine or regular-strength chicken broth
- 1 bottle (8 oz.) clam juice
- 20 to 30 small hard-shell clams, cleaned (see "Cleaning and opening clams," page 88)
- 2 tomatoes, seeded and chopped
- 2 cups cooked rice
  Watercress

Heat oil in a 5 or 6-quart kettle over medium heat. Add onion and garlic and cook, stirring, until onion is soft. Stir in basil, oregano, fennel (if desired), and parsley. Add wine and clam juice; cover, reduce heat, and simmer for about 5 minutes.

Add clams, cover, and steam until clams open (10 to 12 minutes); stir often, pushing unopened clams down into broth. Stir in tomatoes and rice. Cover and cook until heated through.

Ladle clams and broth into individual bowls and garnish with watercress. Makes 4 first-course or 2 entrée servings.

New England Steamed Clams

A bucket of steamed clams is the New Englander's idea of how to begin a lobster dinner. Served simply, with a dipping sauce of melted butter, these clams-in-shell make an equally good appetizer anywhere in the country.

- 2 to 3 small hard-shell clams, cleaned (see "Cleaning and opening clams," page 88)
- ½ cup dry white wine or water
- 2 tablespoons butter or margarine
- ½ cup (¼ lb.) butter or margarine, melted
- 1 lime or lemon, cut in wedges

Arrange clams on a rack in a large kettle; add wine. Cut the 2 tablespoons butter into small cubes and distribute over clams. Cover kettle, place over medium-high heat, and bring to a boil. Steam just until clams open (about 5 to 10 minutes).

To serve, arrange clams in shallow soup bowls; spoon broth over clams. Pour the ½ cup melted butter into small individual serving dishes. Garnish each butter dish with a lime wedge. Makes 4 to 6 appetizer servings.

Creamy Clam Ramekins

Large shells, such as those of the Pismo clam, make dramatic containers for this ambrosial mixture of clams, wine sauce, mushrooms, and cheese. Use individual ramekins if you can't get the shells.

- 6 tablespoons butter or margarine
- ½ cup chopped green onion (including some tops)
- ½ pound mushrooms, sliced
- 1 tablespoon all-purpose flour
- ¼ cup whipping cream
- ¼ cup dry white wine or milk
- ½ cup clam juice (use reserved nectar from clams, or use bottled clam juice)
- 6 tablespoons freshly grated Parmesan cheese
- 2 cups shucked, minced raw clams (Pismo clams are best; you'll need 8 clams in shell, *each* about 4½ inches long—to open, see "Cleaning and opening clams," page 88)
- 3 egg yolks, beaten
- 1 tablespoon lemon juice
  Salt
- ½ cup fine dry bread crumbs

In a large pan, melt 4 tablespoons of the butter over medium heat; add onion and mushrooms and cook until onion is soft and all liquid from mushrooms has evaporated. Stir in flour; cook, stirring, until bubbly. Using a wire whip, gradually stir in cream, wine, and clam juice. Cook, stirring, until bubbly. Add 2 tablespoons of the Parmesan and the clams.

Bring mixture to a boil, stirring. Remove from heat; beat some of the hot mixture into egg yolks, then stir egg mixture into hot mixture in pan. Cook over medium heat, stirring constantly, until thickened (do not boil). Stir in lemon juice; add salt to taste. (Mixture can now be covered and chilled for several hours, if desired.)

Spoon clam mixture evenly into scrubbed Pismo clam shells (mixture will fill 6 to 8 half shells) or individual ramekins (mixture will fill 3 to 4 individual 2-cup ramekins). Melt remaining 2 tablespoons butter; mix with bread crumbs and remaining 4 tablespoons Parmesan cheese until well blended. Sprinkle crumb mixture evenly over clam shells or ramekins.

Arrange shells or ramekins on a baking sheet. Broil about 6 inches from heat until heated through and bubbling (about 5 minutes—10 minutes if mixture is chilled). Makes 3 to 4 servings.

Clams on the Half Shell

From the Spanish maritime tradition comes this zesty seafood hors d'oeuvre: chilled herbed clams on the half shell.

- 3 dozen small hard-shell clams, cleaned (see "Cleaning and opening clams," page 88)
  Boiling water
- 2 tablespoons *each* olive oil and lemon juice
- 1 tablespoon chopped fresh coriander (cilantro)
- 1 clove garlic, minced or pressed
- ¼ cup finely chopped green onion (including some tops)
  Salt, pepper, and liquid hot pepper seasoning

Arrange half the clams in a wide frying pan. Add boiling water (about ½ inch deep); cover and steam over medium-high heat until clams open (about 5 to 10 minutes). Remove clams as they open and set them aside to cool. Repeat until all clams are open and cool.

With a fork, remove clams from shells and place in a bowl. Snap shells apart, saving half of each shell. Cover shells and chill.

In a small bowl, combine oil, lemon juice, coriander, garlic, and green onion. Add salt, pepper, and hot pepper seasoning to taste. Pour marinade over clams; cover and chill up to 24 hours.

To serve, lift clams from marinade and set one in each half shell; arrange shells on a serving platter. Spoon any remaining marinade over clams. Makes 3 dozen appetizers.

Linguine with Clam Sauce

Invitingly Italian: a robust, fresh tomato clam sauce blankets slender pasta strands called linguine. Whole clams in their shells are the garnish. (You'll need some cheesecloth in order to strain the clam juices.)

(Continued on page 92)

Puget Sound's rocky seashore yields up these clams,
swimming in an herbed rice and tomato broth. For dessert, more of nature's bounty—
plump, fresh blackberries and cream. The recipe for
Steamed Clams is on the facing page.

¼ cup olive oil
¼ cup butter or margarine
3 tablespoons finely chopped parsley
1 large clove garlic, minced or pressed
3 medium-size tomatoes, peeled, seeded, and chopped
¼ teaspoon *each* salt and crumbled oregano leaves
⅛ teaspoon pepper
  A few drops liquid hot pepper seasoning
3 to 4 dozen small hard-shell clams, cleaned (see "Cleaning and opening clams," page 88)
2 tablespoons water
  About 6 ounces hot cooked linguine or spaghetti

In a frying pan, heat olive oil and butter over medium-high heat. Add parsley and garlic and sauté, stirring occasionally, for 1 to 2 minutes. Add tomatoes, salt, oregano, pepper, and hot pepper seasoning. Simmer gently, stirring occasionally, for about 10 minutes; then reduce to lowest heat to keep warm.

Meanwhile, put clams and water into a kettle. Heat, covered, just until clams open; remove from heat. Lift clams from kettle and drain briefly (reserve clam juices in bottom of kettle). When cool enough to handle, cut whole clams from shells by severing hinge or adductor muscles (reserve some clams in their shells for garnish, if desired); add shucked clams to warm tomato sauce.

Line a wire strainer·with 1 layer of cheesecloth; pour reserved clam juices from kettle through strainer and add to tomato sauce (discard cheesecloth). Reheat sauce briefly and serve immediately, spooning it over hot linguine and garnishing with reserved whole clams in shell. Makes 4 servings.

Clam Fritters

Light and puffy, crispy outside and meltingly tender inside, full of little clam nuggets, these traditional fritters are served plain or with wedges of lemon.

¼ cup all-purpose flour, unsifted
½ teaspoon baking powder
1 egg
1½ cups minced or ground clams
  Half butter or margarine and half salad oil (about ¼ cup *each*)
  Salt and lemon wedges (optional)

In a bowl, combine flour, baking powder, and egg with clams; mix until batter is well blended. In a wide frying pan, heat butter and oil (¼ inch deep), over high heat until it foams but doesn't brown. Drop clam batter into hot fat by heaping tablespoonfuls, adding as many spoonfuls as will fit without crowding. Cook, turning once, until fritters are browned on both sides (less than a minute on each side). Remove from pan, drain briefly on paper towels, and arrange on warm serving platter; keep warm until all fritters are cooked. Add more butter and oil to pan, if necessary, and repeat process with remaining clam batter.

When all fritters are done, salt to taste, if desired, and serve immediately, garnished with lemon wedges, if desired. Makes about 20 fritters, each about 2 inches in diameter.

Crispy Clam Bits

These golden, clam-filled morsels turn a quick family dinner into a mouth-watering treat. Quick tartare sauce (page 21) makes a perfect accompaniment.

  Salad oil
1 cup corn flake crumbs
1 teaspoon dill weed
2 cans (*each* 10 oz.) whole baby clams, drained well
2 eggs
  Lemon wedges

In a 3-quart pan, heat ½ inch oil to 375° on a deep-frying thermometer. Meanwhile, combine crumbs and dill weed in a bag. In a small bowl, beat eggs slightly; add clams and mix until well coated. Drain briefly. Place clams in crumb mixture, close bag, and shake thoroughly.

Drop about a quarter of the clams at a time into oil and cook until golden brown (about 1 to 2 minutes). With a slotted spoon, lift out clams and drain on paper towels. Repeat process with remaining clams.

Serve immediately, garnished with lemon wedges. Makes 4 to 6 servings.

CRAB

Serving customs vary from coast to coast, but the pleasure of eating fresh crab is the same all across the country. With equal gusto, westerners tuck into a dinner of crab cioppino, soaking up the garlic-rich tomato stew with chunks of sourdough bread, while easterners relish a snack of hot crab cakes or an elegant luncheon of golden soft-shell crabs, sautéed in butter and garnished with lemon wedges.

Crab varieties differ from region to region, though the flesh is universally sweet and delicate, useful in almost any crab recipe. The two principal eastern varieties are rock crabs and blue crabs.

Rock crabs are found only on the northeastern coast and are sold live in shell; they are so small (averaging only ⅓ pound) that three whole crabs make approximately one serving. Blue crabs are the most common eastern variety, caught along the mid and southeastern coasts. They average ¼ to 1 pound (one to three crabs usually make a serving) and are sold live in shell, as well as cooked (and sometimes frozen) in shell. They are also cooked and picked from the shell to be sold as fresh or frozen

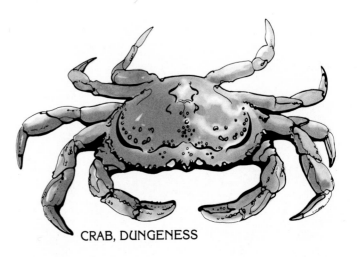

CRAB, DUNGENESS

crabmeat (lump meat and flake meat from the body, claw meat from the legs).

Blue crabs also become the famous delicacy, soft-shell crabs. At a certain stage in growth, the blue crab molts, shedding its shell and developing a new one: this is the soft-shell stage. When sold as soft-shell crabs, the blues are smaller than usual (about 2 oz. to ⅓ pound); two or three crabs make a serving. Soft-shell crabs can be cooked whole, shell and all, with only ·a minimum of preparation (see ''How to prepare soft-shell crabs for cooking,'' page 95).

From the west coast comes the Dungeness crab, sold live in shell; cooked (and sometimes frozen) in shell; and as cooked fresh or frozen crabmeat, picked from the body and claws. Caught in large—though decreasing—numbers off the California, Oregon, and Washington coasts, the Dungeness is larger than its eastern counterparts; it averages 1¼ to 3½ pounds (one large crab serves two people).

The other western crab is the most majestic of all—the Alaska king crab, ranging from 6 to 20 pounds. Caught off the coast of Alaska, king crab appears in markets most often in the form

of legs, cooked and frozen. These legs are sold, in shell or picked from shell, all over the United States.

For the finest, freshest flavor, crab should be bought and kept alive until just before it is cooked and eaten, so that it is cooked only once (if your market usually doesn't carry live crab, you might try ordering it a few days in advance). Reheating precooked crab almost inevitably results in some overcooking of the delicate meat. However, if only cooked crab in shell or cooked (fresh or frozen) crabmeat is available (as in the case of Alaska king crab), either use it in cold dishes that do not

(Continued on page 95)

HOW TO CLEAN & CRACK LIVE & COOKED CRABS

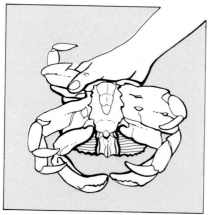

1. Grasp live crab *from rear, firmly holding the last 1 or 2 legs on either side. Place crab with its back down on cutting board. (Rubber gloves will help protect your hands from sharp shells.)*

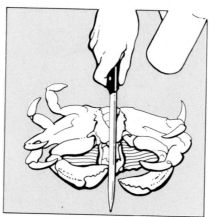

2. Position a heavy, sharp knife, *with blade down, in direct center of crab, between the legs. Using a mallet or hammer, hit back of knife with a hard, quick blow—this will kill crab instantly.*

3. Grasp a front claw *of crab firmly and twist it off, breaking it where claw joins crab's body. Repeat process with other front claw and the legs. If crab is raw, scrub claws and legs, then rinse well.*

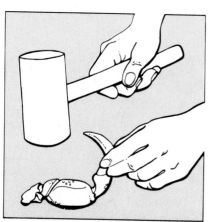

4. Hold a leg or claw piece *on its narrow edge on cutting board and crack the shell of each section of the claw or leg with a mallet. If crab is raw, rinse away loose shell bits.*

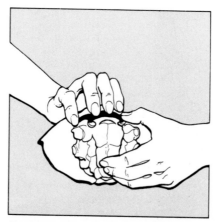

5. Pull off crab's broad back shell *(pry with knife, if necessary). Remove and discard gills and spongy parts under shell—save creamy crab butter, if desired. If crab is raw, rinse body well.*

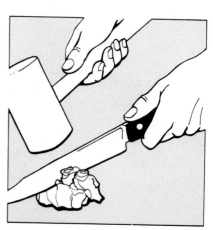

6. Position knife blade *down center of crab's body; tap back of knife with mallet to cut body in half. Repeat to cut each half into 2 or 3 chunks, positioning knife between leg joints. If raw, rinse well.*

Pile chilled cracked crab high on a serving dish, ring it with
whole cooked artichokes, and let your guests help themselves. The lemon butter mayonnaise
and rémoulade sauce (recipes on pages 20–21) go equally well with the artichokes and the crab.
The recipe for Cracked Crab Fest is on the facing page.

...Crab (cont'd.)

require reheating, or add it to a hot dish only at the last moment, cooking *just* until heated through, then serving immediately.

A general rule of thumb in determining serving quantities is that 4 pounds of crab in shell will yield about 1 pound (or four servings) of cooked crabmeat for salads, sandwiches, and casseroles.

Storage. Crabs can be covered with a damp cloth and kept alive in a cool place for up to 12 hours—make sure they are still alive and moving before you cook them. Cooked crabs should be eaten the same day they are cooked or bought, whether fresh or thawed, and should be stored in the refrigerator until served. Crabmeat, if cooked, fresh, and picked from shell, can be wrapped airtight and frozen at 0° for up to 2 months. Thaw only in the refrigerator; do not thaw at room temperature and do not refreeze.

How to cook live crab. When you're planning to serve whole cracked crabs for a crab fest, or when you need cooked crabmeat to use in salads and other dishes, you'll get the freshest flavor by cooking whole live crabs yourself—though you can, if necessary, buy cooked whole crabs or crabmeat. (To cook soft-shell crabs, see "How to prepare soft-shell crabs for cooking," below.)

In a large kettle, bring about 8 quarts water (enough to immerse 3 small crabs or 2 large ones) to boiling with 2 tablespoons salt. Wearing gloves, grasp live crabs as directed in step 1 of "How to Clean & Crack Live & Cooked Crabs" (page 93), and drop into boiling water. Cover kettle and simmer for 5 minutes (for a ⅛-pound rock crab) to 25 minutes (for a 3½-pound Dungeness crab) after water returns to boiling. Lift out crabs with tongs and let cool until you can handle them. Crack and clean each crab as directed in steps 3–6 of "How to Clean & Crack Live & Cooked Crabs" (page 93).

How to prepare soft-shell crabs for cooking. Soft-shell crabs need only minor preparation for cooking; one of their remarkable characteristics is that they can be eaten "shell" and all. Usually crabs will have been cleaned before you buy them (ask the fish dealer if you're not sure). If necessary, you can clean them yourself by gently pulling back points of each crab's back shell, using a knife or sharp implement, and cleaning out spongy sections that lie beneath. Then turn crab over and remove apronlike covering on front.

Soft-shell crabs are best when butter-sautéed, pan-fried, deep-fried, or broiled until lightly browned (see directions in "Basic Methods," pages 14–31) and served with one of the seasoned butters on page 29.

Crab Cioppino

Legend has it that this robust shellfish stew was invented by an Italian in San Francisco; it is traditional to sop up the thick, red, garlicky sauce with lots of extra-sour sourdough bread.

⅓ cup olive oil or salad oil
1 large onion, sliced
1 bunch green onions, sliced (including some tops)
1 green pepper, seeded and coarsely chopped
3 large cloves garlic
⅓ cup lightly packed chopped parsley
1 can (1 lb.) tomato purée
1 can (8 oz.) tomato sauce
1 cup dry white wine or dry red wine
2 cups water
Half a bay leaf
3 teaspoons salt
¼ teaspoon pepper
⅛ teaspoon *each* dry rosemary and thyme leaves
About 5 pounds live whole crabs in shell (large blue crabs or medium-size Dungeness crabs—do not use soft-shell crabs)
1 dozen small hard-shell clams, cleaned (see "Cleaning and opening clams," page 88)
1 pound large raw shrimp or prawns, deveined (see "Shelling and deveining shrimp," page 116)
1 large loaf sourdough or Italian-style bread

In a wide, deep frying pan with a tight-fitting lid, heat oil over medium-high heat; add onion, green onion, green pepper, and garlic; sauté, stirring occasionally, for about 5 minutes. Add parsley, tomato purée, tomato sauce, wine, water, bay leaf, salt, pepper, rosemary, and thyme. Bring to a boil; reduce heat, cover, and simmer gently for about 1 hour. Remove garlic. (You can do this much up to 12 hours ahead, if you wish; cover and chill.)

Clean and crack live crabs (see "How to Clean & Crack Live & Cooked Crabs," page 93); arrange cracked crab pieces

evenly in bottom of a large kettle (at least 8-quart size). Arrange clams evenly over crab; arrange shrimp evenly on top of clams. Heat sauce to simmering; pour over shellfish. Cover and simmer until clam shells are open (20 to 30 minutes).

Serve in wide, shallow soup bowls, arranging some of each shellfish in each bowl and spooning sauce generously over fish; accompany with chunks of bread. Makes about 6 servings.

Cooked crab cioppino. The stew can be somewhat easier to make and eat if you buy whole, cooked, cleaned, and cracked crab (thaw if frozen) instead of live crab; shucked clams instead of clams in shell; and cooked, shelled, and deveined large shrimp or prawns (thaw if frozen), instead of raw shrimp in shell. Prepare recipe as directed above, but cook shellfish in sauce only about 15 minutes or until just heated through. Serve immediately as directed.

Cracked Crab Fest
(Pictured on facing page)

Messy, yet not to be missed—chilled cracked crab is an easy-to-make party pleaser. Feature one of the sauces or a marinade, or serve all the sauces, smörgåsbord-style, and let your guests choose.

Whole crabs in shells, live or cooked, thawed if frozen (allow about 1 to 1¼ lb. of crab in shell per person—soft-shell crabs are not recommended)
Cracked ice
Sauce or marinade (suggestions follow)

If you have purchased live crabs, cook, crack, and clean them at least 2¼ hours before serving time, as directed in "How to cook live crab" (this page) and "How to Clean & Crack Live & Cooked Crabs" (page 93). Let crabs cool; cover and chill for at least 2 hours or until serving time.

If you have purchased cooked crabs, crack and clean them as directed in "How to Clean & Crack Live & Cooked Crabs," page 93; cover and chill until serving time. (If using pungent crab marinade, prepare according to directions—recipe follows. Marinate some or all of the crab.)

Just before serving time, pour an even mound of cracked ice onto a large serving tray (tray should be deep enough to contain water as ice melts). Arrange chilled cracked crabs on ice (lifting from marinade, if used, and draining briefly before arranging on ice). Serve crabs, accompanied by one or more sauces for dipping (suggestions follow), passed in separate bowls at table. Provide guests with nutcrackers and small forks or picks to help extricate crabmeat from shells, and small dishes to hold their choice of sauce. (If using pungent crab marinade on all of the crabs, do not offer a sauce.)

Sauces for cracked crab. Accompany crab with one or more of the following dipping sauces—each serves 4 to 6 people: herbed mayonnaise (see recipe on page 21), rémoulade sauce (page 21), lemon butter mayonnaise (page 20), aïoli (page 20), or skordalia (page 33). For a light, refreshing sauce (one that is also low in calories), serve a Japanese ginger vinegar sauce (recipe follows).

Pungent crab marinade. In a bowl, combine ½ cup *each* salad oil, white wine vinegar, and dry white wine with 1 teaspoon salt, ¾ teaspoon dry mustard, 1 small clove garlic (minced or pressed), and a dash of liquid hot pepper seasoning. Add 1 egg and beat rapidly with a fork until blended.

Add cracked crab pieces; turn to coat well with marinade. Cover dish and chill for 1 hour, stirring several times. Serve as directed above. Makes about 1½ cups (enough to marinate 2 medium-size Dungeness crabs or 4 large blue crabs, cracked).

Ginger vinegar sauce. Combine ½ cup rice wine vinegar or white wine vinegar, 1 tablespoon water, 1 teaspoon peeled, shredded fresh ginger root, and ¼ teaspoon salt. Stir in 2 to 3 tablespoons mirin (sweet rice wine) or cream sherry to make sauce slightly sweet. Makes about ⅔ cup (enough for 4 to 6 servings of crab).

King Crab on the Half Shell

A brief broiling heats these Alaska king crab legs...they're garnished with lemon and sour cream for a special, yet simple family dinner.

4 cooked Alaska king crab legs in shell (about 3 lb. total), thawed if frozen
¼ cup butter or margarine, melted
Seasoned salt
Lemon wedges
Chopped parsley
Sour cream

When crab legs are completely thawed, break at joints (it's advisable to wear gloves—shells have sharp points). With kitchen scissors, cut down both sides of each shell; lift off and discard upper half of shell, leaving meat on lower half.

Turn on broiler. Arrange crab legs, shell side down, in a shallow baking pan and brush crabmeat generously with melted butter. Sprinkle with seasoned salt to taste. Place pan in broiler (adjust height to 6 inches from heat) and broil for 5 minutes or just until heated through.

Serve several pieces (about 1 whole leg) to each person, garnishing with lemon wedges and sprinkling with parsley. Pass a bowl of sour cream at table to spoon over crab. Makes 4 servings.

Crab & Leek Pie

(Pictured on page 99)

Crabmeat and bits of fresh leek in a quichelike cheese custard make the delicate filling of this main-dish pie. For last-minute simplicity, bake the pie shell in advance.

Baked pastry shell (recipe follows)
1½ cups shredded Swiss, Samsoe, tybo, or Gruyère cheese
2 tablespoons butter or margarine
2 leeks
½ pound crabmeat, thawed if frozen, or ½ pound small cooked shrimp
4 eggs
1 cup half-and-half (light cream)
2 tablespoons lemon juice
½ teaspoon grated lemon peel
¼ teaspoon *each* salt and dry mustard
Dash of mace

Sprinkle bottom of pastry shell evenly with half of the cheese (be careful to avoid breaking shell). Split leeks lengthwise and wash thoroughly; cut off and discard coarse green sections of leaves and chop remaining tender stalks.

Preheat oven to 325°. In a frying pan, melt butter over medium-high heat; add leeks and sauté until soft; gently mix with crab and spoon evenly over cheese in pastry shell.

In a bowl, beat eggs with half-and-half, lemon juice, lemon peel, salt, mustard, and mace, and pour over crab mix-

ture. Sprinkle evenly with remaining cheese. Bake for 55 to 60 minutes or until egg mixture is set in center and appears firm when pan is gently shaken. Remove from oven; let cool at least 15 minutes, then serve warm. Or cool to room temperature and serve. Makes 6 servings.

Baked pastry shell. Prepare 1½ times as much pastry as you would normally use for a 9-inch pastry shell (use either a mix or your own recipe). Line a 9-inch pie pan, using extra dough to make a high, sturdy, fluted edge. Chill until ready to bake.

At baking time, preheat oven to 425°. Arrange a piece of foil to cover bottom and sides of pastry; press gently to fit (be careful not to puncture pastry with foil). Fill with dry beans to keep pastry from shrinking. Bake for 10 minutes; carefully remove foil and beans and bake about 5 minutes longer or until lightly browned. Let cool; then cover and keep at room temperature until ready to use (keeps up to 12 hours).

Crabmeat Patties

Similar to the famous Maryland crab cakes, these little patties let the flavor of the crab come through deliciously.

About 20 saltine crackers
2 cups crabmeat, thawed if frozen, or 2 cans (*each* 7½ oz.) crabmeat, drained well
4 teaspoons Worcestershire
⅛ teaspoon liquid hot pepper seasoning
3 tablespoons chopped parsley
1½ teaspoons prepared mustard
3 tablespoons mayonnaise
1 egg
3 tablespoons butter or margarine
Chopped parsley
Lemon wedges

Finely crumble crackers into a bowl; you should have 1 cup crumbs. Flake crabmeat into bowl with crumbs. Add Worcestershire, hot pepper seasoning, parsley, mustard, and mayonnaise. Mix until blended. Add egg and stir until mixture is well blended.

Shape crab mixture into 8 patties. In a frying pan, melt 2 tablespoons of the butter over medium heat. Cook patties until browned (about 3 minutes); add remaining 1 tablespoon butter, turn patties, and cook until browned.

Sprinkle patties with chopped parsley; serve with lemon wedges. Makes 4 servings.

SHELLFISH FOR TWO

With shellfish prices skyrocketing, many of us hesitate to put our savings into shrimp, crab, or scallops. But when only two are dining, there's hardly a more delicious investment.

Oyster & Shrimp Ramekins

A madeira sauce studded with mushrooms sets off oysters and shrimp.

- ⅓ to ½ pound medium-size raw shrimp, shelled and deveined (see directions on page 116)
  Boiling salted water
- 1 jar (10 or 12 oz.) shucked oysters
  About ½ cup milk
- 3 tablespoons butter or margarine
- ½ small onion, chopped
- ¼ pound mushrooms, sliced
- 2 tablespoons all-purpose flour
- 2 tablespoons Madeira or dry sherry
- ¼ teaspoon thyme leaves
  Salt and pepper
  Chopped parsley
  Grated Parmesan cheese
  Hot cooked rice

Drop shrimp into boiling salted water to cover. Cook until shrimp are firm and pink (about 5 minutes), then drain and set aside.

Drain oysters, reserving liquid. Cut oysters into bite-size pieces. In a frying pan over medium heat, add oysters and their liquid and cook until their edges begin to curl (about 3 minutes). Remove oysters and set aside. Measure liquid and add enough milk to make ½ cup; reserve.

Melt butter in frying pan over medium heat; add onion and mushrooms and cook until soft. Sprinkle in flour and cook until bubbly. Gradually blend in milk mixture and cook, stirring, until sauce boils and thickens. Then stir in Madeira, thyme, oysters, and shrimp. Season to taste with salt and pepper.

Spoon mixture into 2 individual ramekins (about 1½-cup size). Sprinkle each with parsley and Parmesan. Broil briefly just until cheese browns. Serve with hot cooked rice. Makes 2 servings.

Scallop Pesto Sauté

Scallops team well with a pesto sauce redolent of basil.

- ½ to ¾ pound scallops (thawed if frozen), cut in half if large
- 3 tablespoons butter or margarine
- 1 carrot, sliced ¼ inch thick
- 1 small onion, cut in 1-inch squares
- 1 small zucchini, sliced ¼ inch thick
- 8 to 10 small mushrooms, halved
- ½ small green pepper, cut in 1-inch squares
  Pesto sauce (recipe follows) or 2 tablespoons thawed frozen pesto
  Grated Parmesan cheese
  Hot cooked rice (optional)

Pat scallops dry with paper towels. Cut scallops in slices about ¼ inch thick. Cover and set aside.

In a frying pan, melt 1 tablespoon butter over medium-high heat. Add carrot and onion and cook, stirring, for 2 minutes. Add another tablespoon butter along with zucchini, mushrooms, and pepper; cook, stirring, until vegetables are just tender-crisp (about 2 minutes longer). Turn vegetables out of pan and keep warm.

Add remaining 1 tablespoon butter to pan, then stir in pesto sauce. Add scallops and cook, stirring, until scallops are just opaque throughout (about 4 minutes). Return vegetables to pan and continue to cook, stirring, until vegetables are hot and coated with pesto sauce.

Turn vegetable mixture into a shallow serving dish and sprinkle with Parmesan. Serve with hot cooked rice, if desired. Makes 2 servings.

Pesto sauce. In a small bowl, mix together 1 tablespoon grated Parmesan cheese, 2 teaspoons *each* dry basil and parsley flakes, and 1 tablespoon olive or salad oil.

Seafood Curry

Exotic spices compound the flavor interest of shrimp, crab, or langostinas (small lobsters found in some markets).

- 1 chicken bouillon cube
- ¾ cup hot water
- 3 tablespoons butter or margarine
- 1 small onion, chopped
- 1 stalk celery, chopped
- ½ small green pepper, seeded and chopped
- 1 teaspoon curry powder
- ⅛ teaspoon ground ginger
- 2 tablespoons all-purpose flour
- ½ cup milk
- ½ to ¾ pound small cooked shrimp, crabmeat, or langostinas (thawed if frozen)
  Hot cooked rice
  Condiments: Salted peanuts, raisins, shredded coconut, chopped hard-cooked egg, crumbled cooked bacon, and Major Grey's chutney.

Dissolve bouillon cube in boiling water and reserve. In a frying pan, melt butter over medium heat; add onion, celery, and green pepper and cook until soft. Stir in curry powder, ginger, and flour; cook until bubbly.

Gradually blend in reserved chicken bouillon and milk; cook, stirring, until sauce boils and thickens. Then stir in your choice of shellfish; cook until heated through (about 2 minutes).

Serve with rice and condiments. Makes 2 servings.

Crab Sandwich on Rye

Serve up hot crab patties on toasted rye, spread with a taste-tingling tarragon sauce. Cabbage salad, tart and tangy, is served alongside.

- ¼ cup butter or margarine
- 2 tablespoons all-purpose flour
- ⅔ cup milk
- 1 pound crabmeat (thawed if frozen), shredded
- Salt
- About ½ cup fine dry bread crumbs
- Piquant tarragon sauce (recipe follows)
- Cabbage salad (recipe follows)
- 8 slices rye bread, toasted and buttered

In a pan, melt 2 tablespoons of the butter; add flour and cook, stirring, over medium heat until bubbly. Using a wire whip, gradually stir in milk; cook, stirring constantly, until mixture boils and thickens. Remove from heat and stir in crab; let cool slightly and add salt to taste.

Divide mixture into 4 parts and form each part into a flat patty, about 3 inches in diameter. Coat each patty with bread crumbs, handling carefully; dust off excess crumbs gently. Line a baking sheet with wax paper; arrange patties in single layer on wax paper. Cover and chill (up to 12 hours if made ahead).

Prepare piquant tarragon sauce and cabbage salad; set aside. In a wide frying pan over medium heat, melt remaining 2 tablespoons butter until it foams but doesn't brown. Promptly add patties and cook, turning once, until heated through (about 2 minutes on each side).

Meanwhile, spread 4 pieces of the rye toast with some of the tarragon sauce. Place a crab patty on each sauce-covered toast; top with remaining toasts. Serve immediately, accompanying each sandwich with some of the cabbage salad. Makes 4 servings.

Piquant tarragon sauce. In a bowl, combine ⅔ cup *each* mayonnaise and sour cream, 4 teaspoons sweet pickle relish, 2 teaspoons grated onion, 1 teaspoon Dijon mustard, and ½ teaspoon tarragon leaves. Set aside ⅔ cup to use in cabbage salad (recipe follows); cover and chill remaining sauce until serving time. Makes 1½ cups.

Cabbage salad. Thinly slice into shreds a small, firm head of cabbage to make about 4 cups. Blend with ⅔ cup piquant tarragon sauce. Cover and chill until serving time.

Crab Pilaf

The Greeks make an excellent pilaf into which they plunge cracked raw crab to cook along with the rice, tomatoes, and quantities of mint.

- About 5 pounds live whole crabs in shell (large blue or medium-size Dungeness crabs—do not use cooked crab or soft-shell crab)
- ½ cup olive oil
- 1 medium-size onion, sliced
- 2 cups water
- 1 can (1 lb.) whole tomatoes
- 1½ teaspoons salt
- ¼ teaspoon pepper
- 1 cup long-grain rice
- 3 tablespoons chopped fresh mint leaves or dry mint

Crack live crabs as directed in "How to Clean & Crack Live & Cooked Crabs," page 93; set aside. Heat olive oil over medium-high heat in a kettle or wide, deep frying pan with a tight-fitting lid. Add onion and sauté, stirring occasionally, until soft. Add water; drain liquid from tomatoes into pan. With a large spoon, press tomatoes through a wire strainer into pan. Add salt and pepper; bring to a boil and add rice, crab pieces, and mint. Reduce heat to low; cover and simmer very slowly for about 45 minutes or until rice is tender.

To serve, spoon crab and rice onto plates; provide nutcrackers and small forks or picks to help diners extricate crab meat from shells; later offer finger bowls or hot damp towels. Makes 4 servings.

Crab & Avocado Crêpes

Wrap fragile pancakes around a creamy, crab-laden filling, and accent them with slices of avocado to make these rich seafood crêpes. You can assemble the crêpes ahead—chill until ready to bake and serve.

- About 1 dozen crêpes (recipe follows)
- 1 pound crabmeat, thawed if frozen
- About 1 cup sour cream
- Butter or margarine
- 3 tablespoons grated Parmesan cheese
- 2 ripe avocados
- 2 tablespoons lemon juice

Prepare crêpes. In a bowl, combine crabmeat and ½ cup of the sour cream; mix until well blended. Spoon about 3 tablespoons of the mixture down center of each crêpe and roll to enclose. Place filled crêpes, seam side down, in a single layer in a buttered shallow baking pan; sprinkle evenly with Parmesan cheese. Cover and chill up to 1 hour if made ahead.

Preheat oven to 400°. Bake, covered, just until heated through (about 10 minutes—20 minutes if chilled).

Meanwhile, peel, pit, and slice avocados. Coat slices with lemon juice to prevent darkening.

Serve crêpes immediately; garnish each crêpe with about 1 tablespoon of the remaining sour cream and several avocado slices. Makes 6 servings.

Crêpes. In a blender, combine 2 eggs, 1½ cups milk, ½ teaspoon salt, 1 cup unsifted all-purpose flour, and 2 tablespoons salad oil; cover and whirl at high speed until smooth. In a crêpe or small frying pan, melt 1 teaspoon butter or margarine over medium-high heat; swirl to coat bottom. Pour in about 3 tablespoons of the batter all at once; quickly tilt pan to coat bottom with a thin layer of batter. Cook until surface is dry and edge is lightly browned; turn and cook other side until lightly browned. Stack crêpes as each is made.

Crab & Red Onion Vinaigrette

The focal point of this sprightly salad is crabmeat, mingled with artichoke hearts, avocado slices, and crunchy marinated onion rings.

- ½ cup olive oil or salad oil
- ¼ cup white wine vinegar
- ½ teaspoon *each* dry mustard and grated lemon peel
- ¼ teaspoon salt
- ⅛ teaspoon pepper
- 1 medium-size red onion, thinly sliced
- Red or romaine lettuce leaves

- 1 pound crabmeat, thawed if frozen
- 1 ripe avocado
- 1 jar (6 oz.) marinated artichoke hearts, drained

In a bowl, combine oil, vinegar, mustard, lemon peel, salt, and pepper. Add onion slices; cover and marinate 4 to 6 hours.

To serve, line a shallow salad bowl with lettuce leaves. With a slotted spoon, lift onion slices from marinade, reserving marinade. Combine onion with crabmeat and arrange on lettuce. Peel, pit, and

(Continued on page 100)

Cooling on the windowsill is an aristocrat of main-dish pies—
crab and leek bits in a quichelike cheese custard, baked to golden perfection.
The recipe for Crab & Leek Pie is on page 96.

...Crab & Red Onion Vinaigrette (cont'd.)
slice avocado. Garnish crabmeat mixture with avocado slices and artichoke hearts. Pour reserved marinade over all. Makes about 4 servings.

Crab Mold with Pineapple & Avocado

Create an easy, yet inviting, salad—individual creamy crab molds shimmering on lettuce leaves, ringed with slices of cool avocado and pineapple.

- **1 envelope unflavored gelatin**
- **¼ cup cold water**
- **½ cup condensed cream of mushroom soup (undiluted)**
- **1 small package (3 oz.) cream cheese, softened**
- **¼ cup *each* mayonnaise and sour cream**
- **1 tablespoon *each* grated onion, lemon juice, and tomato-based chili sauce**
- **6 drops liquid hot pepper seasoning**
- **¼ cup finely chopped celery**
- **¼ pound crabmeat, thawed if frozen**
- **Butter lettuce**
- **1 large avocado**
- **Lemon Juice**
- **1 small pineapple, peeled, cored, and cut in lengthwise wedges**
- **Pitted ripe olives**

Sprinkle gelatin over cold water and let stand until softened (about 5 minutes). In a small pan, heat together the soup, cheese, and gelatin mixture over medium heat, stirring, until gelatin is dissolved.

Remove from heat and let cool to lukewarm; then stir in mayonnaise, sour cream, onion, the 1 tablespoon lemon juice, chili sauce, and hot pepper seasoning. Mix in celery and crabmeat and turn into 4 individual molds or custard cups. Cover and chill until firm (2 to 3 hours).

Dip molds in hot water a few seconds to loosen (do not leave in water too long or allow water to touch gelatin mixture, or salads will melt). Unmold onto individual plates lined with butter lettuce leaves. Peel and slice avocado, sprinkle slices with lemon juice, and divide equally among the plates, arranging slices around each crab mold. Divide pineapple wedges equally among salads, arranging alongside avocado around molds. Garnish with olives and serve immediately. Makes 4 servings.

CRAYFISH

The crayfish is a creature of many talents. It may appear as the exalted ecrevisse—essential in its elegant form and flavor to French "haute cuisine." Or it may take the form of the humble southern crawdad or mudbug, caught with the hands on a lazy afternoon by the swimming hole.

Poached any number of different ways, the meat of this cousin to the lobster has something of the lobster's sweet flavor, though it tastes less rich. Like the lobster, crayfish turns bright scarlet when cooked; it looks somewhat like a miniature lobster too, varying in length from about 3 to 7 inches.

Adaptable to climate as well as cuisine, crayfish inhabit the still or slow-moving year-round streams, rivers, creeks, and canals, the lakes, ponds, and reservoirs all across the country. They are there for the taking, about 190 varieties of them, usually living at a depth of from 1 to 10 feet of water. If you find a trove of them, gather a group of friends and start a "crayfish hunt," using either your hands to catch them, or simple, purchased traps, baited with liver or bacon. (First check with your state fish and game department as to regulations concerning crayfishing.)

If you prefer, you can buy crayfish (or crawfish, as they are often called) in the market in some regions, notably Louisiana, Mississippi, and the Pacific states of Washington, Oregon, and California. In the southern United States, crayfish are sold live in shell or cooked (and sometimes frozen) in shell, or they are cooked, picked from the shell, and sold in 5-pound cans of tail meat. In the West, crayfish are sold live in shell or cooked (and sometimes frozen) in shell.

Sizes of crayfish vary with region and variety, but 10 to 12 crayfish, each about 5 inches long, yield approximately ¼ pound of tail meat, or one serving.

Storage. Keep live crayfish in a cool place, or in the refrigerator, up to 24 hours, covered by damp cloths. Check them over before cooking and discard any that are dead (refrigeration makes them sluggish, but be sure they are still moving). If you buy cooked crayfish or cook it yourself, use it the same day; or if it has not been frozen, you can pick the meat from the shells, wrap it airtight, and freeze it at 0° for up to 2 months. Thaw frozen crayfish only in the refrigerator; do not thaw at room temperature and do not refreeze.

How to eat a whole crayfish. Eating crayfish is not a delicate process—it involves both hands. Put aside your manners and pick up the cooked crayfish with your fingers.

With a gentle twisting motion, break the tail away from the body (or thorax). Most of the succulent meat is found in the tail (if the sand vein has not been removed from the back of the crayfish, pluck it out and discard it). The claws, if you take the trouble to crack them, contain an especially sweet meat. In the body cavity you'll find a treasure of sienna-colored "butter" to eat, and maybe even the delicious bright red egg clusters carried by the female. Once you've enjoyed all the various meats of the crayfish, sip the last tasty juices out of the shells.

Crayfish in Court Bouillon
(Pictured on page 86)

An unforgettable meal: crayfish, poached in wine and herbs, then heaped in a scarlet mound on a platter and served with pots of melted butter or mayonnaise.

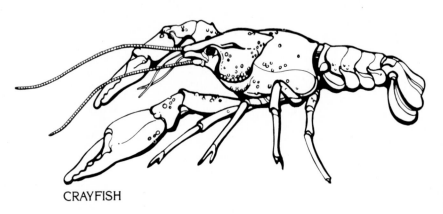

CRAYFISH

Water
2 cups dry white wine
2 medium-size onions, sliced
2 or 3 carrots, sliced
1 lemon, sliced
3 or 4 parsley sprigs
8 to 10 whole black peppers
2 teaspoons salt
1 or 2 bay leaves
   Live crayfish in shell (allow about 10 to 12 crayfish, *each* about 5 inches long, per serving)
   Melted butter, or margarine and mayonnaise

Fill a kettle (6 to 8 qt. size) about ⅔ full of water. Add wine, onions, carrots, lemon, parsley, peppers, salt, and bay leaf. Cover and bring poaching liquid to a boil; reduce heat and simmer for 15 minutes.

Meanwhile, rinse crayfish to remove any mud or silt. Remove sand vein just before cooking, if desired (this is not a process for the squeamish): Grasp behind pinchers and turn stomach side up (you may wish to wear gloves for this). The tail has 3 sections; twist the center section, snapping the shell; then gently pull out sand vein and discard.

Bring poaching liquid to vigorous boil. Uncover and drop in as many as 2 dozen crayfish, one at a time, big ones first. Push them down into liquid to kill quickly. When liquid returns to a boil, cook 5 minutes or until bright red. Lift out with slotted spoon, draining briefly; transfer to a warm serving platter. Repeat process until all crayfish are cooked, adding water, if necessary, to maintain volume of liquid.

Serve crayfish as soon as they are cool enough to handle, accompanied by small individual dishes of melted butter and mayonnaise in which to dip crayfish.

LOBSTER
(Pictured on page 102)

Many would agree that the scarlet lobster is the king of shellfish, with meat so succulent and sweet that it needs no embellishment to make it mouthwateringly delicious—except perhaps a saucer of melted butter or a dab of homemade mayonnaise. Boil it or broil it in the shell, say the lobster-lovers, then tuck in your bib and enjoy it without further ado. (To be appreciated at its best, the lobster should be alive until you cook it, so that it maintains the height of moist tenderness.)

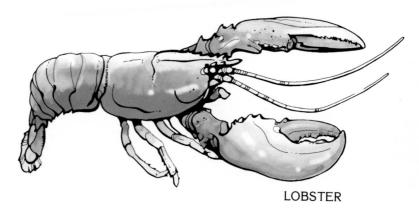

LOBSTER

Two kinds of lobster are available in United States markets; the best known is the northeastern lobster, caught in traps off the New England coast. These shellfish, with their distinctively large, meaty anterior claws, are sold live all along the east coast and in specialty shops as far west as Washington, Oregon, and California. (In the East, the meat of this lobster is also sold cooked, either in the shell or picked from the shell.)

On the southwest coast of the United States is found the second variety of lobster, known as the spiny Pacific or rock lobster. Sold live in southwestern markets (you can order it a few days ahead in northwestern or inland western markets), this lobster has all its meat concentrated in the tail, and its front claws are almost insignificant. From these lobsters (and spiny lobsters imported from other countries, such as Mexico and Australia) come the frozen lobster tails and frozen whole lobsters found in markets across the country.

Most lobster tails are uncooked when frozen, so when thawed, they must be cooked before you eat them. Whole lobsters are usually cooked before freezing (you can tell by the bright red or orange color), so you need only thaw the meat to use it in cold dishes or just heat it through to use it in hot ones.

A miniature variety of lobster called langostinas is also found in American markets, usually sold cooked, shelled, and frozen. They are about as large as medium shrimp and are ready to eat when thawed; use them in salads or as you would any cooked lobster meat.

Storage. Live lobsters can be kept up to 12 hours in a cool place, covered with damp cloths (check to make sure they're alive and moving before cooking). If you buy cooked lobsters (or cook live ones), they should be eaten the same day. However, you can pick the cooked, fresh meat from the shell, wrap it airtight, and freeze it at 0° for up to 2 months. Thaw it in the refrigerator; do not thaw at room temperature and do not refreeze.

How to cook live lobster. Both the live spiny and the live northeastern lobster can be boiled and cleaned, then served hot with melted butter or chilled and served with mayonnaise or another cold fish sauce (see recipes on pages 20 and 21). Live northeastern lobster can be killed, cleaned, split, and then broiled (though this method is not for the squeamish, it results in the most succulent and tender broiled lobster); live spiny lobsters are easier to handle if boiled first, then cleaned, split, and broiled just until reheated.

Boiling live lobster. In a large kettle, bring to boiling enough water to cover lobsters generously; add about 1 tablespoon salt for each quart water. Grasp each lobster from behind the large front claws or front legs (you may wish to wear gloves when handling sharp, spiny lobsters). Plunge lobsters head first into boiling water. Bring water back to a boil; reduce heat, cover, and simmer about 7 minutes for 1-pound lobsters or 10 minutes for 2-pound ones. Remove lobsters and plunge into cold water to stop the cooking; rinse and drain.

Cleaning and serving boiled lobster. With a heavy, sharp knife, split lobster from end to end through its heavy shell. Remove small sac (stomach) that lies just behind head, and pull out intestinal vein, which runs down to end of tail. Do not discard coral-colored roe (if any) or yellow liver. Crack claws of northeastern lobsters. Twist off and discard spiny lobster legs. If you wish to remove all meat from spiny lobster at once, grasp tail and body and bend shell backwards at joint to break; pull meat out of tail.

(Continued on page 103)

Like scarlet warriors, these handsome northeastern lobsters
defy comparison for their commanding appearance and succulent meat. Simply boil them
(see boiling instructions on page 101) and then enjoy them with melted butter,
steamed corn, raw vegetables, and crusty rolls.

Serve warm, freshly cooked lobsters with melted butter or margarine mixed with lemon juice to taste, if desired (use about 2 teaspoons lemon juice to ¼ cup butter). If you have lobster with roe, you can remove roe when cleaning and beat it into soft butter or margarine (use about ¼ to ½ cup butter with roe of each lobster); serve in place of melted butter. You can also chill lobsters in their shells for an hour or so and serve them with plain mayonnaise, herbed mayonnaise (see page 21), or lemon butter mayonnaise (see page 20). Or you can remove meat from shells and use it to make salads or other cold dishes.

To eat, use a lobster cracker or nutcracker to crack the big claw shells of northeastern lobsters. Break off small legs of either type of lobster and suck out juices and morsels of meat inside. Use a fork to extract tail meat from shell, easing it out gently; then cut it with a knife and fork into bite-size pieces.

Broiling live northeastern lobster. Hold lobster on its back and kill instantly by inserting tip of a sharp knife between tail section and body shell, cutting to sever spinal cord. Split lobster lengthwise and remove stomach and intestinal vein as directed in "Cleaning and serving boiled lobster," page 101. Place split lobster on broiler pan, meat side up. Brush meat generously with melted butter or margarine, or spread with whipped lemon butter (see page 29). Place in broiler, about 4 inches from heat, and broil for 10 to 12 minutes or until meat is lightly browned. Serve immediately.

How to cook frozen lobster tails. Since lobster tails are usually frozen uncooked, you must either boil or broil them before serving (they should be completely thawed before cooking).

Boiling lobster tails. In a large kettle, bring to boiling enough water to cover lobster tails; add 1 tablespoon salt for each quart of water. Plunge thawed tails into water; when boiling resumes, cover kettle and simmer about 5 minutes for 4-ounce tails; add 1 minute for each additional ounce. Remove and plunge into cold water to stop cooking; drain. Serve hot, with melted butter or margarine; or let cool, chill, and serve cold or use in salads and other cold dishes.

Broiling lobster tails. Using kitchen scissors, cut along inner edges of soft undershell of thawed lobster tails, clipping off the many fins along outer edges. Peel back soft undershell and discard. Bend overshell back, cracking some of the joints to prevent curling. Arrange on broiler pan, shell side up,

and broil, about 5 inches from heat, for 4 minutes. (If lobster tails are large, split them lengthwise into 2 servings each.) Turn over and spread meat with whipped lemon butter (see page 29) or brush generously with melted butter or margarine; broil, meat side up, about 5 minutes longer. Serve immediately.

How to heat precooked lobster. If you buy whole, frozen, precooked lobster, or have leftover cooked lobsters on hand, you can reheat them by broiling or barbecuing. If frozen, thaw lobsters completely; then split and clean them as directed in "Cleaning and serving boiled lobster," page 101.

Broiling cooked lobster. Spread each half of the split, cleaned lobster with whipped lemon butter (see page 29) or brush with melted butter or margarine. Broil, about 4 to 5 inches from heat, for about 4 minutes or just until lobster is heated through.

Barbecuing cooked lobster. About 30 to 45 minutes before you plan to begin cooking, ignite about 6 to 8 long-burning briquets for each pound of lobster. Spread each half of the split, cleaned lobsters with melted butter or margarine or whipped lemon butter

PREPARING LOBSTER TAIL FOR BROILING

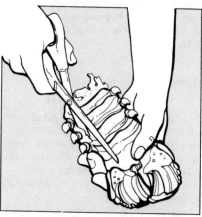

1. To prepare lobster tail *for broiling, cut along edges of tail's undershell with kitchen scissors. As you cut, be sure to clip off the many fins along outer edges.*

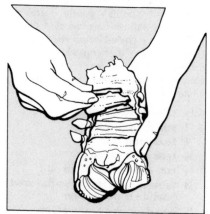

2. Working toward tail end, *peel back soft undershell; discard. Bend tail backward, cracking some of the joints of the overshell to prevent curling while broiling.*

SPLITTING & CLEANING A WHOLE LOBSTER

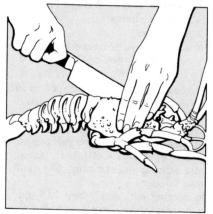

1. To prepare cooked lobster *for cleaning and serving, split northeastern or spiny Pacific lobster in half through length of shell. (You can also split raw northeastern lobster for broiling.)*

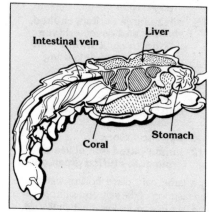

2. Clean cooked lobster *by removing small sac (stomach) that lies just behind head and pulling out intestinal vein that runs down to end of tail. Save coral roe (if any) and yellow liver to serve with lobster.*

(see page 29); wrap each half completely in foil.

When coals are covered with gray ash, arrange in single, solid layer to underlie entire area to be used on grill. Knock off gray ash and let burn down until moderately hot (about 5 to 10 minutes). Adjust grill height to 4 to 6 inches above coals. Place lobster pieces, shell side down, on grill to fit over coals. Cook just until heated through (about 15 minutes). Unwrap from foil and serve immediately.

Lobster Paella Salad

A garland of lemon-marinated lobster tails and jumbo shrimp surrounds this version of Spanish paella. Here, the traditional saffron-flavored rice pilaf is served as a chilled salad, bathed in a tangy tarragon dressing with pimentos, capers, and anchovies. It's ideal for an elegant summer dinner. Serve with a dry white wine.

2¼ cups boiling water
1 cup long-grain rice
1 teaspoon salt
⅛ teaspoon saffron
⅓ cup olive oil or salad oil
3 tablespoons tarragon-flavored white wine vinegar
¼ cup chopped green onion (including some tops)
2 tablespoons chopped pimentos
1 tablespoon capers, drained
1 small can (2 oz.) anchovy fillets, drained and chopped
6 cooked lobster tails, split in half lengthwise (see "How to cook frozen lobster tails," page 103)
1½ dozen large shrimp, cooked, shelled, and deveined (see "How to cook shrimp" and "Shelling and deveining shrimp," page 116)
    Shellfish marinade (recipe follows)
    Butter or romaine lettuce leaves
6 large tomatoes
12 jumbo pitted ripe olives or pimento-stuffed green olives

In a large pan, place boiling water, rice, ½ teaspoon of the salt, and saffron; cover and simmer over low heat until rice is barely tender, 20 to 25 minutes (do *not* overcook—rice should be slightly firm).

Meanwhile, combine oil, vinegar, remaining ½ teaspoon salt, green onion, pimentos, capers, and anchovies. Pour dressing over hot rice and mix lightly with a fork. Cool, cover, and chill at least 4 hours.

Meanwhile, gently loosen lobster meat from shells with a fork, then replace meat in shells. Arrange lobster tails and shrimp in a single layer in a shallow pan. Prepare shellfish marinade; pour over shellfish. Cover and chill several hours, turning occasionally.

To serve, line a large tray with lettuce leaves; mound rice mixture in center of lettuce. Without cutting quite through, core tomatoes and cut in wedges. Lift lobster tails and shrimp from marinade; arrange, along with tomatoes, around mound of rice mixture on tray. Scatter olives over salad. Makes 6 servings.

Shellfish marinade. In a bottle, combine ½ cup olive oil or salad oil, 3 tablespoons lemon juice, and ½ teaspoon dry mustard; shake marinade ingredients until well blended.

Lobster Newberg

For a delectable brunch or luncheon entrée, serve morsels of tender lobster or langostinas enveloped in a smooth, delicate sherry cream sauce. This version works well with leftover lobster meat.

For a heartier meal, you could serve the Newberg over rice.

    About 1 pound cooked lobster meat or 2 cups langostinas, thawed if frozen
3 tablespoons butter or margarine
½ teaspoon salt
¼ teaspoon *each* pepper and paprika
    Dash of cayenne
1 cup half-and-half (light cream)
⅓ cup dry sherry
2 egg yolks
4 slices warm buttered toast, cut in half diagonally, or 4 baked patty shells

Cut lobster meat into ¾-inch slices or chunks (if using langostinas, leave whole); set aside.

In a pan, melt butter over medium-low heat; add ¼ teaspoon of the salt, pepper, paprika, cayenne, and lobster meat. Cook, stirring occasionally, just until heated through.

In another pan, slowly heat half-and-half to scalding (just beginning to bubble at edges); stir in sherry. Using a wire whip, beat egg yolks slightly; add hot half-and-half mixture to yolks, beating rapidly and constantly. Return mixture to pan and cook, stirring, over low heat until slightly thickened (do *not* boil);

add remaining ¼ teaspoon salt.

Pour sauce over lobster and mix thoroughly. Serve on toast slices or heaped high in baked patty shells. Makes 4 servings.

Lobster à l'Américaine

A dollop of cognac and a bouquet of herbs lend subtle seasoning to this classically elegant lobster dish. You'll need a small square of cheesecloth and a long piece of string to make the herb bouquet.

3 live northeastern lobsters (*each* 1 to 2 lb.)
2 parsley sprigs
1 bay leaf
1 teaspoon thyme leaves
1 tablespoon olive oil or salad oil
1 tablespoon butter or margarine
½ cup chopped onion
½ cup chopped celery
½ cup chopped carrot
2 tablespoons cognac
1 cup dry white wine
1 cup consommé
2 cups peeled, seeded, and diced tomatoes
2 tablespoons finely chopped parsley

Boil, split, and clean lobsters, as directed in "Boiling live lobster," and "Cleaning and serving boiled lobster," page 101. Reserve roe (if any) and liver. Remove legs and break in half. Cut tail meat, shell and all, into 1-inch sections; crack claws.

Make an herb bouquet by tying together in a piece of cheesecloth parsley sprigs, bay leaf, and thyme. Tie cheesecloth with a long string for easy removal from pan.

In a wide frying pan, heat oil and butter over medium-low heat. Add onion, celery, carrot, and herb bouquet and cook until soft. Add lobster pieces (do not add roe or liver); cook just until heated through (do *not* overcook).

Add cognac to pan and set aflame by holding a match close to pan edge as soon as liquor is added (be sure pan is *not* beneath a ventilating exhaust or flammable items); shake pan gently until flame dies.

Remove lobster and keep it warm. Add wine, consommé, and tomatoes to pan and bring to a boil. Reduce heat; cover and simmer for 15 minutes. Discard herb bouquet. Return lobster to pan, along with roe and liver, and cook just until heated through.

Arrange on a warm serving dish; sprinkle with chopped parsley. Serves 6.

MUSSELS

A familiar sight to Americans on either coast is a rocky shoreline covered with ranks of crescent-shaped dark blue mollusks called mussels. These shellfish are not only beautiful; they are delicious, as the French, who eat them with gusto, will attest. You can buy them in stores, live in shell, or collect them off the rocks yourself and take them home to steam just as you steam clams.

How to collect mussels. Though mussels are a nutritious, easy-to-find food, westerners should be cautious in collecting them—on the Pacific coast, mussels may be dangerous from May 1 through October. During these months, beaches are posted with quarantine signs. Do not eat (or drink the juice from) mussels from the Pacific coast during this time or at any time that such quarantine signs are posted.

If you're on the eastern shore, though, or in the off-quarantine season in the West, it's easy to help yourself to the plentiful mussels. At low tide, hunt for them where there are outcroppings of rock exposed to the open, pounding surf along the coast; they will have attached themselves to the rocks with tough, brown hairlike byssus or "whiskers." Pry them off the rocks with a crowbar or screwdriver. Don't take home any that have gaped open, because these are dead. Put your catch in pots or pails and cover with damp seaweed to take home.

Storage. Live mussels, covered with damp cloths or seaweed and kept in a cool place, will last up to 24 hours. Check to make sure shells are tightly shut before cooking; discard any that are open. Serve mussels as soon as they are cooked; or, after cooking, cut hinge or adductor muscles from shell; remove mussel (discard shells), cover, and chill to use cold in salads or other cold dishes (do not store longer than 1 day). Shucked mussels that have never been frozen can be placed in an airtight container and kept at 0° for up to 4 months. Thaw only in refrigerator; do not thaw at room temperature and do not refreeze.

How to prepare mussels for cooking. Clean mussels by scraping off any barnacles; then scrub them with a stiff brush under running water, and they are ready to be cooked.

How to steam mussels. Most recipes for mussels call for steaming them to open the shells. Place mussels (prepared as directed) in a large kettle containing about ½ inch of water; bring water to boiling and steam mussels, tightly covered, over medium-high heat, until shells open (about 5 minutes). Mussels can be served immediately with a pitcher of melted butter (hold each mussel by the byssus or "whiskers" to dip in butter, then bite mussel away and discard byssus) or they can be used in other recipes (try some of the clam recipes, substituting mussels for clams).

Moules Marinière or Provençale

(Pictured on page 107)

Out of the Gallic enthusiasm for mussels came these two ideas for steaming and seasoning—one with simple herbs and wine, the other lively with garlic and tomatoes, à la provençale.

> **3 tablespoons butter or margarine**
> **1 small onion, chopped**
> **1 clove garlic, minced or pressed**
> **1 cup dry white wine or regular-strength chicken broth**
> **½ cup lightly packed minced parsley**
> **⅛ teaspoon pepper**
> **2 to 3 quarts live mussels in shells, cleaned (see "How to prepare mussels for cooking," preceding)**
> **Melted butter**

In a large kettle (about 4-qt. size or larger), melt the 3 tablespoons butter over medium heat. Add onion and garlic and cook, stirring occasionally, until soft. Add wine, parsley, and pepper; bring mixture to a boil. Add mussels, cover, and simmer gently until mussels have opened (about 5 to 8 minutes)—discard any that don't open.

With a slotted spoon, transfer mussels to individual serving bowls; pour cooking liquid evenly over servings. Accompany with small individual dishes of melted butter for dipping mussels. To eat, bite mussel away from byssus as directed in "How to steam mussels," preceding. Makes 2 to 3 servings.

Moules provençale. Prepare preceding recipe, but increase garlic to 3 cloves, minced or pressed. Cook onion, garlic, and ½ cup chopped celery in the butter until soft, as directed above. Add 1 can (1 lb.) whole tomatoes and their liquid and ⅛ teaspoon cayenne; simmer, covered, for 15 minutes. Then add wine, parsley, pepper, and finally mussels, cooking as directed.

Stuffed Mussels

A sprinkling of pine nuts adds crunch to these flavorful crumb-stuffed shellfish, served in their colorful, dark blue shells.

> **About 3 dozen large mussels, cleaned and steamed (see "How to prepare mussels for cooking" and "How to steam mussels," this page)**
> **½ cup (¼ lb.) butter or margarine**
> **1 cup chopped onion**
> **4 cups soft bread crumbs**
> **¼ teaspoon freshly ground black pepper**
> **¼ teaspoon *each* thyme leaves and marjoram leaves**
> **¼ cup pine nuts**
> **Topping (recipe follows)**

Remove mussel meat from shells and reserve shells and ¼ cup of the cooking broth. Chop mussels and set aside.

Preheat oven to 350°. In a frying pan, melt butter over medium-low heat. Add onion and cook until soft. Transfer onion to a bowl and add mussels, bread crumbs, pepper, thyme, marjoram, and reserved cooking broth; mix thoroughly.

Prepare topping. Pack mussel mixture into 18 of the largest half shells and sprinkle each with pine nuts. Cover each shell with topping.

Arrange stuffed mussels in a large shallow baking pan. Bake for 10 minutes or just until tops are well browned; serve immediately. Makes 6 to 8 servings.

Topping. Mix together ½ cup melted butter or margarine, 1 cup fine cracker crumbs, and ¼ cup finely chopped parsley.

MUSSELS

OCTOPUS

Along the shores of the Mediterranean, the exotic octopus is a familiar part of the menu, prepared in a variety of ways. In the U.S., it is less well known, but it's available in large seafood markets and Oriental and Italian shops. It may be sold whole and fresh, but frozen octopus is more common, sometimes whole and often in the form of one large leg. A fresh or frozen uncooked octopus requires precooking (directions follow).

Storage. Fresh octopus, raw or precooked, can be frozen, wrapped airtight, at 0° for up to 2 months. (A whole octopus is usually so large that it is a good idea to separate meat into meal-size portions before wrapping, so that it can be thawed bit by bit, as needed.) Frozen octopus should be thawed in refrigerator; do not thaw at room temperature and do not refreeze.

How to precook fresh or frozen octopus. Rubber gloves are recommended when precooking octopus, as it has been known to cause temporary skin rash. Select a 1 to 5-pound uncooked octopus; thaw if frozen. If octopus is whole, slit open head cavity and discard interior. Cut away and discard beak (between legs); wash octopus.

Separate legs and head and drop both into a large kettle, filled with enough boiling salted water to cover octopus meat. Cover and simmer gently until skin can be peeled or stripped from flesh (usually about 30 minutes). Let octopus cool in cooking water.

Mediterranean Octopus Stew

Slow braising in a seasoned tomato broth steeps tender octopus meat in the flavors of Provence.

- **2 tablespoons salad oil**
- **½ cup green onion, thinly sliced (including some tops)**
- **2 medium-size tomatoes, peeled and diced**
- **1 tablespoon finely chopped parsley**
- **1 clove garlic, minced or pressed**
- **¼ teaspoon thyme leaves**
- **⅛ teaspoon dry rosemary**
- **2 cups precooked diced octopus (see "How to precook fresh or frozen octopus," preceding)**
- **¾ cup dry white wine**
  Salt

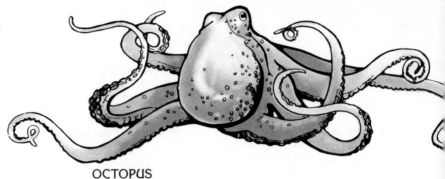

OCTOPUS

Preheat oven to 325°. In a wide frying pan, heat oil over medium-high heat. Add onion, tomatoes, parsley, garlic, thyme, and rosemary, and sauté, stirring occasionally, until vegetables are soft. Add octopus and wine and stir to blend. Pour mixture into a shallow 1½-quart baking dish; bake, uncovered, for 2 hours, stirring occasionally. Salt to taste and serve hot. Makes 4 servings.

OYSTERS

To some Americans, oysters should be savored raw supped from the half shell; to others, they are best immersed in an aromatic stew or fried to a crusty brown. Whether you prefer your oysters bare or clad in seasonings and sauces, there are plenty of varieties from which to choose.

From the east coast come the eastern oysters, small and choice, sold both east and west, live in shell or shucked (removed from shell). These are a prime variety for serving raw on the half shell (see directions in "Cleaning and opening oysters," below, and recipe in "Fish in the Raw," page 61).

The main western varieties are the native Olympia oysters, distinctively flavored and available shucked, packed fresh in small bottles (excellent served raw—see recipe in "Fish in the Raw," page 61), and the large Pacifics, which originated in Japan and are sold shucked, also packed fresh in jars. Graded according to size, Pacifics are choicest when extra small (over 144 oysters per gallon—sometimes called "petit-points"); following that are sizes ranging from small (97 to 144 per gallon), to medium (65 to 96 per gallon), and large (not more than 64 per gallon).

Storage. Live oysters in shell can be covered with damp cloths, and kept in a cool place up to 24 hours; gaping shells that do not close when touched indicate oysters are dead and should be discarded. Shucked oysters should be eaten the day they are bought; if they are fresh, though, they may be wrapped airtight and frozen at 0° for up to 4 months. Thaw them in the refrigerator; do not thaw at room temperature and do not refreeze.

Cleaning and opening oysters. When you buy oysters in shell, you'll need to know some techniques for opening them in order to serve raw or to extract meats for use in other recipes.

First scrub shells well with a stiff-bristled brush under cold running water; then drain. Put an oyster, cupped side down, on a firm surface. Force blade of a strong, narrow-bladed knife into bill (curved side opposite hinge end of shell) and follow bottom contour of shell until you cut adductor muscle (less effort is required with Pacific and eastern oysters if you break off about ⅜ inch or so of bill with a hammer to make a gap between shells—rinse bits of shell off with cold water before inserting knife blade). Pull off top shell of oyster, cut shellfish free, and serve it raw from bottom shell or in a dish (see "Fish in the Raw," page 61) or use shucked oysters for cooking.

Poaching oysters. Cooked oysters are often called for in recipes; a simple poaching makes them useful in cocktails, salads, and many other dishes.

Combine 2 cups water with 1 teaspoon salt and ½ teaspoon pepper in a small frying pan. Bring to boiling; add 1 to 2 cups shucked oysters (see "Cleaning and opening oysters," preceding) into hot liquid and simmer (do not boil) over low heat for 4 to 6 minutes or until oysters become plump and slightly firm and the edges curl; drain and use in hot dishes or cover and chill to use cold.

(Continued on page 108)

Blue-black shells are steamed to reveal brilliant-hued—
and delicious—mussels inside. Dip the mussels in melted butter, and eat;
savor, too, the wine-based broth of this dish, called Moules Marinière.
The recipe is on page 105.

…Oysters (cont'd.)

(Serve these poached oysters as you might raw ones—see recipe in "Fish in the Raw," page 61.)

Oyster Salad

This cool, pastel luncheon salad combines plump fresh oysters with capers and crisp celery bits in a lightly clinging mayonnaise sauce. Serve it with French bread and a light white wine.

- **1 jar (10 or 12 oz.) shucked oysters, drained**
- **1 tablespoon lemon juice**
- **1 teaspoon *each* brown sugar, prepared mustard, and prepared horseradish**
- **¼ teaspoon liquid hot pepper seasoning**
- **½ cup mayonnaise**
- **1 cup finely chopped celery**
- **¼ cup capers and their liquid**

Poach oysters as directed in "Poaching oysters," page 106. Drain and spread on a plate in a single layer. Cover and refrigerate for 1 hour or until thoroughly chilled.

In a bowl, combine lemon juice, sugar, mustard, horseradish, hot pepper seasoning, and mayonnaise; mix until well blended. Cut chilled oysters into bite-size pieces. Add to mayonnaise mixture along with celery and capers; mix well. Makes 4 servings.

Hangtown Pie

Golden fried oysters and scrambled eggs make Hangtown fry—the deluxe meal of the California Gold Rush days. Put them in a toasty-warm pie crust and they become that old-time favorite, Hangtown pie.

- **Baked 8 or 9-inch pastry shell (directions follow)**
- **1 jar (10 or 12 oz.) shucked oysters, drained**
- **All-purpose flour**
- **1 egg**
- **1 tablespoon water**
- **Fine dry bread crumbs or cracker crumbs**
- **¼ cup butter or margarine**
- **2 tablespoons salad oil**
- **4 to 6 eggs, slightly beaten**
- **2 tablespoons half-and-half (light cream) or milk**
- **2 tablespoons minced chives (fresh, frozen, or freeze-dried)**
- **½ teaspoon salt**
- **⅛ teaspoon pepper**
- **Lemon wedges and dill pickles (optional)**

Prepare pastry shell (directions follow) and keep warm; or, if pastry shell has been made ahead and is at room temperature, place on a baking sheet in a 250° oven while preparing other ingredients.

Pat oysters dry with paper towels. Coat with flour; shake off excess. Beat the 1 egg slightly with water in a shallow pan; spread crumbs on a sheet of wax paper. Dip each oyster in egg to coat all sides; drain briefly and roll in crumbs to coat all sides. Arrange coated oysters in single layer on wax paper within reaching distance of range.

In a wide frying pan, heat 2 tablespoons of the butter and the 2 tablespoons oil over medium heat until it foams but doesn't brown. Promptly add oysters and cook, turning once, until browned on both sides (about 4 minutes on each side). Remove from pan and keep warm.

Meanwhile, thoroughly blend the 4 to 6 eggs together with half-and-half and chives; add salt and pepper. Melt the re-

maining 2 tablespoons butter over medium-low heat in a small frying pan; add egg mixture; scramble until eggs are softly set.

Remove warm pastry shell from oven; spread egg mixture evenly in bottom. Arrange oysters on top. Cut in wedges and serve immediately, garnished with lemon wedges and pickles, if you wish. Makes 4 to 6 servings.

Baked pastry shell. Prepare pastry for an 8 or 9-inch pastry shell (use either a mix or your own recipe). Line an 8 or 9-inch pie pan, making a fluted edge. Chill until ready to bake.

At baking time, preheat oven to 425°. Arrange a piece of foil to cover bottom and sides of pastry; press gently to fit (be careful not to puncture pastry with foil). Fill with dry beans to keep pastry from shrinking. Bake for 10 minutes; carefully remove foil and beans and bake about 5 minutes longer, or until lightly browned. Use warm, if oysters and eggs are ready, or cover and keep at room temperature (keeps up to 12 hours in a dry place).

Oyster-Dill Soufflé

Nuggets of oyster float in a golden, frothy cloud of egg. Flavored with dill, this airy soufflé is equally appropriate for a light family supper or a special dinner gathering, and it's surprisingly easy to whip up.

- **Butter or margarine**
- **1 jar (10 or 12 oz.) shucked oysters and their juices**
- **About ½ cup half-and-half (light cream) or milk**
- **5 eggs**
- **¼ cup butter or margarine**
- **¼ cup all-purpose flour, unsifted**
- **¾ teaspoon salt**
- **½ teaspoon dill weed**
- **⅛ teaspoon pepper**
- **Dash of liquid hot pepper seasoning**

Preheat oven to 350°. Generously butter a 1½-quart soufflé dish or other round casserole with straight sides.

Cut oysters into small pieces, about ¼-inch square; turn oysters and their juices into a pan. Bring to a simmer over medium heat and cook to release any remaining oyster juices (about 1 minute); drain, reserving juices. Set oyster pieces aside. Measure juices and add enough half-and-half to make 1 cup liquid; set aside.

Separate eggs and set them aside. In pan, melt the ¼ cup butter over medium

OYSTERS

heat; stir in flour and cook, stirring, until bubbly. Remove from heat and, using a wire whip, gradually stir in the oyster-liquid mixture. Add salt, dill weed, pepper, and hot pepper seasoning. Return to heat and cook, stirring constantly, until thickened. Remove from heat and beat in egg yolks; add oyster pieces and mix until well blended.

Beat egg whites until they hold short, distinct, moist-looking peaks. Fold about half the egg whites thoroughly into yolk mixture, then gently fold in remaining egg whites.

Pour mixture into soufflé dish. Bake for about 35 minutes, until soufflé is lightly browned and appears set in center when dish is gently shaken. Serve immediately. Makes 4 to 6 servings.

Oysters Meunière in French Rolls

For an after-theater party or a special luncheon, these simple oyster-stuffed rolls are ideal—French-inspired, they are informal, yet elegant.

4 French rolls
3 tablespoons butter or margarine, softened
1 tablespoon *each* lemon juice and dry white wine
¼ teaspoon *each* salt and crumbled tarragon leaves
1 jar (10 or 12 oz.) shucked oysters, drained
2 tablespoons whipping cream
Parsley or watercress sprigs

Preheat oven to 450°. Slice a "lid" off the top of each roll and pull out most of the soft bread inside rolls (save soft crumbs for other purposes). Spread 2 tablespoons of the softened butter inside hollowed rolls and on lids. Set rolls and lids on a baking sheet and toast in oven until lightly browned (allow 5 to 10 minutes for rolls; lids will brown faster than rolls).

Meanwhile, in a frying pan, melt remaining 1 tablespoon butter; add lemon juice, wine, salt, and tarragon. Add oysters (cut into bite-size pieces, if large) to pan. Cook over medium heat until bubbly and oysters are firm with curled edges (about 5 minutes). Dividing equally, spoon oysters into toasted French rolls; cover rolls with foil and set aside.

Boil pan juices over high heat, stirring and scraping, until reduced to ¼ cup. Stir in cream and heat, stirring to blend with pan juices. Spoon evenly over oys-

ters; place each roll on a serving plate and garnish with parsley or watercress; arrange a roll lid to the side of each roll. Makes 4 servings.

Oyster Crisp

Try a savory combination of oysters layered with bacon and cheese, then smothered in cream and buttered crumbs—it's rich, but worth every bite.

1 pint (1 lb.) shucked oysters, with their juices
¼ teaspoon salt
⅛ teaspoon pepper
⅛ teaspoon ground or freshly grated nutmeg
6 strips bacon, cooked until crisp, then crumbled
1 cup shredded Swiss cheese
1 cup whipping cream
½ cup coarsely crushed saltine crackers
2 tablespoons butter or margarine

Preheat oven to 400°. Grease a shallow 1½-quart baking dish. Arrange oysters evenly in dish, pour their juices over them. Sprinkle salt, pepper, and nutmeg evenly over oysters. Scatter crumbled bacon over oysters; then top with cheese. Pour cream evenly over all; then cover evenly with cracker crumbs and dot with butter. Bake, uncovered, for 20 minutes. Makes about 4 servings.

Mexican Oyster Stew

Fiesta-bright and tasty, this intriguing, chili-flavored oyster soup is garnished with stuffed green olive slices.

3 tablespoons butter or margarine
1 medium-size onion, chopped
2 tablespoons chopped green pepper
2 tablespoons all-purpose flour
2 teaspoons chili powder
½ teaspoon *each* dry mustard and oregano leaves
2 cups milk
1 bottle (8 oz.) clam juice
¼ cup dry sherry or milk
1 jar (10 or 12 oz.) shucked oysters, with their juices
About 10 pimento-stuffed green olives, sliced

In a 3-quart pan, melt butter over medium heat; add onion and green

pepper and cook until soft (about 5 to 10 minutes). Stir in flour, chili powder, mustard, and oregano and cook, stirring, until bubbly. Using a wire whip, gradually stir in milk, clam juice, and sherry; cook, stirring, until mixture is bubbly.

Cut oysters into bite-size pieces, if large; stir oysters and their juices into soup and cook, stirring occasionally, for about 3 minutes or until oysters are firm with curled edges.

Ladle hot soup into mugs or small bowls and garnish each with sliced olives. Makes 5 cups.

SCALLOPS

The scallop has an unusual trait: it can propel itself along the ocean floor simply by opening and shutting its hinged shell—a characteristic that requires a hefty hinge (or adductor) muscle. It is this adductor muscle that we enjoy as "scallop meat," tender, slightly sweet, and delicate.

All the scallops sold in the United States are caught off the east coast (or imported from Australia), removed immediately from their shells, and frozen for transportation. (The shells are often sold separately, prepared for use as individual heat-and-serve dishes.) Both western and eastern markets sell frozen scallops.

Two varieties of scallops are available, distinguished mainly by size. The smaller size (and reputedly the more tender) is the bay or cape scallop; the larger and more common variety is the sea scallop. The two can be used interchangeably in the same recipes.

Storage. Frozen scallops can be wrapped airtight and kept at 0° for up to 3 months. They must be thawed before cooking; do this in the refrigerator. Do not thaw at room temperature and do not refreeze.

Coquilles St. Jacques au Gratin

A luscious cheese sauce, bubbling hot and thick with mushrooms, enfolds tender scallops in this make-ahead entrée. It will be an elegant addition to your dinner party repertoire.

(Continued on page 111)

Esteemed by many cultures as a wonderful delicacy,
raw oysters on the half shell are an elegant appetizer anywhere when served
with a spicy cocktail sauce and lemon wedges.
The recipe for Raw Oyster or Clam Cocktail is on page 61.

  2 pounds scallops (thawed if frozen), cut in bite-size pieces if large
  About 1 cup regular-strength chicken broth
  ¼ cup butter or margarine
  ¾ pound mushrooms, sliced
  1 tablespoon lemon juice
  1 large onion, finely chopped
  6 tablespoons all-purpose flour, unsifted
  ½ cup whipping cream
  ⅛ teaspoon ground nutmeg
  1½ cups shredded Swiss cheese
  ¼ cup lightly packed minced parsley
  Salt

In a pan, combine scallops and 1 cup of the broth and bring to a boil; reduce heat, cover, and simmer gently for about 5 minutes or until scallops are just opaque throughout. Remove from heat; let scallops cool in liquid. Drain cooled liquid into a pint measuring cup. Add broth, if necessary, to make 2 cups liquid; reserve. Cover scallops and chill.

In a wide frying pan, melt 2 tablespoons of the butter over medium-high heat and add mushrooms and lemon juice. Cook, stirring, until mushrooms are golden brown and all liquid is evaporated. Pour into a small bowl and set aside.

To frying pan, add remaining 2 tablespoons butter and the onion. Cook over medium-high heat, stirring, until onion is soft but not browned. Stir in flour and cook until bubbly. Remove pan from heat and, using a wire whip, gradually stir in reserved scallop liquid. Return to heat and bring to a boil, stirring; cook until thickened (about 10 minutes). Add mushroom mixture, cream, nutmeg, and ½ cup of the cheese; stir until blended. Cover sauce and chill.

When sauce is cold, stir in scallops along with parsley and salt to taste. Di-

vide scallop mixture equally among 4 to 6 individual 2-cup ramekins (or use scallop shells, commercially prepared for baking) and sprinkle remaining 1 cup cheese evenly over top, dividing equally among ramekins. Cover and chill until ready to bake (up to 24 hours).

Preheat oven to 400°. Bake, uncovered, until bubbling and edges are beginning to brown (about 12 to 15 minutes). Makes 4 to 6 servings.

Stir-fried Chinese Scallops

Bright green edible-pod peas and tender scallops are tossed quickly in a hot wok or frying pan, mingled with a rich oyster sauce. Buy the oyster sauce in Oriental markets.

  2 tablespoons oyster sauce
  2 teaspoons cornstarch
  1 teaspoon soy sauce
  ¼ teaspoon sugar
  ½ pound scallops, thawed if frozen, sliced thickly across the grain
  2 tablespoons butter or margarine
  1½ cups whole edible-pod peas, thawed if frozen
  ¼ cup chopped green onion (including some tops)
  Hot cooked rice

In a bowl, combine oyster sauce, cornstarch, soy, and sugar. Pat scallops dry with paper towels and stir into oyster sauce mixture; set aside.

In a wok or wide frying pan, melt butter over medium heat. Add peas and onion and stir-fry until vegetables are almost tender (about 3 to 4 minutes). Add scallop mixture; raise heat to high and stir-fry for about 3 minutes or until scallops are just opaque throughout and sauce is slightly thickened. Serve immediately, spooning over hot cooked rice. Makes about 4 servings.

Broiled Ginger-Honey Scallops

Scallops acquire flavor depth from a pungent, spicy-sweet marinade; coat them in sesame seed after broiling, if you wish.

  ¼ cup sesame seed (optional)
  3 tablespoons lemon juice
  2 tablespoons salad oil
  1 tablespoon *each* honey and soy sauce
  ¼ teaspoon ground ginger
  1 small clove garlic, minced or pressed
  1 pound scallops (thawed if frozen), cut in bite-size pieces if large

If using sesame seed, heat a frying pan over medium heat; add seed and toast until golden, stirring frequently to prevent scorching. Set seed aside.

In a mixing bowl, combine lemon juice, oil, honey, soy, ginger, and garlic; add scallops and mix until well coated with marinade. Cover and chill for at least 3 (and up to 6) hours, stirring frequently.

Lift scallops from marinade (reserve marinade) and, dividing evenly, thread on 4 metal or wooden skewers. Broil about 3 inches from heat, turning occasionally and basting with reserved marinade, just until opaque throughout (about 3 to 5 minutes).

If sesame seed is used, spread on a piece of wax paper; after broiling, turn each skewer over in seed to coat scallops evenly. Serve immediately. Makes 4 servings.

Tarragon Butter-sautéed Scallops

A brisk stir in the sauté pan and these scallops, flavored with an herbed mushroom butter, are ready to serve.

  6 tablespoons butter or margarine
  ½ teaspoon tarragon leaves
  3 tablespoons chopped shallots or white part of green onion
  2 cups sliced mushrooms
  1 pound scallops (thawed if frozen), cut in bite-size pieces if large
  2 tablespoons dry white wine
  Chopped parsley
  Lemon wedges

In a wide frying pan, melt butter over medium-high heat. Add tarragon, shal-

(Continued on page 114)

SCALLOPS

SEAFOOD BISQUES & CHOWDERS

Whether you're planning an elegant soirée or an informal family get-together, a classic shellfish soup makes a wonderful centerpiece for your meal.

Shellfish Bisque

A bisque is any creamy rich soup made from meat or fish, but especially shellfish. For this recipe you may use shrimp or crab, but the base is the same —cream of potato soup. So we present the cream of potato soup recipe first, followed by directions for transforming the soup into the specific shellfish bisque of your choice.

Cream of Potato Soup

¼ cup butter or margarine
1 large onion, chopped
1 cup chopped celery, including some tops
3 or 4 medium-size thin-skinned potatoes, peeled and cut in ½-inch cubes (about 4 cups total)
¼ cup finely chopped parsley
   About ½ teaspoon salt
   About ¼ teaspoon pepper
1 quart regular-strength chicken broth (or 4 chicken bouillon cubes plus 1 quart water)
1 quart milk
3 teaspoons cornstarch
¼ cup water
   Salt and pepper
   About 2 tablespoons butter or margarine
   Finely chopped parsley

In an 8 to 10-quart kettle, melt the ¼ cup butter over medium heat; add onion and celery and cook, stirring occasionally, until onion is soft (about 10 minutes). Add potatoes, the ¼ cup parsley, ½ teaspoon salt, ¼ teaspoon pepper, and chicken broth; cover and cook until potatoes are tender (about 30 minutes).

Stir in milk and cook, covered, until soup is thoroughly hot, but not boiling. In a cup, combine cornstarch and water until smooth; stir into soup and continue cooking, uncovered, until soup boils and thickens (about 5 minutes).

Taste and add more salt and pepper, if needed.

To serve, pour soup into a tureen and float a generous pat of butter (about 2 tablespoons) on soup's surface. Sprinkle soup with chopped parsley. Makes 6 to 8 servings.

Shrimp bisque. Prepare cream of potato soup (above), adding 1¼ pounds small cooked shrimp or 2 packages (12 oz. *each*) frozen shrimp, partially thawed, just before adding cornstarch mixture. Continue cooking as directed.

Crab bisque. Prepare cream of potato soup (above), but add 1 whole bay leaf along with potatoes, and stir in 1 pound crabmeat, thawed if frozen, just before adding cornstarch mixture. Continue cooking as directed.

Party Bisque

A welcome choice for any large gathering is this generous blend of clams, crab meat, and shrimp, swimming in a rich, wine-flavored bisque. To retain the freshest flavor possible, it's best if made the day of the party.

1¼ cups butter or margarine
1 cup all-purpose flour
4 cans (7½ oz. *each*) minced clams
½ gallon (8 cups) milk
1 pint (2 cups) half-and-half (light cream)
1 bunch green onions, finely chopped
2 pounds crabmeat, thawed if frozen
1 pound small cooked shrimp
1 cup dry white wine
⅓ cup dry sherry
   Parsley sprig for garnish
   Assorted condiments: sieved hard-cooked egg yolks and egg whites (about 8 eggs), ¾ cup chopped chives, and ¾ cup chopped macadamia nuts

In a 6-quart pan over medium heat, melt ¾ cup of the butter. Blend in flour and cook about 2 minutes. Drain liquid from clams (reserve clams) and add

liquid to pan, stirring until blended. Slowly stir in milk and half-and-half, and cook, stirring, until sauce is thickened. Remove from heat.

In a wide frying pan over medium heat, cook onions in remaining ½ cup butter until limp. Add crab, shrimp, and drained clams; cook, stirring gently, until seafood is hot. Add seafood to soup mixture and stir in white wine and sherry. Cook over medium heat until hot.

Turn into a heated tureen or other large serving bowl or casserole. Garnish with a parsley sprig. Surround with small bowls of condiments. Makes about 16 servings.

Hearty Clam Chowder
(Pictured on page 126)

A soup to satisfy almost any appetite, this creamy main-dish chowder abounds with clam morsels, chunks of potato and other vegetables, and crispy bits of bacon.

4 strips bacon, diced
⅓ cup chopped green onion (including some tops)
5 medium-size potatoes, peeled and cut in ½-inch cubes
2 tablespoons chopped green pepper
1 stalk celery, sliced
1 carrot, thinly sliced
1 clove garlic, minced or pressed
2 cups water
1 teaspoon salt
½ teaspoon pepper
1 teaspoon Worcestershire
4 drops liquid hot pepper seasoning
2 cups shucked, chopped raw clams, with their nectar (see "Cleaning and opening clams," page 69)
2 cups half-and-half (light cream)

In a large kettle over medium heat, cook bacon, stirring occasionally, until crisp. Add green onion, potatoes, green pepper, celery, carrot, and garlic. Pour in water; add salt, pepper, Worcestershire, and hot pepper seasoning. Bring to a boil; reduce heat, cover, and simmer 15 minutes or until potatoes are tender.

In a separate pan over medium heat, cook clams in their own nectar, stirring occasionally, for 3 minutes or until tender. Add clams to vegetable mixture; add half-and-half and stir until well blended. Heat just until piping hot (do not boil). Serve immediately. Makes 4 servings.

Mussel Chowder

A rich and creamy chowder makes a fine background for steamed mussels.

Steamed mussels (directions follow)
¼ **cup butter or margarine**
1 **large onion, chopped**
1 **stalk celery, thinly sliced**
½ **pound mushrooms, sliced**
1 **bay leaf**
½ **teaspoon paprika**
1 **can (about 14 oz.) chicken broth**
1½ **cups half-and-half (light cream)**

Remove cooked mussels from shells, clipping and discarding beards. Strain cooking liquid through several thicknesses of cheesecloth; discard vegetables. Measure 1½ cups liquid and set aside (if necessary, add water to make 1½ cups, or boil to reduce liquid to this amount).

In a 3-quart pan over medium heat, melt butter. Add onion, celery, and mushrooms and sauté, stirring, until onion is soft (about 10 minutes). Stir in bay leaf, paprika, chicken broth, and reserved mussel liquid; bring to a boil. Reduce heat, cover, and simmer for 15 minutes. Remove bay leaf. Stir in half-and-half and mussels, cover, and cook over low heat just until heated through (do *not* boil). Makes 4 to 6 servings.

Steamed mussels. In a large pan, melt 3 tablespoons butter over medium heat; add 1 small onion (chopped) and 1 clove garlic (minced or pressed) and cook, stirring occasionally, until soft. Stir in 1 cup dry white wine or regular-strength chicken broth, ½ cup lightly packed minced parsley, and ⅛ teaspoon pepper; bring mixture to a boil. Add 2 quarts live mussels in shells, cleaned (see "How to prepare mussels for cooking," page 105). Cover and simmer gently until mussels have opened (about 5 to 8 minutes)—discard any that don't open.

New England Fish Chowder

The combination of salmon blended with your choice of white-fleshed fish makes this chowder a favorite.

2 **strips bacon**
1 **large onion, chopped**
1 **clove garlic, minced or pressed**
2 **cups water**
½ **cup dry white wine**
1 **bay leaf**
2 **whole allspice**
3 **chicken bouillon cubes**
½ **pound salmon steak**
½ **pound halibut, cod, rockfish, or haddock**
¼ **cup all-purpose flour**
¼ **cup water**
2 **cups milk**
   Dash of ground nutmeg
   Salt and pepper
   Chopped parsley (optional)

In a 4-quart or larger pot over medium heat, cook bacon until crisp. With a slotted spoon, lift out bacon. Remove and discard all but 2 tablespoons of the drippings from pan.

Add onion and garlic; cook, stirring, until onion is soft. Add the 2 cups water, wine, bay leaf, allspice, and bouillon cubes; bring to a boil. Reduce heat, cover, and simmer for 20 minutes.

Add fish, cover, and simmer until fish flakes (about 10 minutes for fresh fish). Lift fish out with a slotted spoon. Remove and discard skin and bones; coarsely flake fish and set aside.

Mix flour and the ¼ cup water until smooth; gradually stir into soup. Cook over medium heat, stirring constantly, until soup thickens. Stir in milk, return bacon and fish to soup, and cook over medium heat, stirring often, until soup is heated through. Add nutmeg, and sprinkle with salt and pepper to taste.

Remove and discard bay leaf and allspice before serving. Garnish with chopped parsley, if desired. Makes 4 servings.

Mixed Seafood Chowder

Another must for your shellfish soup repertoire is this good American chowder, featuring almost every kind of seafood available.

5 **strips bacon (or ⅓ lb. salt pork), diced**
1 **large onion, chopped**
⅓ **cup chopped parsley**
1 **clove garlic, minced or pressed**
1 **bottle (8 oz.) clam juice**
1 **cup water**
1 **chicken bouillon cube**
2 **large potatoes, peeled and cut in ½-inch cubes**
½ **pound scallops, thawed if frozen, cut in 1-inch chunks**
1 **pound fish fillets, cut in 1-inch pieces**
2 **cups *each* milk and half-and-half (light cream)**
1 **can (10 oz.) baby clams**
½ **pound small cooked shrimp**
   Salt and pepper
   Paprika
   Butter or margarine

In a 5-quart or larger kettle, cook bacon over medium heat until crisp. With a slotted spoon, lift out bacon and reserve. Discard all but 2 tablespoons of the drippings.

Add onion, parsley, and garlic; cook, stirring occasionally, until soft. Add clam juice, water, bouillon cube, and potatoes. Cover, reduce heat, and simmer until potatoes are almost tender (about 15 to 20 minutes). Add scallop chunks and fish pieces; cover and simmer until fish flakes readily when prodded with a fork (about 6 to 12 minutes).

Add milk, half-and-half, clams, shrimp, and reserved bacon. Cook, uncovered, over medium heat, stirring occasionally, just until hot (do not boil). Add salt and pepper to taste.

Turn soup into a serving bowl. Sprinkle lightly with paprika and float a generous pat of butter (about 2 tablespoons) on soup's surface. Makes 6 to 8 servings.

lots, and mushrooms; cook, stirring frequently, until mushrooms are tender.

Pat scallops lightly with paper towels. Push mushroom mixture to one side of pan and add scallops. Cook scallops, turning with a wide spatula, for about 4 minutes or until scallops are just opaque throughout. Sprinkle wine over scallops and cook 1 minute longer.

Combine scallops and mushroom mixture; spoon into individual scallop shells or ramekins, if desired. Sprinkle each serving with chopped parsley and garnish with lemon wedges. Serve immediately. Makes 3 servings.

Creamed Scallops with Grapes

Pastel delicacy—flaky patty shells are heaped with scallops and glossy green grapes in a mild curry cream sauce.

Court bouillon (recipe follows)
1½ pounds scallops (thawed if frozen), cut in bite-size pieces if large
¼ cup butter or margarine
1 medium-size onion, chopped
¼ cup all-purpose flour, unsifted
1 tablespoon curry powder
1¼ cups half-and-half (light cream)
1 teaspoon lemon juice
4 hard-cooked eggs, diced
1 cup seedless green grapes
Salt and pepper
Dash of nutmeg
6 baked patty shells or hot cooked rice

Prepare court bouillon. Bring to a boil, add scallops and simmer, uncovered, for about 5 minutes or until scallops are just opaque throughout. Lift scallops and seasonings from bouillon with a slotted spoon; set scallops aside and discard seasonings. Pour bouillon through a wire strainer; return to pan and boil rapidly, uncovered, until reduced to about 1 cup; reserve.

In a frying pan, melt butter over medium heat; add onion and cook until soft. Stir in flour and curry powder and cook until bubbly. Remove from heat, using a wire whip, gradually stir in reserved court bouillon and the half-and-half. Return to heat and cook, stirring, until bubbly and thickened. Remove from heat and stir in lemon juice, scallops, eggs, and grapes; season to taste with salt, pepper, and the dash of nutmeg. Return to medium heat and cook, stirring,

just until heated through.

To serve, spoon mixture into patty shells, dividing equally; pass any remaining scallop mixture in a serving bowl. Or serve scallop mixture over rice. Makes 6 servings.

Court bouillon. In a pan, combine 1 bottle (8 oz.) clam juice, 1 can (about 14 oz.) regular-strength chicken broth, 1 bay leaf, 4 whole cloves, 6 whole black peppers, and ½ teaspoon crumbled thyme leaves. Bring to a boil, reduce heat, and simmer for 5 minutes.

Scallop & Bacon Skewers
(Pictured on facing page)

Delicate yet distinctively flavored scallops are skewered with bacon and broiled to perfection.

12 strips bacon
2 pounds scallops, thawed if frozen
6 tablespoons butter or margarine, melted
1 teaspoon *each* dry chervil and paprika

Arrange bacon strips on a rack in a rimmed pan. Broil about 6 inches from heat until partially cooked. Drain on paper towels and cut into 1½-inch pieces.

Alternately thread bacon and scallops on 8 metal or wooden skewers. Combine butter with chervil and paprika; brush on bacon and scallops. Broil 6 inches from heat, turning occasionally and brushing with butter mixture, until bacon is crisp and scallops are opaque throughout (10 to 15 minutes). Makes 6 to 8 servings.

Garlic Scallop Sauté

Scallop-lover's pleasure and garlic-lover's joy—the sweet, tender shellfish sauté in a moment and are served up in a sauce strongly flavored with the bold bulb.

1 to 1½ pounds scallops, thawed if frozen
3 tablespoons olive oil
3 to 4 tablespoons minced or pressed garlic
¼ cup chopped parsley
Salt
Lemon wedges

Pat scallops lightly with paper towels and slice thinly across the grain. In a wide

frying pan, heat oil over medium heat. Add scallops and cook, turning with a wide spatula, for about 4 minutes or until scallops are just opaque throughout.

With a slotted spoon, lift scallops from pan and set aside, leaving juices in pan.

Raise heat to high and boil juices, stirring frequently to prevent burning, until caramel in color (juices will spatter). Reduce heat to medium-high and add garlic, parsley, and scallops; stir just until heated through; sprinkle with salt to taste. Serve immediately, garnished with lemon wedges. Makes 3 or 4 servings.

SHRIMP

The shrimp is a small creature, as even its name suggests (in Middle English, the word "shrimpe" meant "puny person," and in Swedish, the term "skrympa" means "to shrink"). Yet the shrimp is probably the most popular of all seafood sold in the United States. It is delicious: sweet, tender-crisp, and delicate. It is lovely: curving, rosy shapes with pure white inner flesh. It cooks quickly and is low in calories. It is useful served hot or cold, plainly or elaborately dressed; as an appetizer, main dish, sauce ingredient, or garnish; in salads, or sandwiches.

Though shrimp are caught on all coasts (northern shrimp in New England, Pacific ocean shrimp on the west coast, southern shrimp in the Gulf), many of the shrimp sold in United States markets are imported in frozen form.

Since there is practically no meat on the head sections of shrimp, the heads are removed and discarded before the shrimp reach the market. The shrimp we buy are actually only the tail sections of the shellfish.

Shrimp are available raw or cooked (raw shrimp are often called green shrimp in retail stores, though they actually look more gray than green), in shell or shelled, and you can buy them either fresh or frozen.

Biologically speaking, all sizes of shrimp belong to the same group of Crustacea; for the most part, they can be used interchangeably in recipes. However, they are sold by size; the plentiful tiny ocean shrimp, which are almost always sold shelled and cooked, come 150 to 180 shrimp to a pound (this size of shrimp is the one referred to when "small cooked shrimp" are called for).

(Continued on page 116)

For a favorite—and very easy—hors d'oeuvre
or main dish, skewered scallops and bacon are brushed with seasoned butter,
then broiled to mouth-watering perfection.
The recipe for Scallop & Bacon Skewers is on the facing page.

...Shrimp (cont'd.)

Small shrimp are 45 to 65 shrimp to a pound, medium ones average 30 to a pound, and large (sometimes called "jumbo" or "prawns") are 6 to 15 per pound.

In order to estimate serving quantities, remember that 2 pounds raw shrimp in shells will yield about 1 pound cooked, shelled and deveined meat (about four main-dish servings). If you purchase cooked shrimp in shell, you will need about 1¼ pounds to yield 1 pound of shelled meat.

Storage. Shrimp, fresh or thawed, should be cooked and eaten the same day it is purchased. Frozen shrimp can be kept at 0° up to 3 months, wrapped airtight. Thaw only in the refrigerator; do not thaw at room temperature and do not refreeze.

Shelling and deveining shrimp. If you purchase raw shrimp in shell, you will probably have to peel the shells off the shrimp before you cook them, and you will have to remove the sand vein that runs down the back of each shrimp, just under the surface of the flesh.

To shell shrimp, first remove legs. Then open shell lengthwise down belly of shrimp and peel it back gently, starting at head end. Once shell has been freed from entire body except tail, you can either cut body-shell off, leaving tail-shell in place, or you can gently tug tip of tail-shell free and pull whole shell away from shrimp meat.

To maintain the most attractive appearance, devein shrimp with a skewer

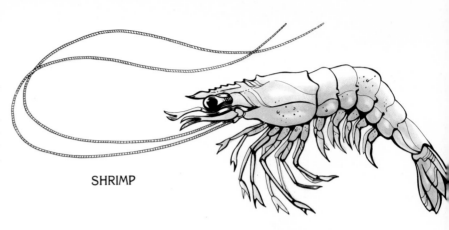

SHRIMP

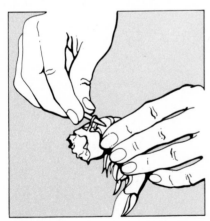

Devein raw shrimp *by inserting slender sharp skewer beneath sand vein that runs down shrimp's back (insert between joints of shell if shrimp is unshelled). Carefully lift skewer to pull vein out (should it break, repeat at another point along back).*

before they are cooked (either before or after they have been shelled). Insert a slender sharp skewer or pick beneath the vein (which appears as a dark line running down center of back) in about the middle of back (between joints in shell, if shrimp is unshelled) and very carefully lift skewer, pulling vein out. If vein should break, insert skewer somewhere along remaining length of vein and repeat process in several places, if necessary. Or, if appearance is unimportant and shrimp are shelled, make a shallow cut lengthwise down back of each shrimp and rinse out sand vein.

How to cook shrimp. Many recipes call for cooked shrimp; here's how to do it yourself. Bear in mind that the general rule of fish cookery applies to shrimp as well: *don't overcook.* Long cooking will toughen and shrink shrimp. You can cook shrimp before or after shelling (if you plan to use cooking liquid for a soup or sauce, cook shrimp in their shells to give extra shrimp flavor to liquid).

For 1 to 2 pounds of shelled or unshelled raw shrimp, bring to a boil 1 quart water with 2 tablespoons salt (or 1 quart basic poaching liquid; see recipe on page 28). Add shrimp and simmer gently (do not boil) for 5 to 8 minutes, depending on size of shrimp. Drain; use shrimp hot or cover and chill. If shrimp have not been shelled or deveined before cooking, shell as directed and devein by making a shallow cut lengthwise down back of each shrimp and rinsing out sand vein.

California Shrimp Salad

Display dainty little shrimp in this lovely salad, bright with bits of tomato and avocado, flakes of coconut, and a lemony oil-and-vinegar dressing.

1 **pound small cooked shrimp**
  Oil and vinegar dressing (recipe follows)
1 **cup sliced green onion (including some tops)**
1 **avocado, peeled, pitted, and diced**
1 **medium-size tomato, peeled and diced**
1 **cup shredded fresh coconut (or ½ cup packaged flaked unsweetened coconut)**
  Iceberg lettuce (about ½ medium head)

Place shrimp in a bowl and pour oil and vinegar dressing over them; turn to coat shrimp well. Marinate, covered, in refrigerator for 1 or 2 hours. Set aside 1 cup of marinated shrimp. To remaining shrimp, add onion, avocado, tomato, and coconut; mix gently.

Line a shallow salad bowl or 4 individual salad plates with outer lettuce leaves. Shred enough of remaining lettuce to make 3 cups and arrange evenly in bowl or on plates. Heap shrimp salad on lettuce. Scatter reserved shrimp over top. Makes about 4 servings.

Oil and vinegar dressing. Combine in a bowl or jar ¼ cup *each* olive oil, salad oil, and white wine vinegar; add 2 tablespoons lemon juice, ½ teaspoon garlic salt, ¼ teaspoon *each* salt and liquid hot pepper seasoning, and ⅛ teaspoon seasoned pepper. Mix until blended.

Fantail Shrimp

For an elegant yet deceptively simple way to serve deep-fried shrimp, take a tip from the Japanese: turn each shrimp inside out so that the tail fans wide and the shrimp, when cooked, becomes a graceful golden butterfly.

Garnish the shrimp with bright yellow lemon wedges, or offer a dipping sauce

—tempura sauce (page 23), shellfish cocktail sauce (page 21), or quick tartare sauce (page 21).

Salad oil
1 pound large raw shrimp in shell
2 eggs
1½ teaspoons sugar
½ teaspoon salt
¼ teaspoon pepper
¼ cup all-purpose flour

In a wok or deep frying pan, heat 2 inches oil to 375° on a deep-frying thermometer.

Leaving tail shells on, wash, shell, and devein shrimp, as directed in "Shelling and deveining shrimp," page 116. Cut a slit through each shrimp, starting about ½ inch from head end and running to within about ½ inch of tail shell. Pull tail through slit gently, so that tail fans out and shrimp forms a butterfly shape.

In a bowl, beat eggs slightly; add sugar, salt, pepper, and flour. Mix until well blended. Dip shrimp, one at a time, in egg mixture to coat all sides; then gently lower into hot oil. Cook 3 or 4 shrimp at a time until golden brown (about 2 to 3 minutes on each side). With a slotted spoon, lift out shrimp and drain briefly. Keep warm until all shrimp are cooked. Serve immediately. Makes 4 servings.

Baked Shrimp with Feta

In the waterfront tavernas of Piraeus, shrimp are served in a thick tomato sauce, laced with partially melted chunks of salty Greek cheese.

1 cup water
1 tablespoon lemon juice
2 pounds medium-size raw shrimp in shell
3 tablespoons olive oil
1 medium-size onion, finely chopped
2 cans (each 8 oz.) tomato sauce
1 tablespoon each cornstarch and water
½ teaspoon oregano leaves
3 ounces feta cheese, cut in ½-inch cubes (for milder flavor, substitute cream cheese)

In a large pan, bring water and lemon juice to a boil. Add shrimp, cover, and simmer just until shells turn pink (about 3 to 4 minutes after simmering begins). Drain off liquid and reserve. When shrimp are cool enough to handle, shell and devein (see "Shelling and deveining shrimp," facing page); set aside.

Meanwhile, preheat oven to 350°. Heat oil in a wide frying pan over medium-high heat; add onion and sauté until soft, stirring occasionally. Add reserved shrimp liquid and the tomato sauce and bring to a boil.

Blend cornstarch with water and stir mixture into tomato sauce. Simmer, stirring, until sauce is thickened. Mix shrimp and oregano into sauce until well blended, then spoon mixture equally into 4 greased ramekins. Divide feta cubes equally among ramekins, tucking them into shrimp mixture. Bake, uncovered, for 15 minutes or until hot and cheese melts. Makes 4 servings.

Iced Shrimp in Dill Marinade

A crisply refreshing way to start the meal—shrimp marinated in lemon and dill, served with crunchy rye wafer bread.

2 pounds large raw shrimp in shell, deveined (see "Shelling and deveining shrimp," facing page)
½ cup lemon juice
3 tablespoons finely chopped onion
2 teaspoons sugar
1 teaspoon each dill weed and salt
¼ teaspoon ground allspice
Fresh dill or parsley sprigs (optional)
Lemon wedges
Rye wafer bread

Cook shrimp as directed in "How to cook shrimp," facing page. Drain off liquid; reserve ¾ cup of liquid and discard remainder. Shell shrimp (see "Shelling and deveining shrimp," facing page) and discard shells.

Combine reserved cooking liquid, lemon juice, onion, sugar, dill weed, salt, allspice, and shrimp. Cover and chill for at least 4 hours (or until next day). Drain off and discard marinade. Serve shrimp from a well-chilled or ice-filled container. Garnish, if you like, with fresh dill or parsley sprigs. Serve with lemon wedges and rye wafer bread. Makes 6 appetizer servings.

"Scampi-style" Shrimp

Like real Italian scampi, these tender shrimp sauté briefly in hot lemon-garlic butter, with a dash of lemon peel and a pinch of parsley.

About ¾ pound medium-size raw shrimp, shelled and deveined (see "Shelling and deveining shrimp," facing page)
6 tablespoons butter or margarine
1 tablespoon minced green onion
1 tablespoon olive oil or salad oil
4 to 5 cloves garlic, minced or pressed
2 teaspoons lemon juice
¼ teaspoon salt
2 tablespoons minced parsley
¼ teaspoon grated lemon peel
Dash of liquid hot pepper seasoning
Lemon wedges

Pat shrimp dry on paper towels; set aside. In a wide frying pan, melt butter over medium heat. Stir in onion, oil, garlic, lemon juice, and salt; cook until bubbly.

Add shrimp to pan and cook, stirring occasionally, until shrimp turn pink (about 5 minutes). Blend in parsley, lemon peel, and hot pepper seasoning; turn into serving dish. Garnish with lemon wedges. Makes 2 servings.

Curried Shrimp

Mildly spicy, a thick creamy vegetable sauce blankets whole shrimp in this classic curry.

1 pound medium-size raw shrimp, shelled and deveined (see "Shelling and deveining shrimp," facing page)
¼ cup butter or margarine
⅓ cup chopped onion
¼ cup chopped green pepper
3 tablespoons all-purpose flour
1 clove garlic, minced or pressed
1 teaspoon curry powder
2 cups half-and-half (light cream)
1 tablespoon lemon juice
½ teaspoon salt
⅛ teaspoon each ground ginger, pepper, and chili powder
Hot cooked white or brown rice
Major Grey's chutney, chopped green onion, chopped hard-cooked egg (optional)

Cook shrimp as directed in "How to cook shrimp," facing page. Drain and set aside.

(Continued on page 119)

Olé! Not one but two lively Mexican treats—
guacamole and marinated shrimp—beckon party guests. With hot sauce,
lime wedges, and tortilla chips, all combinations are possible.
The recipe for Mexican Shrimp Appetizer is on the facing page.

...Curried Shrimp (cont'd.)

In a pan over medium heat, melt butter; add onion and green pepper and cook until soft (about 5 minutes). Add flour, garlic, and curry powder; cook, stirring, until bubbly. Remove from heat and, using a wire whip, stir in half-and-half, lemon juice, salt, ginger, pepper, and chili powder.

Return to medium heat and cook, stirring, until thickened. Add shrimp and heat through. Serve at once, or set over hot water to keep warm (it keeps well up to about 2 hours). Serve over hot rice; if desired, pass serving bowls of chutney, onion, and egg at table, to garnish curry. Makes about 6 servings.

Basque Shrimp & Clam Paella

Clams popping from their shells and heaps of juicy shrimp characterize this distinctive Basque version of the classic paella. Serve it with a fresh green salad.

   6 green onions
   ¼ cup butter or margarine
   1 large clove garlic, minced or pressed
   1½ cups long-grain rice
   ⅛ teaspoon saffron
   1 can (10 oz.) whole baby clams
   1 bottle (8 oz.) clam juice
   3 cups regular-strength chicken broth
   1 teaspoon honey
   1 bay leaf
   1 pound medium-size raw shrimp, shelled and deveined (see "Shelling and deveining shrimp," page 116)
   ½ cup chopped parsley
   1½ dozen small hard-shell clams, cleaned (see "Cleaning and opening clams," page 88)
   Lemon wedges

Preheat oven to 350°. Thinly slice white part of green onions (slice some tops and reserve). In a shallow, 4-quart casserole that can be used over direct heat, melt butter over medium heat. Add white onion slices and garlic and cook until soft. Add rice and saffron; cook, stirring, until rice is lightly browned (about 5 minutes).

Drain baby clams and measure liquid; add enough water to make 1 cup. Set clams aside. Add liquid to casserole, along with clam juice, 1 cup of the chicken broth, honey, and bay leaf; bring to a simmer.

Bake casserole, covered, for 30 minutes or until liquid is absorbed. Remove from oven; stir in 1 more cup of the chick-en broth and arrange shrimp on top. Bake, covered, for 10 minutes longer. Remove from oven; stir in remaining 1 cup broth, baby clams, parsley, and green onion tops. Push hard-shell clams into rice.

Bake, covered, 15 minutes longer or until clams open. Serve with lemon wedges. Makes 4 to 6 servings.

Mexican Shrimp Appetizer

(Pictured on facing page)

Lime peel and juice add zest to these refreshing marinated shrimp; serve them with guacamole and crisp tortilla chips for an unusual appetizer.

   1½ pounds medium-size shrimp, cooked, shelled, and deveined (see "Shelling and deveining shrimp," and "How to cook shrimp," page 116)
   ¼ teaspoon grated lime peel
   ¼ cup *each* lime juice and dry white wine
   ½ cup catsup
   Salt
   3 or 4 drops liquid hot pepper seasoning
   Guacamole (recipe follows)
   Bottled hot sauce, tortilla chips, and lime wedges

Place shrimp in a deep bowl. Add lime peel, lime juice, wine, catsup, salt to taste, and hot pepper seasoning; stir until blended. Pour over shrimp and toss to coat completely. Cover and chill at least 4 hours or until next day. (Shrimp can then be served cold or at room temperature.)

Prepare guacamole. Mound in center of a round serving plate. Drain shrimp and arrange around edge of plate. Serve with crisp tortilla chips, hot sauce, and lime wedges. Makes 10 to 12 appetizer servings.

Guacamole. Cut 2 large ripe avocados in half, remove pits, and scoop out pulp. Coarsely mash pulp with a fork. Stir in 2 to 3 tablespoons lemon or lime juice, ½ teaspoon salt, and several drops of liquid hot pepper seasoning. (Or for a smooth dip, whirl avocado mixture in blender.)

Bahia Shrimp Sauté

Brazilians make an exotic stir-fry dish of succulent pink shrimp and lightly cooked vegetables, permeated with a pungent blend of spices and garnished with peanuts and toasted coconut.

   1 bunch spinach (about ¾ lb.)
   ¼ cup packaged flaked unsweetened coconut
   3 tablespoons salad oil
   1 pound medium-size raw shrimp, shelled and deveined (see "Shelling and deveining shrimp," page 116)
   1 medium-size onion, chopped
   1 clove garlic, minced or pressed
   1 package (9 oz.) frozen cut green beans, thawed
   ¼ teaspoon *each* ground ginger, ground cumin seed, ground coriander, crushed red pepper, and paprika
   Salt and pepper
   ¼ cup dry-roasted peanuts

Cut off and discard spinach stems; rinse leaves well, pat dry, and cut into short shreds; set aside. In a wide frying pan or wok over medium heat, toast coconut, stirring, until golden; lift out, set aside.

To pan or wok, add 2 tablespoons of the oil and the shrimp; stir-fry until shrimp turn pink (about 5 minutes). With a slotted spoon, lift out shrimp; set aside. Add remaining 1 tablespoon oil to pan; stir in onion and garlic and cook, stirring occasionally, until onion is soft.

Stir in green beans, ginger, cumin, coriander, red pepper, and paprika. Stir-fry for 3 minutes. Add spinach and cook, stirring, 1 minute; then return shrimp to pan and cook just until heated through (about 1 minute longer). Season to taste with salt and pepper; sprinkle with coconut and peanuts. Makes 4 servings.

Dilled Shrimp & Cheese Rolls

A mouthwatering shrimp salad mixture melts with cheese inside hot sesame rolls; top with an olive and a curl of shrimp.

   1½ pounds medium-size raw shrimp, shelled and deveined (see "Shelling and deveining shrimp," page 116) or 1½ pounds small cooked shrimp
   ¾ cup diced tybo, Gruyère, Samsoe, or Swiss cheese
   ¼ cup sliced green onion (including some tops)
   ¾ teaspoon salt
   ½ teaspoon dill weed
   ⅓ cup mayonnaise
   1½ teaspoons white wine vinegar
   6 sesame seed sandwich rolls, split and buttered
   6 pimento-stuffed green olives

(Continued on page 122)

BUILDING A SIMPLE SMOKER

Convert a garbage can to a smoke oven? Unusual idea, perhaps, but in fact it's quite simple, and the resulting smoker can do just about anything that a regular smokehouse can. (If you plan to do a lot of smoking, though, it's best to buy a smoke oven.)

The smoker consists of a standard-size metal garbage can outfitted with an electric hot plate. The hot plate ignites a pan of wood chips that smolder up to 3 hours at a controlled rate and at temperatures you can regulate. The smoke and heat produced by the wood chips are contained in the covered can, where they circulate around fish (placed on racks or hung on hooks above the hot plate), cooking and smoking the fish at the same time. Once the chips are ignited, the smoker needs occasional checking.

Fish with moderate fat content, such as salmon, sablefish, butterfish, and eel, benefit notably from the curing and smoking process, acquiring a pleasant, smoky taste that enhances the original flavors of the fish, yet leaves them moist and tender.

Making the smoker

Most hardware stores carry everything you'll need to put the oven together: a 32-gallon galvanized garbage can (galvanized can will not emit toxic gases at low temperatures used in smoking); a single-element hot plate with a heat control knob; a mercury oven thermometer; one or more wire racks (the kind used for cooling cakes; do *not* use galvanized refrigerator racks); two ⅜-inch steel bars to support the racks; a metal pie pan; 15 feet of asbestos-wrapped HPD 14-gauge, 3-wire cord; a 3-prong plug; and a ¼-inch dowel as a stem extension for the hot plate's control knob.

You'll also need some heavy wire to fashion a spacer loop between hot plate element and pie pan (make a ring of wire and crimp three 1-inch legs into it—the ring stands on the hot plate and supports the pie pan), as well as to make several S-shape hooks for hanging whole fish.

With a cold chisel or large spike, punch 2 sets of holes to accommodate rack bars (1 set about 4 to 6 inches and 1 about 10 inches from top) and 1 hole *each* for knob stem and electric cord of hot plate. Use electrical tape to mask the jagged edges of the hole that the cord passes through.

Since each hot plate is different, you'll have to use ingenuity to extend the heat control knob to the outside of the can. We removed the knob, glued one end of a short ¼-inch dowel inside it, and pushed the other end of the dowel into the knob stem.

Important: Since hot plates are designed for indoor use, you need to add an insulated cord with a third ground wire to protect against shock. Open the hot plate and detach the 2-wire cord from the screws; discard cord. Attach 2 of the wires of the asbestos-wrapped

HPD cord to the screws. Secure the third (green) ground wire to the metal body of the hot plate by twisting wire around a part of the body, or by soldering or screwing wire to body. Also secure a piece of wire from the metal hot plate body to the can itself with a sheet metal screw. Plug the cord into a 3-hole grounded outlet. Use the smoker oven only on dry surfaces and be careful to keep the cord dry, too.

If a fire starts in the can, unplug the hot plate immediately. If a fire extinguisher is needed, use only the dry chemical type suited for electrical fires.

Operating the smoker

For wood chips, use any hardwood. Pure hickory or blends of hickory and other woods are the most readily available, though; you'll find them at feed and fuel stores and some hardware stores. Buy the smallest chips available.

If chips are larger than kidney beans, whirl them, a few at a time, in an electric blender.

Put 2 to 4 cups finely chopped wood chips in the metal pie pan and place directly on the hot plate element. Turn the hot plate to its highest setting. As soon as the chips produce enough smoke to fill the can (about 3 to 5 minutes), lift out the pan, protecting your hands. Place the spacer loop around the element and set the pan on top (the loop should hold the pan about 1 inch above the element to prevent chips from flaming).

Insert rack bars—choose the level that will hold your fish well above the pan of chips and still allow the can to be tightly covered. Place wire rack (or racks) containing fish across the bars and place oven thermometer on racks. Or, if racks are not to be used, hang fish from rack bars, using S-hooks (see directions that follow for whole trout, catfish, and mullet), and place thermometer in bottom of can, protecting your hands from the heat. Cover can tightly with lid. Reduce heat as directed for specific fish. Wait about 10 minutes, then check thermometer and make further adjustments as necessary to keep the temperature steady.

Smoking fish

Catfish, trout, butterfish, eel, haddock, mullet, sablefish, and salmon are all particularly good candidates for smoking. The directions that follow include cooking methods for fillets and steaks, whole butterfish, and larger whole fish such as trout, catfish, and mullet.

Fillets and steaks. Prepare a salt brine (enough for about 12 pounds of fish) as follows: in 2 quarts of water, dissolve 1 cup salt and 1½ cups sugar; add 3 tablespoons coarse ground pepper and 2 or 3 bay leaves. Cover fish with brine and allow to stand 3 to 6 hours in refrigerator. Drain fish, rinse in cold water, then allow to stand on racks, uncovered, until dry (about 30 minutes).

If using fillets, place them, skin side down, on a double thickness of cheesecloth and cut away excess cloth, following outline of fish. Rub wire rack with salad oil; place prepared fillets (cheesecloth side down) or steaks directly on rack. For additional flavor, lay a branch of fresh herbs such as bay, dill, rosemary, or tarragon on surface of fish.

Follow operating directions (preceding); when chips are ignited and spacer loop is in place, adjust hot plate control knob to about medium-high heat (thermometer in can should read 170°). Smoke fish for 1½ to 3½ hours (the thicker the pieces, the longer they take to cook; allow about 1½ hours for ½-inch-thick pieces, 2½ hours for 1-inch-thick pieces, and 3½ hours for 1½-inch-thick pieces) or until fish flakes readily when prodded in thickest portion with a fork. Serve hot or cold.

Whole butterfish. Small whole butterfish can be smoked on wire rack just as steaks are. Buy dressed butterfish or clean and scale them yourself (see directions on page 7). Cut 2 or 3 shallow slashes in both sides of each fish; then cover and soak fish in salt brine (as for fillets and steaks, preceding). When fish are drained and dry, oil wire racks and place fish directly on rack on their sides. Smoke according to directions that precede. Serve hot or cold.

Whole trout, catfish and mullet. Clean up to 12 whole trout, catfish, or mullet (each not more than 12 inches long and about 1-pound size—see directions for cleaning on page 7). Scale mullet, if necessary (see directions on page 7) or skin catfish, leaving heads on (see directions on page 39). Rinse fish thoroughly in cold water. Cover and soak fish in salt brine (as directed for fillets and steaks, preceding). When fish are drained and dry, insert S-hooks through gills and out mouth of each fish (use 2 hooks for each fish). Insert rack bars at level that will hold fish above pan of chips; hang fish from rack bars by S-hooks. Following directions that precede, smoke for about 1

hour or until fish flakes readily when prodded in thickest portion with a fork. Serve hot or cold.

Storing smoked fish

The process of curing and smoking has an added advantage besides flavor: it helps to retard spoilage. So after you've smoked your fish, you can keep it, covered, up to 2 weeks in the refrigerator, or wrap it airtight in freezer paper or heavy-duty foil and freeze it at 0° for up to 2 months.

Smoked Fish in Caper Cream Sauce

Capers add a touch of tang to this creamy smoked fish dish. Serve it with crisp toast points for brunch or heap it in patty shells for a delectable luncheon entrée.

- 1 to 1½ pounds smoked fish, hot from the smoker
- 2 tablespoons butter or margarine
- 2 tablespoons all-purpose flour
- 1 cup half-and-half (light cream)
- 1 tablespoon drained, chopped capers
- 4 baked patty shells or 4 slices warm buttered toast, cut in half diagonally

Using two forks, gently flake fish into bite-size pieces while hot, removing and discarding any bones or skin. Cover and keep fish warm while you make caper cream sauce.

Melt butter in a pan over medium-low heat; stir in flour and cook, stirring, until bubbly. Remove from heat and, using a wire whip, gradually stir in cream. Add capers; return to heat and cook, stirring constantly, until thickened (about 5 to 10 minutes). Stir in fish; cook just until heated through. Avoid overcooking.

Serve immediately, mounded in patty shells or spooned into individual ramekins and garnished with toast pieces. Makes 4 servings.

Preheat oven to 350°. If using raw shrimp, cook as directed in "How to cook shrimp," page 116. Let cool; reserve 6 shrimp for garnish and coarsely chop remainder. If using small cooked shrimp, reserve 18 for garnish; coarsely chop remainder. You should have about 2½ cups chopped shrimp.

In a bowl, combine shrimp, cheese, onion, salt, dill weed, mayonnaise, and vinegar; mix until well blended. Spread bottom halves of sandwich rolls with shrimp mixture, dividing equally. Arrange tops of rolls on top of mixture and wrap each sandwich individually in foil.

Bake for about 20 minutes or until cheese begins to melt. Unwrap and serve; garnish top of each sandwich with an olive and 1 medium-size or 3 small shrimp, threaded on a wooden pick. Makes 6 servings.

Szechwan Shrimp with Bamboo Shoots

Szechwan cuisine favors distinctively piquant seasonings for shrimp: a tart sweet and sour sauce, pungent with garlic and ginger, and a generous scattering of sliced green onions.

> 1 **pound medium-size raw shrimp, shelled and deveined (see "Shelling and deveining shrimp," page 116)**
> 2 **tablespoons cornstarch**
> 2 **stalks celery, cut in ½-inch lengths**
> ½ **can (8½ oz.) sliced bamboo shoots, drained**
> 3 **cloves garlic, minced or pressed**
> 1½ **tablespoons finely minced fresh ginger root**
> ¼ **cup chopped green onion (including some tops)**
> ¼ **cup vinegar**
> 2 **tablespoons soy sauce**
> 5 **teaspoons sugar**
> **About 3 tablespoons salad oil**
> **Hot cooked rice**
> **Sliced green onion**

Slice shrimp in half lengthwise; mix with cornstarch until well coated. Set aside.

Combine celery, bamboo shoots, garlic, ginger, and the ¼ cup chopped green onion; set aside. In another bowl, stir together vinegar, soy, and sugar.

In a wok or wide frying pan, heat 2 tablespoons of the oil over medium-high heat until oil ripples when pan is tilted. Add shrimp, a few at a time, and stir-fry until shrimp turn pink (about 5 minutes). With a slotted spoon, lift out shrimp; set aside.

Add remaining 1 tablespoon oil to pan, if needed, and add bamboo shoot mixture. Stir-fry for 1 minute; stir in vinegar mixture and when it boils, return shrimp to pan. Mix just until blended. Serve immediately over hot cooked rice. Garnish with sliced green onion. Makes 3 or 4 servings.

SQUID

Say "squid" and many Americans grimace, imagining a horrifying, tentacled monster of the deep. But Mediterranean, Oriental, and Mexican cooks realized long ago that squid (also called inkfish or calamari) is harmless—in fact, delicious—to eat, and they soon made it the focus of many tantalizing recipes.

Those cooks discovered that squid is as adaptable and appetizing tossed in a simple oil and vinegar dressing as it is when elegantly stuffed and served in a flavorful tomato sauce. From them, we learn that it can be served hot or cold, in any number of different ways, with a host of different seasonings. A fine-textured, snowy flesh and a flavor and tenderness much like abalone's (though at a fraction of the cost) contribute to the squid's appeal.

One of the most inexpensive shellfish available in U.S. markets, squid is sold coast to coast (it is caught off the north and mideastern coasts and the western coast) in whole form, fresh or frozen. It must be cleaned and prepared before cooking (see page 125), but the process is quite simple. Once cleaned, the entire squid is edible.

Storage. Fresh, cleaned squid can be frozen (and frozen squid can be kept frozen), wrapped airtight, at 0° for up to 2 months. Thaw it in the refrigerator; do not thaw at room temperature and do not refreeze.

Ricotta-stuffed Squid

Plump little squid mantles, stuffed full of cheese and parsleyed crumbs, make a hearty dish when simmered in a thick tomato sauce.

> 1 **pound large squid, thawed if frozen**
> ½ **pound ricotta cheese**
> ½ **cup *each* grated Parmesan cheese and lightly packed chopped parsley**
> 2 **cloves garlic, minced or pressed**
> ⅓ **cup fine dry bread crumbs**
> 1 **tablespoon butter or margarine**
> ⅓ **cup chopped green onion (white part only)**
> 2 **cans (*each* 14½ oz.) pear-shaped tomatoes**
> 1 **teaspoon beef stock base (or 1 beef bouillon cube, crushed)**
> ⅛ **teaspoon pepper**
> **Chopped parsley**
> **Lemon wedges**

Clean squid (see "How to Clean & Prepare Squid for Cooking," page 125). Set mantles aside and chop bodies and legs. Mix ricotta, Parmesan, the ½ cup parsley, garlic, bread crumbs, and chopped squid until well blended; set aside.

In a frying pan over medium heat, melt butter; add green onion and cook until soft. Add tomatoes and their liquid (break up tomatoes with a spoon), beef stock base, and pepper. Simmer, uncovered, for about 30 minutes or until thickened.

Meanwhile, preheat oven to 300°. Using a small spoon or your fingers, stuff squid hoods with cheese mixture, dividing cheese mixture evenly between them and filling them well.

Arrange stuffed squid hoods in a shal-

(Continued on page 124)

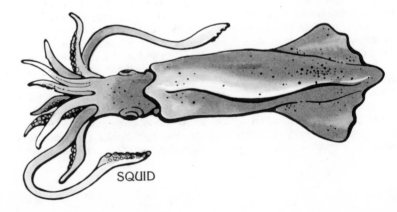

SQUID

Tender squid and a mélange of vegetables
cook quickly in a wok for this Squid & Vegetable Stir-fry.
The recipe is on page 124.

...Ricotta-stuffed Squid (cont'd.)

low 1½-quart baking dish and pour tomato sauce evenly over them.

Bake, uncovered, for 30 minutes or until squid is tender when pierced. Garnish with parsley and lemon wedges. Makes about 4 servings.

Deep-fried Squid

Tempting to youngsters and oldsters alike, these nutty golden curls and rings of tender squid make an intriguing and inexpensive main dish for family gatherings.

    2 pounds squid, thawed if
       frozen
       Garlic salt
       About 1 cup *each* fine dry
          bread crumbs and
          all-purpose flour, unsifted
       Salad oil

Clean squid (see "How to Clean & Prepare Squid for Cooking," page 125), keeping hoods separate from legs and bodies. Cut hoods crosswise in ¼ to ½-inch-wide slices, forming rings. Drain hood rings and squid legs and bodies on paper towels, still keeping hoods separate; sprinkle all the squid with garlic salt. Combine bread crumbs and flour; spread mixture in a shallow pan or on wax paper.

In a wok or deep pan, heat 1½ inches salad oil to 375°. Coat hood rings with crumb mixture; shake off excess. Lower a slotted spoonful of coated rings into hot oil and cook for only about 30 seconds or until lightly browned (squid becomes very tough if overcooked). Lift from oil with slotted spoon and drain on paper towels; keep warm.

Repeat process with remaining rings; then coat legs and bodies with crumb mixture, shake off excess, and continue as directed for rings (legs should be cooked for about 30 seconds also; they tend to spatter fat, so have a lid handy to cover pan loosely). Always allow oil to return to 375° before each addition. When all the squid is cooked and drained, serve immediately. Makes 4 to 6 servings (12 appetizer servings).

Squid & Vegetable Stir-fry

(Pictured on page 123)

Tossed quickly in a hot pan, these tidbits of squid, mushrooms, celery, and green pepper mingle with garlic and fresh ginger to make an Oriental mélange.

    1 pound squid, thawed if frozen
       Sauce mixture (recipe
          follows)
    3 tablespoons salad oil
    2 cloves garlic, minced or
          pressed
    2 teaspoons finely minced fresh
          ginger root
    1 medium-size onion, thinly
          sliced
    ¼ pound mushrooms, sliced
    1 cup sliced celery
    1 green pepper, seeded and
          thinly sliced

Clean squid (see "How to Clean & Prepare Squid for Cooking," facing page). Slit hoods in half lengthwise; then cut crosswise into ¾-inch-wide strips. Leave bodies and legs whole, or cut each into 2 or 3 pieces. Prepare sauce mixture and have all ingredients assembled and ready for cooking.

In a wok or 12-inch frying pan, heat 2 tablespoons of the oil over high heat. Add garlic, ginger, and onion and stir-fry for 1 minute. Add mushrooms and stir-fry until mushrooms are limp (about 2 minutes). Remove mixture from pan and set aside.

Heat remaining 1 tablespoon oil in pan. Add squid and cook, stir-frying, for about 1 to 2 minutes or until pieces curl. Add celery and pepper and stir-fry for 2 minutes more. Return mushroom mixture to pan, add sauce mixture, and cook, stirring, until sauce thickens. Makes 4 servings.

Sauce mixture. Blend 1½ tablespoons cornstarch with 2 tablespoons soy sauce, 1 teaspoon *each* sugar and vinegar, and ½ cup regular-strength beef broth.

Insalata di Mare

Invitingly fresh and lemony fragrant, this Roman "salad of the sea" combines snowy poached squid with clams and shreds of lemon peel.

    1 pound squid, thawed if
          frozen
       Water
    1 can (10 oz.) whole clams
       Peel of 1 small lemon (pared
          thinly with a vegetable
          peeler), cut in very thin
          strips
    ¼ cup lemon juice
    ⅓ cup olive oil
    2 tablespoons minced parsley
       Salt and pepper

Clean squid (see "How to Clean & Prepare Squid for Cooking," facing page). Leave bodies and legs whole, but cut hoods crosswise in ½-inch-wide slices to form rings.

In a pan, bring a quantity of water (enough to cover squid) to a boil over highest heat. Drop in squid and cook just until edges begin to curl (about when boil resumes—if you overcook squid, it will be very tough). Drain at once and set aside.

Drain liquid from clams into a pan; set clams aside. Add lemon peel to clam liquid and bring to a boil; remove from heat and stir in clams and cooked squid. Chill, covered. When cool, stir in lemon juice, oil, parsley, and salt and pepper to taste; mix until well blended. Serve chilled, but not ice cold. Makes 3 servings (6 appetizer servings).

Squid Stuffed with Curry Rice

The surprise inside these tempting little squid bundles is a rice stuffing seasoned with curry and flecked with crisp bacon bits.

    2½ pounds squid, thawed if frozen
    5 tablespoons olive oil or
          salad oil
    3 shallots, finely chopped, or
          white part of 1 bunch green
          onions, finely chopped
    3 pounds tomatoes, peeled,
          seeded, and chopped
    1 teaspoon *each* thyme leaves
          and lemon juice
    4 cloves garlic, minced or pressed
    1 bay leaf
    ½ teaspoon *each* salt and sugar
    3½ tablespoons dry white wine
    ½ cup water
       Curry rice stuffing (recipe
          follows)

Clean squid, as directed in "How to Clean & Prepare Squid for Cooking," page 125. Set hoods aside; chop bodies and legs for stuffing (see below).

In a large pan, heat 2 tablespoons of the oil over medium-high heat. Add shallots and cook until soft. Stir in tomatoes, thyme, lemon juice, garlic, bay leaf, salt, sugar, wine, and water. Bring to a boil; reduce heat and simmer, uncovered, for 10 minutes. Set aside.

Prepare curry-rice stuffing. Stuff each hood to within 1 inch of top. Weave a wooden pick or small skewer across top of each hood to secure.

In a large frying pan, heat remaining

3 tablespoons oil over medium-high heat. Add stuffed squid hoods and cook, turning, until golden on all sides (about 8 minutes). Reduce heat to low; spoon tomato mixture over squid. Simmer, covered, for 1 hour or until squid is very tender when pierced with a fork.

With a slotted spoon, lift out squid and arrange on a serving platter; carefully remove picks. If necessary, thin sauce with a few tablespoons water. Spoon about half the sauce over squid and pass remaining sauce at the table. Makes about 6 servings.

Curry rice stuffing. Cook ½ pound sliced bacon until crisp; drain and crumble. In a large frying pan, heat 2 tablespoons olive oil or salad oil over medium-high heat. Add 6 large shallots or 1 small onion, chopped, and chopped squid bodies and legs. Cook until shallots are soft (2 to 3 minutes). Remove pan from heat. Add 2½ cups cooked long-grain rice, 3 cloves garlic (minced or pressed), ½ cup chopped parsley, 1 teaspoon salt, 1 beaten egg, 1 teaspoon curry powder, and bacon. Mix until blended.

Squid Sauce with Spaghetti

A departure from your everyday meat-based spaghetti sauce, this recipe offers an easy and inexpensive way to go Italian with squid.

- 1 **pound squid, fresh or frozen and thawed**
- 1 **large onion, chopped**
- 1 **large clove garlic, minced or pressed**
- ½ **medium-size green pepper, seeded and chopped**
- 3 **tablespoons olive oil or salad oil**
- 1 **can (about 1 lb.) Italian-style tomatoes**
- ½ **teaspoon** *each* **chervil, dry basil, and salt**
- ¼ **teaspoon** *each* **dry rosemary and pepper**
- 2 **tablespoons chopped parsley**
- 8 **ounces spaghetti or vermicelli Boiling salted water**

Clean squid (see "How to Clean & Prepare Squid for Cooking," this page). Finely chop hoods and bodies and place in a colander to drain. You should have 1¼ to 1½ cups meat.

In a wide frying pan over medium-high heat, cook onion, garlic, and green pepper in oil until limp. Drain liquid from tomatoes into pan; coarsely chop tomatoes, then add to pan with chervil,

basil, salt, rosemary, pepper, and parsley. Reduce heat and simmer, uncovered, stirring occasionally, for about 20 minutes or until slightly thickened. Add squid and simmer until squid is tender (7 to 10 minutes).

Meanwhile, following package directions, cook spaghetti in a large kettle of boiling salted water until al dente; then drain. Arrange spaghetti on a serving dish, ladle sauce over it, and serve. Makes 4 servings.

HOW TO CLEAN & PREPARE SQUID FOR COOKING

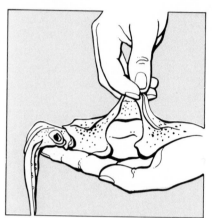

1. Holding a squid *under running water, peel off and discard all of the transparent, speckled membrane from the hood, exposing the pure white meat of the hood.*

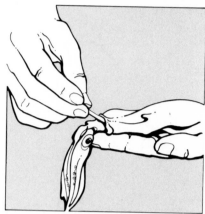

2. Carefully pull out *the long, transparent, sword-shaped shell from inside the hood and discard it. (This "sword" is what makes the squid a shellfish.)*

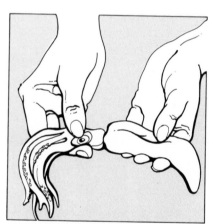

3. Gently separate *body from hood. Strip off and discard all material that easily comes free from body, including ink sac. (If sac breaks, rinse body to remove ink.) Discard contents of hood; rinse inside.*

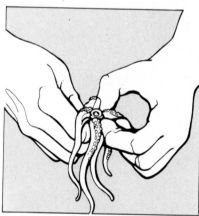

4. Turn body upside down *so that tentacles are spread open to expose center. Squeeze body gently to pop out the hard, parrotlike beak from between the tentacles.*

Assemble a host of fresh ingredients to prepare
Hearty Clam Chowder, the most traditional of traditional American soups.
The recipe is on page 112.

INDEX